Punching the Clock

Punching the Clock

Adapting to the New Future of Work

JOE UNGEMAH

OXFORD
UNIVERSITY PRESS

OXFORD
UNIVERSITY PRESS

Oxford University Press is a department of the University of Oxford. It furthers
the University's objective of excellence in research, scholarship, and education
by publishing worldwide. Oxford is a registered trade mark of Oxford University
Press in the UK and certain other countries.

Published in the United States of America by Oxford University Press
198 Madison Avenue, New York, NY 10016, United States of America.

Library of Congress Cataloging-in-Publication Data
Names: Ungemah, Joe, 1976– author.
Title: Punching the clock : adapting to the new future of work / Joe Ungemah.
Description: New York, NY : Oxford University Press, [2021] |
Includes bibliographical references and index.
Identifiers: LCCN 2020039404 (print) | LCCN 2020039405 (ebook) |
ISBN 9780190061241 (hardback) | ISBN 9780190061265 (epub) |
ISBN 9780190061272
Subjects: LCSH: Work—Psychological aspects. | Employees—Psychology. |
Psychology, Industrial. | Industrial sociology.
Classification: LCC HF5548.8 .U54 2021 (print) | LCC HF5548.8 (ebook) |
DDC 306.3/60112—dc23
LC record available at https://lccn.loc.gov/2020039404
LC ebook record available at https://lccn.loc.gov/2020039405

DOI: 10.1093/oso/9780190061241.001.0001

1 3 5 7 9 8 6 4 2

Printed by Sheridan Books, Inc., United States of America

Contents

The Future of Work in a Post-Pandemic World   vii

1. Imitation   1
   *The short and troubled history of Uber's corporate culture, how
   aggression toward a Bobo doll unlocked the rules of role modeling,
   and when unconscious bias becomes reality*

2. Connection   16
   *Attachment sets the stage, a tour of the Love Lab, the magic ratio,
   and how the Four Horsemen predict the success of relationships in
   and out of the workplace*

3. Reward   32
   *Reinforcement of behavior, B. F. Skinner's ruthless quest for learned
   helplessness, the ways casinos play on basic human urges, and
   what pre-school children can teach us about restraint*

4. Choice   47
   *Why people sometime feel paralyzed by decisions, how looking
   after a houseplant can lead to a longer life, and when small decisions
   stacked up to cause the Hindenburg disaster*

5. Confidence   61
   *Captain Chesley Sullenberger's crash on the Hudson, Nick Leeson's
   single-handed destruction of Barings Bank, and what Major League
   Baseball salaries can tell us about ego threat*

6. Power   74
   *What the Stanford Prison Experiment and the 2016 Academy Awards
   together reveal about direct and indirect types of power on employee
   relations and inclusiveness*

7. Helping   89
   *Why people will help in some circumstances and fail to act in others,
   as explained by the brutal murder of Kitty Genovese and an unusual
   bus accident in London*

8. Intent 101

The 1934 field study of a Chinese couple seeking a hotel, recent woes at Airbnb, and how personal connections can resolve the disconnect between intent and action

9. Obedience 115

Stanley Milgrim's experiment that uncovered how authority overpowers good intentions and the implications it has for whistle-blowing on unethical or illegal behavior

10. Conformity 129

Individuals caving to the crowd, groupthink during the Bay of Pigs fiasco, and how groups can change even the deepest held opinions

11. Identity 142

The North Pond Hermit, how social labels and group memberships define personal identity, and the story of one employee who can be said to "Bleed Blue"

12. Conflict 155

Sherif's Robbers Cave experiment; the Troubles of Northern Ireland; and how social mobility, group categorization, and self-esteem fan the flames of group conflict

13. Misdirection 168

The tale of a famous spirit photographer, the psychological tricks used by con-men, and how cognitive biases worked against spotting and reacting to the COVID-19 crisis

Further Reading 179
Index 187

The Future of Work in a Post-Pandemic World

9,020. This is the number of days a newly graduated college student can expect to work in his or her lifetime based on average life expectancy and retirement age. Put into perspective, work makes up just over 30% of everything we will ever do. The only activity that overshadows this level of commitment is really not an activity at all, but rather the time we spend asleep. On average, we sleep 10,608 days or 35% of our lifetime, taking account of the drop in sleeping hours from a high of 13 hours for infants to a low of 7 hours for seniors. Considering that two-thirds of our lives are caught up either working or asleep, this leaves precious little time for everything else we value and enjoy, including the time we spend with family and friends. Just from a time perspective, working could be considered the trait that best describes what it means to be human.

Yet this is not how the vast majority of workers would describe their existence. Roughly only a third of the workforce would describe themselves as highly engaged in the work that they do. The rest of us trudge through the day, doing tasks that may pay the bills but leave us hollow inside. When the BBC asked for examples of the most boring jobs their readers experienced, the examples were telling. Jane from Yate dreams of peas, "I tested the temperature of frozen peas for a whole summer. I used to dream about endless rivers of little green balls." Pete's story is not too different, "I put pepperoni on 14,000 pizzas per day at a factory in Nottingham. If the conveyer belt broke down, we made smiley faces on the pizzas with the pepperoni. So, if you ever see a smiley pizza, that's why." At least Jane and Pete had tangible jobs, which is different from Jon who lives in London: "I was once employed through the summer as 'someone to talk to.' It was a small architectural company that only had three employees. When I queried why there was so little work to do, they told me it was just refreshing to have someone else to talk to and discuss ideas with."

If it isn't the job itself that makes you tune out, it is likely the people that you work with. In a poll sponsored by Samsung of 1,000 office workers, employees reported losing 22 minutes a day to unwanted distractions caused by their colleagues, such as moaning or eating loudly. Almost a third of those surveyed had left a previous job because their colleagues became too irritating, far outpacing physical workplace environment or technology limitations as key reasons to quit.

Potentially, some of these frustrations might disappear as the world of work moves to more virtual and tenuous forms of employment. Greater numbers of people are adapting to the *gig economy*, broadly characterized by workers cobbling together multiple jobs or becoming independent contractors who are not tied into traditional employment relationships. These workers are inserting themselves into a workplace increasingly dominated by the "Future of Work," where routine tasks are augmented by robotic process automation while straightforward decisions are increasingly being made by artificial intelligence. The physical workplace is changing, too, with open-plan, flexible designs carrying names like "neighborhoods" replacing offices and cubicles. Not only are these new workplaces cheaper to operate, with their smaller physical footprint per employee, but they are also said to address the changing needs of employees to interact with and collaborate across a broader range of coworkers. Not every office will take it to the extreme of installing a fire pit or a tunnel-slide between floors, but perceptions about what constitutes a workplace are evolving. Propelling technological and environment changes further are the attitudes of new workers. Fresh graduates are putting increased priority on building skills (potentially for the next gig) and doing fulfilling work in a vibrant community of collaborators, as opposed to climbing the career ladder or seeking personal wealth.

The momentum building toward this vision of the Future of Work was unexpectedly accelerated in early 2020, fueled by a pandemic that forced the closure of workplaces and the rapid deployment of new ways of working. According to the World Health Organization (WHO), COVID-19 was first reported in Wuhan, Hubei Province, China, on 31 December 2019, as a cluster of pneumonia cases. Thirteen days later, the first case outside of China was confirmed by officials. On 30 January 2020, the WHO declared the novel coronavirus a Public Health Emergency of International Concern, recognizing the severity of both the illness and its potential to spread through human-to-human transmission. At this point, China had reported 8,141 confirmed cases and 171 deaths. With spread intensifying, especially in Italy and Iran, the WHO declared COVID-19 a pandemic on 11 March 2020, and, with it, countries around the world began to enact stay-at-home orders and encourage social distancing.

Within days, workplaces were turned upside down. Nonessential workers and consumers alike were told to stay at home, placing incredible pressure on small businesses to remain financially solvent. Many businesses were unable or unwilling to fully adopt to online only or curb-side pickup, deciding instead to shutter and lay off workers. By the middle of April, unemployment in the United States surged beyond 20 million (in comparison, the Great Recession of 2008 recorded job losses of 8.7 million). Even big businesses cut pay, furloughed workers, or closed operations to stymie financial losses. Beyond differences between industries or business size, the pandemic's effects on employees are disproportionate. According to the Bureau of Labor Statistics, more than half of information workers (e.g., IT professionals, consultants, or middle management) can work from home, but only 1 in 20 service workers can do the same. Workers who make cars, cook food, or clean hospitals depend on a defined workplace and therefore are not eligible for remote working. Bubbling below the surface is a socioeconomic disparity, with these jobs held predominantly by people of color or those without college degrees. Heidi Shierholz from the Economic Policy Institute, as quoted by *The Washington Post*, states, "A lot of people who have highly paid, white-collar jobs that are computer-focused can adjust to this crisis without a lot of pain. And then there's a much larger group that can't adjust without a lot of pain to themselves and their families." For workers who were able to transition to remote working, an experiment into the Future of Work was undertaken that would challenge both the technological infrastructure and the social bonds that tie together coworkers and the customers they serve.

Such a major transformation would be unthinkable just 15 years ago, as pointed out by Rory Cellan-Jones of the BBC. In 2005, YouTube, Facebook, and Twitter were in their infancy, while the iPhone was 2 years from commercial launch. Online shopping accounted for only 3% of purchases, while video-chat was a novelty, relying on high-end equipment that was out of reach in the mainstream. Even if the applications existed, stable and fast internet was another matter, with only a fraction of households connected to broadband service. For example, approximately 8 million households in the United Kingdom had a broadband connection that reached speeds of 10 Mbps, while another 7 million people were reliant on dial-up connections. Broadband speeds today are on average five times faster, making the possibility of widescale video conferencing a reality.

During the COVID-19 pandemic, an estimated 30% of the workforce found themselves squirreled away in makeshift home offices. A few weeks prior to the pandemic, these home offices could have been laundry rooms or attic spaces, but they were converted quickly to become the locus of household economic activity. Tethered to their computers and mobile phones, the need for collaboration exploded as employees navigated how best to work remotely and simultaneously deal with the economic meltdown caused by the pandemic. IT departments scrambled to add bandwidth and plug holes in their video conferencing and file-sharing infrastructure. In an initial review of internet usage, peak traffic surged by between 10% and 30% from pre-pandemic levels, with the high end dominated by countries that mandated distance learning for children. The pandemic was a real-life test on the minimal conditions needed for remote working at scale. Even before the pandemic, some of the business requirements were obvious, such as having a high-speed internet connection, standardized company-issued equipment, and software that would allow multiple users to collaborate on documents. Other requirements appeared only after the pandemic was under way and when systems were put under stress, such as security holes in video conferencing technology or failures of virtual private networks to handle the increased user load.

Yet the harder and more subtle challenges of remote work were not technology-related, but rather dug at the core of human interaction. Interacting with coworkers and customers virtually, even with the best technology, does not replicate the improvisational nature of face-to-face contact. Conference calls do not provide the same opportunities for rapport building or social connection when compared to sharing lunch with a colleague or walking the corridors of someone else's work environment. This point was demonstrated by Ctrip, a Chinese travel agency, in an experiment on home working for its 16,000 employees. After initially witnessing higher satisfaction and productivity among call center staff, the effects reversed dramatically over time due to a constant feeling of loneliness. This finding aligns with research by Google on its most productive workers, which discovered that psychological safety was a key determinant of productivity. Writing about this study, Derek Thompson of *The Atlantic* states, "Almost everything that doesn't feel like work at the office is what makes the most creative, most productive work of the office possible." It is not hard to imagine that after a few months in quarantine, workers might have wished for all those unwanted coworker annoyances that distracted them for 22 minutes each day.

Through necessity, COVID-19 provided the opportunity for companies to challenge core concepts about what constitutes a workplace. In some instances, companies went further to reimagine how the work itself got done, taking the opportunity to re-evaluate how data and automation might provide a better operating model and anticipating that the business environment was likely forever altered by the pandemic. Matt Mullenweg, CEO of Automattic (parent company of WordPress and Tumblr), was quoted by *The Guardian* as saying "This is not how I envisioned the distributed work revolution taking hold. . . . Millions of people will get the chance to experience days without long commutes, or the harsh inflexibility of not being able to stay close to home when a family member is sick. . . . This might be a chance for a great reset in terms of how we work."

To fully adjust, companies and employees must first realize that the Future of Work is a different type of work and does not follow the same rules as the traditional workplace. Beyond the ambiguity caused by the transition to new social norms about how to do work, a long-term and permanent swing toward the gig economy involves abundant and temporary relationships. Workers will not be given the time to develop deep relationships with a stable group of colleagues. Instead they will be forced to establish rapport quickly with a revolving door of colleagues, finding ways to work collaboratively from the start, which might be a fatal flaw for the new work environment. Unlike technology, worker behavior is driven by psychological drives and biases that have emerged over millennia. Social patterns and meaningful relationships take time to develop, which is at odds with the most extreme versions of the Future of Work. The workplace, just like any other social environment, is dictated by subtle laws that will resist change even with the most advanced technology.

To help navigate the Future of Work in a post-pandemic world, this book calls on some of the very best psychological research to explain our decisions and relationships at work. It explores how leaders can build confidence and yield their power to either beneficial or disastrous consequences. It also discusses how to make better connections with our workmates to ensure that relationships don't go off the rails. It answers why we sometimes hesitate to help a colleague, fail to make an important decision, or succumb to temptation or peer pressure. The book dives deep into our psyche, addressing how our personal identity draws lines with whom we interact and why we take favorites even when we promise to be inclusive.

Each topic is discussed by making connections between seemingly unrelated topics, with the intent of challenging how much we know about our own impulses and those of our coworkers. Many of the implications of the research are spelled out (e.g., how diversity and inclusion or whistleblowing policies face an uphill challenge), yet there are many more implications to be found in these stories. This is especially true when considering that we are still just experimenting with the Future of Work and a true transition to a gig economy. It is hoped that by treating the workplace like any other social environment, a firmer understanding of worker behavior can be reached, which in turn will allow for more productive and enjoyable relationships. Some of the lessons might be worthy enough for us to take a slight breather before heading full speed into the Future of Work. Considering that we spend 30% of our lifetime at work, which is more time than in any other conscious activity, it seems that we are all vested in making the workplace experience the very best it can be.

1

Imitation

Less than a decade from its founding, Uber reinvented the taxi industry. By connecting riders and drivers via technology, Uber provided assurance that a passenger's ride would be on time, in a roadworthy car, and with greater professionalism than what the incumbent taxi companies were offering. From start-up to becoming a megalith valued at $70 billion and operating in 70 countries, Uber and its founder, Travis Kalanick, were on top of the world. Despite the ingenuity involved in transforming a stale and forgotten industry into one of the high-tech elite, the company has been plagued by a rash of sexual harassment cases that, in hindsight, stem from the very behaviors that resulted from Uber's aggressive expansion and success. Core values like taking bold bets, being obsessed with the customer, and "always be hustlin'" created a "bro'" culture that has proved difficult to unwind.

The *New York Times* conducted a series of 30 interviews with existing and past employees to investigate how deep-rooted sexism was in the company. The interviewees did not disappoint, with reported incidents like groping of female employees at a company retreat, homophobic slurs being slung at a subordinate during a heated debate, and threats to beat another employee with a baseball bat. These examples underlie a company culture where employees were pitted against each other while the company turned its full attention to the bottom dollar. Uber's "bro'" culture can best be illustrated by a company party in 2015. A lucky group of employees were invited to the Palms Hotel in Las Vegas, where they attended a private concert by Beyoncé and took part in hard drinking and gambling. Some employees took the party further by openly using cocaine in the bathrooms. The night was topped off with four separate incidents of groping and one particularly spirited employee stealing a bus and taking it for a joy ride. Employees were acting less like representatives of a multibillion dollar company and more like brothers from the local chapter of a college fraternity.

What makes Uber's story more shocking was senior management's awareness and complete dismissal of accusations about misconduct. A senior Uber executive back in 2014 suggested that investigative journalists who pried into

Punching the Clock. Joe Ungemah, Oxford University Press (2021). © Oxford University Press.
DOI: 10.1093/oso/9780190061241.003.0001.

Uber should themselves be put under investigation. Kalanick was not immune to the culture he created, but rather he set the tone by jokingly calling himself a "boober" for his ability to attract women now that he led a multibillion dollar company. He surrounded himself with like-minded executives who reportedly patronized an escort bar in South Korea in 2014 as part of a business trip.

Uber's culture hit a tipping point in February 2017, when Susan Fowler, a site-reliability engineer, detailed extensive harassment and bullying in a personal blog. Shortly after her hiring, Fowler was propositioned for sex by her new manager: "It was so clearly out of line that I immediately took screenshots of the chat messages and reported him to HR." Instead of immediate action, Fowler was ignored, "Upper management told me that he 'was a high performer' and they wouldn't feel comfortable punishing him for what was probably 'just an innocent mistake on his part.'" Instead of treating all employees equally, Uber sided with the assailant, putting the star performer's comfort above that of his victim's.

Fowler's personal experience was common practice at Uber, where misbehaving employees were moved around the company rather than reprimanded as long as they were performing well. Promoting a "star" culture, where the best employees are shielded from scrutiny, turned reckless when mixed with gender imbalances. With a 66% to 34% split between men and women (with only 15.1% female representation in core jobs like engineering and product management), a bro culture that tolerated bad behavior was born. Kalanick's initial response to Fowler's blog was to open an internal investigation, asking Board Member Arianna Huffington and Eric H. Holder, former US Attorney General, to review harassment cases and Human Resource's handling of them. Kalanick apologized during a 90-minute all-hands meeting stating that "I am authentically and fully dedicated to getting to the bottom of this."

Although initially believing that Uber only had a handful of bad apples, the investigation proved otherwise. A total of 215 cases of misconduct were investigated, resulting in 20 employee terminations and 31 employees given a warning and mandatory training. The 20 terminations included senior executives and were a direct result of sexual harassment, discrimination, unprofessional behavior, retaliation, bullying, and physical safety issues, with almost all representing the San Francisco headquarters. Such decisive action by a company was unprecedented, proving without doubt the systemic issues within the culture and the company's need to address them. Yet considering that only 5–15% of sexual harassment cases are typically reported, the extent of harm at Uber was likely much, much higher.

Things quickly became personal for Kalanick as leader and founder of Uber, when he was asked to resign on 20 June 2017. Investors were wary of Kalanick's leadership style and his ability to change from entrepreneur to business leader. Despite its size, Uber had not yet made a profit and was facing a number of regulatory, oversight, and intellectual property (IP) ownership challenges. With pressures mounting, investors lost faith that Kalanick was providing proper oversight and therefore was placing the company at considerable risk. One investor, Benchmark Capital, went so far as suing Kalanick for allegedly sabotaging the search for a replacement CEO. At his final all-hands meeting, Kalanick described the past 6 months at Uber as the most difficult of his life and admitted that he made many mistakes. Kalanick left to a standing ovation but in his wake stood a battered company.

Uber's bro culture didn't pop out of nowhere. The disruptive, ultra-macho behaviors of its founder created an environment that allowed sexual harassment to flourish. With a lack of female representation in key positions, allegations of misconduct were quickly dismissed and the accusers discredited. Taking the cue that sexual harassment was an ignored, if not an accepted, cultural norm, male employees were free to do what they wanted. Employees of either gender who found the culture disquieting probably concluded that it was easier to leave than to fight for what was right. Sadly, Uber's story is not alone as an example of a toxic culture. Fox News's recent firings of Bill O'Reilly and Roger Ailes, who independently racked up a half dozen sexual harassment and verbal abuse allegations each, demonstrate a similar combination of a star culture in a male-dominated workplace. Kalanick, like Ailes or O'Reilly, acted as a role model for what is permissible and accepted in a social environment, which can run contrary to what we know to be ethical and right. If his behavior was not blatantly copied by employees, it was enough to silence them.

Learning How to Be a Bully

It is beautiful spring day and the weather is perfect for lunch outside in your local park. As you unwrap your sandwich, you begin to observe the children playing around you. In many ways, the playground is the perfect microcosm in which to learn about human behavior. Under the slides, a handful of kids are engaged in collaborative play, filling pails of sand, building a mini-world, destroying it, and then pretending to bring the remains to the city dump. Over at the swings, another child is playing alone, swinging on her tummy and flying as a super hero. Close by, a parent is having a tough time convincing his son that it is time to leave; what was a perfectly fun morning at the park will be ending in tears. In the middle of the playground, over by the rings, an altercation has caught your eye. A group of three kids have decided to bully an unfortunate child. One can only imagine what minor transgression set the whole thing off, but the situation is in full swing now with words, pushes, and screams. Parents helicopter in to put out the fire and begin to heap apologies on each other, explaining that they have no clue where their child learned such behavior.

This question about the origin of behavior intrigued a particular group of psychologists who believed that social learning was the primary determinant of personality and future behavior. If some individual displayed aggressive tendencies, the psychologists contended that it was because that person had been exposed to a violent environment in the past and, potentially, were rewarded for acting aggressively before. Equally, parents and other authority figures might have simply ignored the aggression or failed to punish it in a consistent or effective way. This pattern of observation, experience, and reinforcement was thought sufficient enough to set a person up for aggressive tendencies without the need for any type of intrinsic aggressive personality characteristic that would have existed at birth.

In 1961, a group of researchers led by Albert Bandura at Stanford University set out to establish the influence of social learning on behavior by exploring aggression in children. They were particularly interested in whether role models could encourage aggression without directly recognizing or punishing the children's actions. Moreover, they wanted to see if the observed aggression would transcend into a new environment, where the original role model was no longer present. The study, which has been etched into history as the "Bobo doll study," set in motion an ongoing political debate and a series of congressional hearings about the power of television and other forms of media to cause violence among children.

The researchers recruited a gaggle of 72 children from the University of Stanford Nursery School, aged between 3 and 5 years, with an even split between girls and boys. The study began by inviting each child individually into a playroom, set up with an activity table. Being the 1960s, children were given geometrical potato prints to play with and a highly colorful sticker book of animals, flowers, and western-themed characters. Forty-eight of the children encountered an adult on their journey to the playroom who was invited by the experimenter to play in the same room as the children. The adult was seated at a table at the opposite side of the room and provided an array of tinker toys, a mallet, and an inflated Bobo doll that stood at 5 feet tall.

The adult role model varied depending on the experimental condition. Half of the children witnessed a role model who acted aggressively, while the other half witnessed the adult engaged in nonaggressive play. As an additional level of complexity, half of the children were assigned an adult who was the same sex as themselves, whereas the other half had a role model of the opposite sex. Together, these experimental variables allowed the researchers to test out whether children would imitate the aggression and/or nonaggression of the role model in a novel environment, as well as whether gender differences played a part in the modeling of behavior, especially as aggression is typically seen as a masculine trait. To control for any preexisting differences in the aggression among the children, the researchers gathered ratings about their typical behavior at the nursery school, specifically how often they displayed physical aggression, verbal aggression, aggression against inanimate objects, and aggressive inhibition (whether the children had a tendency for pent-up emotions).

The adult role models acted initially the same for every child by playing with the tinker toys, but, after approximately 1 minute, the aggressive models changed tactics. The role model turned attention to the Bobo doll, turning it first on its side then sitting on it and punching it repeatedly in the nose. The role model proceeded to strike the doll in the head with the mallet, followed by tossing the doll in the air and kicking it around the room. The sequence was repeated three times to ensure that it sunk in for the observing children, whose mouths were probably wide open in shock at such unprovoked and poor behavior by an adult. Accompanying the physical aggression, the role model also laid on the verbal assaults, such as "Sock him in the nose," "Hit him down," and "Throw him in the air." There were also two nonaggressive comments used by the role model, specifically "He keeps coming back for more" and "He sure is a tough fella."

For the children assigned to the nonaggressive role model, playtime was uncomplicated. The adult continued to play with the tinker toys while the child was allowed to make potato stamps to their heart's desire. After 10 minutes, the experimenter came for the children, said goodbye to the role model, and brought the child to another game room. In this second room, the children were given a completely new set of toys to play with, which were seen as prized possessions for a 1960s child: a fire engine, train, jet fighter, cable car, spinning top, and complete doll set. The purpose of this second room was not to reward the children but rather to use the toys as a means of frustrating them and eliciting aggression. The researchers were concerned that previous research had found that witnessing a violent act tends to decrease aggression in the observer. Thus, creating some frustration would level-set the children across the experimental conditions.

To create frustration, the toys were taken away from the kids as soon as they became engrossed in play. Worse, the experimenter told them that these were the very best toys and were being reserved for some other group of special kids. The children were then ushered into a third room, one that, although in the same building, provided a sufficiently different environment for the experiment to be conducted. With all the shuffling around, the experimenter stayed in the new playroom to provide a sense of security for each child. In the room was a set of aggressive-themed toys, including an inflated 3-foot Bobo doll, a mallet and peg board, two dart guns, and a tether ball with a face on it. There was also a set of nonaggressive toys, including a tea set, crayons, a ball, three bears, two dolls, cars and trucks, and farm animals. Each child was allowed to play uninterrupted for 20 minutes before the end of the experiment. All the while, the researchers observed the children's behaviors from behind a one-way mirror.

The 20-minute play time was broken into 5-second increments during which the researchers watched and recorded the children's actions. This provided 240 opportunities for a child to be witnessed as being aggressive. The researchers watched for three forms of imitation: specifically whether the child reenacted the physical aggression, the verbal assaults ("Sock him in the nose"), or the nonaggressive statements ("He sure is a tough fella"). They also watched for partial imitation (e.g., hitting something else with the mallet rather than Bobo's head, or sitting on Bobo but not hitting him). Other aggressive acts that were not imitated were additionally recorded, such as punching Bobo, yelling at Bobo, or shooting darts at Bobo and other objects in the room. All these aggressive acts were recorded alongside nonaggressive play and, for particularly bored children, no play whatsoever.

As predicted, children who witnessed an adult role model attack Bobo were found to imitate the behavior when given a chance. The highest amount of physical imitation occurred in boys who witnessed an aggressive male role model. They copied the behavior 25.8 times on average (against a total of 240 opportunities). This was accompanied by imitation of the verbal abuse at 12.7 times on average. When the boys observed an aggressive female role model, their imitation dropped to 7.2 times for physical aggression and 2 times for verbal aggression. Girls showed a different pattern. When watching a female role model, their imitative verbal abuse was the highest of any group, at an average of 13.7 instances. Yet the male role model had a greater effect on whether girls imitated the physical abuse, at 7.2 instances rather than 5.5 instances on average with a female role model.

Beyond the directly imitative behavior, the sex of the role model influenced both partial imitation and the overall amount of aggression observed in the children. Specifically, the male role model had a significant influence on the children's behavior. Boys who observed aggressive male models scored highest, racking up 131.8 instances of aggression (55% of the total play time), as compared to boys who observed either the female role model (31% of their total play time) or no role model whatsoever (30% of their total play time). Male role models also played a part at tamping down aggression across both boys and girls. Nonaggressive male role models reduced the number of aggressive instances to 62 for boys (26% of total play time) and 8.7 for girls (4% of total play time), as compared to the girl's control group with 36.5 instances (15% of their play time).

The researchers surmised that the influence of the male role model was in part due to how aggression is widely viewed in society. Specifically, physical aggression (especially when the research was conducted) is considered a masculine trait and, therefore, the children took more notice of the male role model's behavior. Such a conclusion was strengthened by some of the spontaneous remarks of the boys who witnessed an aggressive female role model, such as "Who is that lady? That's not the way for a lady to behave," or "You should have seen what that girl did in there. She was acting like a man. I never saw a girl act like that before." This is in stark contrast to the approval shown for the aggressive male role model by both boys, "He's a good socker, he beat up Bobo. I want to sock like him," and girls, "That man is a strong fighter. . . . He's a good fighter like Daddy."

Yet this pattern of imitation fell down when considering examples of verbal aggression, where there was greater imitation of same-sex role models (girls imitated the female role models and boys imitated the male role models). Interestingly, the amount of verbal abuse shoveled at Bobo did not differ significantly between boys and girls, suggesting that this type of aggression is not linked to views of masculinity, but rather that children take their social cues based on the sex of the adult role model.

The Bobo doll study effectively demonstrated that aggressive behaviors were learned and imitated without any specific reward or punishment of behavior. Observing an aggressive role model sends a message that aggression is permissible and thereby lessens inhibitions about reacting in a similar way when frustrated. In a follow-up study, the research team explored whether the same effects would be encountered when viewing a video of a role model rather than witnessing aggressive behavior in person. They found that the live role model held more sway over children's behavior than a person on film, yet both were more powerful than a cartoon character. Yet even the cartoon produced more aggression than children exposed to either a nonaggressive role model or no role model whatsoever.

If the results of the Bobo doll study are considered more broadly than children's play, they reveal how a bullying culture can develop and thrive at work or in society. Aggression toward peers, direct reports, or even third parties (like contractors, vendors, or even customers) is learned through exposure and without any explicit training. Humans have a tendency to imitate the behavior of others and, in the absence of any direct feedback, these behaviors take on a life of their own. This is especially true for work environments where no direct confrontation or punishment occurs to put bad behavior in check. What this study shows is that ignoring aggression can be as influential as rewarding it. Role models provide a glimpse at what is acceptable in a given social environment, and their example is absorbed by the people observing them.

The implication for leaders is obvious. Staff are taking their cues from their leaders, and if the target behavior is one of aggression, then it can be anticipated that others will act aggressively. This can be expected whether that leader is being observed in person, on the phone, or through recorded media. Interestingly, the type of leader might also affect what behavior gets copied. Styles and actions that have a masculine quality are likely transferred to a greater extent by male role models, whereas other behaviors that are sex neutral are role modeled and imitated more broadly. Depending on the relative diversity of an organization, this difference between the sexes could have significant effects. Based purely on the numbers, male-dominated workplaces can be anticipated to have greater chances of imitated aggression, thus providing extra support to those who call for more diverse workplaces. More interestingly, they would also have the greatest chances of imitated nonaggression given the right set of male role models.

The Pygmalion Effect

The Bobo doll study sits at the extreme end of a continuum where interaction between the role model and a student was minimized to the greatest extent possible. Beyond saying hello in the hallway, the adult playmate had virtually no interaction with the children. The role model kept to a specific, timed script, ignoring cues from the children about whether they were paying attention or interested in the treatment of Bobo. Reality is very different, with role models and students playing off each other and giving each other feedback about how well the role model's behavior is accepted and responded to. It is easy to forget that role models, too, are looking for approval and acceptance, even if these needs are being veiled behind a confident and authoritative persona.

Recognizing the power that role models wield on learners, especially with children and young adults, Robert Rosenthal sought to explore how prior expectations held by a role model could create a self-fulfilling prophecy. Specifically, personal biases transform into covert and subtle cues that build up, unintentionally creating the exact thing that the bias was based on. Known as the *Pygmalion effect*, it got its name from the Greek sculptor Pygmalion who did such a great job at rendering a sculpture of a woman that he eventually fell in love with her. Unlike a typical portrait, the artwork preceded the subject. Also called the *experimenter expectancy effect*, this bias can have profound implications for the social sciences and is why blinded treatments of experimental groups, independent observation and scoring, and other safeguards are put in place when conducting a research study.

Rosenthal was intrigued by how teachers' expectations of their students played out in real scholastic achievement. At the time of the research, it was common practice for elementary school teachers to receive their students' general IQ scores beginning in the first grade. Despite plenty of criticism about what IQ is and how important it is for success in life, IQ is one of the most persistent and profound concepts in psychology. Even if a teacher disagreed with the notion of IQ, it would be hard for him or her to ignore the test score, especially if it could provide useful information about whether a student would likely struggle with a topic. Rosenthal suspected that a relatively benign use of IQ to help students in need was only one possible scenario and instead believed that teachers were applying the information more widely. Against their best attempts to maintain fairness in how they allocated time or recognized achievement, Rosenthal thought it was inevitable that bias would creep into teacher behaviors toward students.

Partnering with Lenore Jacobson at the South San Francisco Unified School District, the researchers administered a measure of IQ called the Tests of General Ability to all children attending a single elementary school in a large town of primarily lower middle-class families. The test was largely independent of school-learned skills in writing, reading, or arithmetic and measured general verbal and reasoning ability. It was also a lesser known test and therefore provided a better cover for the experiment. The school's 18 teachers (16 women and 2 men) were told that the test was called the Harvard Test of Inflected Acquisition and could predict which students would likely experience a period of blooming in the coming academic year due to enhanced learning abilities.

The school was divided up by grade into first through sixth grades. Within each grade, the children were assigned one of three classrooms depending on their scholastic achievement (above average, average, or below average). In each of the classrooms, the experimenters chose 20% of the students at random to make up the experimental condition. The teachers of these students were told that they scored highly on the test and would undergo substantial intellectual gains during the upcoming academic year. Nothing more differentiated the children in the experiment—just the simple labeling of a specific set of children as special.

At the end of the academic year, all the children were retested with the same test battery to see what actually happened. Since all the children were starting from different places, not only in terms of test scores from the first administration but also in their level of academic achievement, a change score was created for each student. The score from the retest was compared to the initial test score to provide an indication of progress, which in turn was used to compare whether children randomly designated as special would outperform their peers. The results were striking. The children randomly designated as special showed the greatest improvement in test scores. Children who teachers anticipated to bloom during the academic year did indeed grow 12.2 points in their IQ, as compared against an 8.4-point improvement for the rest of the children. The change was also more widespread. Approximately 80% of the special children showed improvement against approximately 50% from the control group.

It is important to note that the children themselves were never explicitly told how they scored on the test, yet the effects were found nonetheless. The effects were most marked for the youngest children, those attending first and second grades. In one of the first-grade classrooms, the special children gained 24.8 points (recall that the overall jump for special children was 12.2 points). More than twice the number of special children than the control group gained 20 IQ points, while more than four times the number of special children gained 30 IQ points. Digging deeper into the results to ensure the purity of their study, the researchers explored any potential side effects caused by differences between teachers or the way the retest was conducted. The researchers were pleased to see a positive correlation between gains made by special children and the control children within the same classroom, meaning that teachers who had the greatest positive effect on test scores did so universally with all their students.

To explain the greater gains by young children, the researchers proposed that both the teacher and the student played a role. Specifically, a student's reputation in the school may not be as concrete with younger children because teachers would not have had as much time to form an opinion about each child's ability. This would likely have made the test scores more meaningful and believable for the teachers. Additionally, the way that teachers communicate to younger children (e.g., giving more frequent and consistent encouragement) might open up the possibilities for greater influence. Switching to the child's role, younger children might be more susceptible to their teachers' influence and react more strongly to their cues about personal capability. Additionally, younger children may pay more attention to the social cues given by their teachers, looking for subtler signs of approval and encouragement.

Follow-up research on Rosenthal's original design recorded how teachers' expectations of intellectual capability transcended into cues that resulted in real differences in achievement. Videos of teacher–student interactions discovered that the teachers acted in consistent and subtle ways. Teachers interacting with special students smiled more, made more eye contact, and reacted more favorably to the students' comments in class. In turn, the special students were more likely to report enjoying school and working harder on their studies, creating the exact difference set in motion by the teachers' expectations. Explicit changes in the amount of time or quality of instruction provided to the special children were not necessary for the teachers to have lasting effects on their students' scholastic achievement.

The implications for Rosenthal's research are profound. Expectations of others, whether grounded in reality or completely fabricated, will change our behavior in ways that are nearly impossible to control. Our nonverbal behaviors slip out and communicate who we like and dislike, even if our conscious actions are telling a different story. When mixed together with social stereotypes on characteristics like gender, ethnicity, or age, a host of social mechanisms are put in motion that create the exact situations that our values toward fairness and objectivity aim to avoid. Late in his career, Rosenthal reviewed all the subsequent studies on expectancies, finding that the Pygmalion effect was alive and well across contexts: "the expectations of psychological researchers, classroom teachers, judges in the courtroom, business executives, and health care providers can unintentionally affect the responses of their research participants, pupils, jurors, employees, and patients."

Specific to the workplace, employee reputation can make or break a career. This reputation could include characteristics ranging from the quality of their work to how easy they are to work with or their level of capability. For example, if an employee fails to deliver a good-quality product, even if caused by factors outside of his or her personal control, he or she might be branded as a poor performer. Coworkers might begin to avoid approaching the employee to take part in special projects or to hoard highly prized customer accounts, reducing the number of opportunities to only those projects or customers that no one else wants. Now dealt with a trickier workload, the cards are stacked against the employee, creating a vicious self-fulfilling prophecy of failure. A similar pattern can occur with personal interactions. If an expectation is set that both coworkers are a pleasure to work with, they will likely start their interaction openly, setting them down a path for a productive relationship.

Such expectancy effects are more pronounced for new employees, where one's reputation outpaces any truly observable performance (much like the first- and second-graders in Rosenthal's research). Either new to the organization or fresh to a work team, managers and colleagues will search for cues about what to expect from each other and will likely rely on any available data points to help guide their interaction. Thanks to a world filled with social media, a snapshot of a future colleague or customer can be found in minutes, thus opening the door to a self-fulfilling prophecy about how much we share in common and whether we will value their skills and experience or enjoy in their company. Potentially more dangerous are the labels that organizations provide to their star employees, designating them as either High Potentials or Most Valued Employees. Over years of carrying such a designation, organizations tend to forget the original context behind the employee's success. Often personal performance has as much to do with being in the right place at the right time as it does with any unique employee trait. Yet with the inordinate attention and resources given to High Potentials, a virtuous self-fulfilling prophecy is put in place that will make good on the employee's status as someone special.

All Eyes on the Leader

There is a constant exchange between individuals and the social environment that surrounds them. Cues are given and received about what constitutes socially desirable behavior and at times can conflict with each other or bump up against established cultural norms. In the case of Uber, Kalanick's words and actions gave the impression that treating women differently than men was absolutely fine and potentially could even score bonus points in the bro culture that permeated the company. Wide-scale sexual harassment prevailed, with Human Resources and fellow male employees turning a blind eye to the plights of female colleagues. They might have known that sexual harassment was occurring, but it was easier to think of each incident as episodic rather than accept that the company culture itself was toxic.

In many ways, the scale of Uber's misconduct is predictable. The combination of a male-dominated company with a high-stakes, high-reward culture paves the path toward devaluing women and encouraging sexual harassment. Following the script laid down by psychologists, Kalanick and his leadership team acted as role models for aggressive behavior. Even without directly sanctioning sexual harassment, employees were able to observe Kalanick's words and actions to see what would be punished or rewarded. It is also worthwhile to note that verbal and physical harassment, like the physical aggression shown with the Bobo dolls, is amplified by male role models. With only 15% of key positions held by women, Uber's story plays directly into what we know about imitation: specifically, that physically aggressive behavior is best demonstrated by male role models.

Such overt role modeling is not the only way to change employee behavior. Rosenthal demonstrated that subtle cues, like eye contact and listening more intently, slip out from authority figures and can set in motion a self-fulfilling prophecy. High-potential employees develop into strong performers simply because they are given cues that they are special. Equally, poor performers can develop from continual messaging about their inadequacies. In this way, women who cut their teeth in a male-dominated vocation like IT can face undue challenges simply because of the social stereotypes surrounding gender differences in engineering and technology. The Pygmalion effect is in part to blame for the demographic imbalances experienced by Uber and across the high-tech industry. Girls interested in a scientific or engineering career may begin to doubt their ability simply due to the subtle cues sent by the authority figures around them. Teachers may send inadvertent cues to the boys while a lack of visible female role models might indicate that scientific or engineering jobs are not desirable for girls. In turn, these cues set up a chain reaction in which girls either become disinterested in the subject matter or doubt their abilities, which can lead to a failure to recover from setbacks or undue caution in trying something new. Direct discrimination like that experienced in Uber is not necessary to create a bro culture. Women may simply self-select out of it.

In all the preceding discussion, the focus has been on the negative consequences of role models and imitation of a leader's behavior. It is easy to forget the positive effects that the nonaggressive male role model had on Bandura's children. Equally, positive expectations by leaders about their subordinates can create a virtuous self-fulfilling prophecy that pushes individuals to excel. Leaders thus have great power to shape a culture, regardless of what type of culture it ends up being. When Dara Khosrowshahi became CEO of Uber in 2017, he pledged to turn the company around with his personal motto of "do the right thing." He then proceeded to replace members of the executive team, eliminated mandatory arbitration provisions, tied executive compensation to diversity goals, and increased transparency into how well the company was addressing ongoing safety and harassment concerns. Despite these actions and spending half a billion dollars on marketing, the reputational damage of Uber's bro culture seems unflappable. Customers appear reticent to return to Uber, with the company's main rival, Lyft, estimated to have doubled its market share since 2017. Uber drew a line under the crisis in late 2019, by settling with the Equal Employment Opportunity Commission, which "found reasonable cause to believe that Uber permitted a culture of sexual harassment and retaliation." A $4.4 million fund was created to pay current and future victims of sexual harassment while at work. Uber also agreed to be monitored for 3 years to safeguard any future transgressions. With Travis Kalanick's influence on the company fading away and the emergence of a very different leadership style in Dara Khosrowshahi, only time will tell whether Uber's cutting-edge technology can move beyond its bro culture and deliver on its promise to "ignite opportunity by setting the world in motion."

2
Connection

After grabbing your drink, you head to last available table at the local coffee shop. Not long after sitting down, the conversation of the two people next to you grabs your attention. You normally avoid eaves-dropping, but their discussion has an awkward mixture of friendliness, formality, and power. It quickly becomes obvious that this is no ordinary casual conversation between two friends, but rather an annual performance review with a manager who is attempting to reset a troubled relationship with a direct report. Work has not been great for the two of them; the employee has missed client deadlines, shows up late, and is in free-fall from the good graces of his coworkers.

The manager initially dances around these concerns, fishing around for the reasons behind the noticeable change in performance from the prior year. They talk about how the employee seems to avoid attempts by coworkers to help, preferring to work independently and ignoring professional standards for peer reviews of his client work. Equally, the employee has not offered to support anyone else in recent memory, despite expectations for a collaborative team environment.

The conversation is going nowhere, and the employee's one-word responses are starting to visibly irritate the manager. Frustration builds up to the point where the manager deviates from the facts and launches into a personal attack over a client meeting last week. The conversation is going badly now as the employee becomes defensive and blames someone named Barbara in production. The manager lets go with a slip of the tongue, providing the employee a glimpse of the lack of personal respect the manager holds for him. Abruptly, the manager stands up, closes the meeting with a stern warning, and walks away just in time to miss the smirk that appears on the employee's face. The lack of respect was mutual.

Maybe it was the employee's tendency to close down under stress rather than seeking help that first caused the breakdown in the relationship. Alternatively, it could have been the awkward balance between criticism and praise by the manager that led to the employee's defensiveness and then the manager's contempt. Either way, what this short vignette illustrates is that

Punching the Clock. Joe Ungemah, Oxford University Press (2021). © Oxford University Press.
DOI: 10.1093/oso/9780190061241.003.0002.

there is a lot more that goes on behind the scenes in every personal relationship, and, if the roles could be understood, the path to a complete breakdown might be avoided.

A Strange Situation

Our interest in and ability to hold deep relationships with others originate early in life, stemming from our very first relationships. As babies begin to explore the world around them, they look to their primary caregivers for both comfort and encouragement. Whether or not they feel capable and confident to move about their environment depends in part on the relationships that they have formed with the people who are best able to look after them and protect them from danger. The power of these early relationships extends far beyond the toddler years, into childhood and adulthood, by putting in place patterns of expectations and behavior that define how an individual engages with others. In fact, it was observing two older children at a school for maladjusted children that led John Bowlby to begin questioning how a baby's relationship with his or her mother could imprint itself on future relationships. The theory that he created, supported by the experimental work of Mary Ainsworth, confirmed the power of early parental relationships on an individual's ability to effectively engage in all sorts of social relationships.

Support for attachment theory came initially from observations of the real world. Bowlby focused on the fallout created when parents were separated from their children, which was both undeniable and easily recognized. Mary Ainsworth took a slightly different path, taking advantage of her family's relocation to Uganda in 1953 to embark on some opportunistic field research. Ainsworth set out to observe infant–mother interactions at home, enlisting 26 families to be observed every 2 weeks for 2 hours per visit for up to 9 months. What Ainsworth was looking for were cues about maternal sensitivity to infant needs and the resulting patterns of infant behavior. Specifically, she noticed that mothers who were perceived as more sensitive to their baby's needs had children who cried less and were more content to explore the environment around them. Ainsworth built on these foundations in her second observational study, this time in Baltimore. In 1963, Ainsworth recruited 26 families who had yet to give birth, asking them to participate in 18 home visits that ended just before the child's fifth birthday. Each visit lasted 4 hours, during which Ainsworth relied on observing the family going about their normal routine.

Evident in the data was a pattern of behavior between mother and baby during the first 3 months that, once formed, remained consistent and stable. Mothers differed strongly on how well they reacted to their baby's needs in terms of noticing a need, finding the appropriate response, and resolving it promptly. Across feeding and playing, some mothers worked in unison with their babies, orchestrating their moves like a well-rehearsed dance. For example, when engaged in play, these mothers would watch and adjust their behavior to elicit rounds of bouncing, smiling, and cooing from the babies, whereas other mothers were out of sync with their babies, resulting in stunted sessions. Similar to what she discovered in Uganda, good maternal sensitivity led to less crying and greater exploration.

To build the scientific case for what was becoming known as *attachment theory*, Ainsworth set up the Strange Situation experiment. The experiment aimed to create the ideal conditions to study the balance between exploration and security. The situation unfolded across eight episodes with a fixed order across all participants, with most episodes lasting 3 minutes. Mother and baby pairs individually entered a room with an open floor space that measured approximately 9 feet square. At one end of the room was a child's chair and toys. On the other side of the room was a chair for the mother, as well as a chair that was reserved for a stranger. Upon entering, the child was placed in the middle of the floor facing the toys and allowed to play as he or she wished. Episode 1 lasted approximately 30 seconds and involved an experimenter providing an introduction to the study. The experimenter left the room, which initiated Episode 2. The mother sat in the chair and held back from participating with her baby. For his or her part, the baby was allowed to play. Episode 3 saw the introduction of a woman (the stranger), who entered the room and sat opposite to the mother. The stranger initially sat quietly in her chair, then conversed briefly with the mother, followed by approaching the baby to engage in play.

The mother then got up from her chair and left the room, initiating Episode 4. Depending on the reaction of the child, the stranger would either leave the child alone or encourage him or her to explore and play. In those instances where the child completely broke down, the episode was cut short from the allotted 3 minutes. Episode 5 saw the reunion of the baby with his or her mother. The mother came to the doorway and paused to allow a spontaneous response by the child. Once inside, the mother encouraged the child to explore the toys again. First the stranger, then the mother slipped out of the room for Episode 6 (with the mother saying a quick "bye-bye" to ensure the baby knew he or she was being left alone), allowing the child to play. The stranger re-entered in Episode 7 and would vary her behavior depending on what the child was doing. The experiment ended with Episode 8, closing with a second reunion between mother and child.

Across all episodes, the situation was purposely adjusted to continually tip the balance in favor of either exploration or security. The baby's behavior was watched intently to see how he or she reacted to both the stranger and an empty room, as well as how closely he or she sought security from his or her mother. Behind a one-way mirror, two observers dictated a narrative of what they witnessed, set to a 15-second timer. Initially, 23 pairs of mothers and their babies took part in the laboratory study. They were also observed at home, with visits lasting approximately 4 hours and occurring every 3 weeks. To bolster their findings, a second group of participants was added to the study, involving 33 mother–baby pairs; unlike the original group, these participants were not observed at home.

The researchers looked over the data and attempted to find evidence for how babies interacted with their mothers. Specifically, they looked for and classified examples of where babies either sought or avoided proximity with their mothers as well as whether they wished to maintain or break off contact. Moreover, they evaluated the strength of these behaviors. For example, running across a room was seen as different in intensity to reaching an arm out for his or her mother. Additionally, the experimenters documented examples of distress (crying and searching for the mother) and exploration of the toys or the room.

At odds in the Strange Situation was the baby's conflicting needs of seeking protection and comfort against exploring and learning about the environment. In response to the Strange Situation, Ainsworth found evidence for three primary ways babies cope with this conflict. Group A (sometimes referred to as Insecure Avoidant) tended to show little or no interest in seeking proximity with their mothers. Such babies do not cling or resist being put down and, in some situations, snub their mother's attempt to connect. They are equally nonchalant with the stranger. If they show distress, it is when they are left completely alone. Group B (sometimes referred to as Secure) react warmly to the reunification with their mothers, with a tossup of whether they cry or smile at seeing their mother return. They show clear interest in both proximity and contact with their mothers and find the loss of the mother more concerning than simply being left alone. In regard to the stranger, they show clear preference for interacting with their mothers rather than with the stranger. Group C (sometimes referred to as Insecure Resistant) was much more varied in its composition, held together by a range of maladaptive behavior. Babies in this group either failed to explore the situation or did so begrudgingly, not enjoying the play they were engaged in. What held them in common was an awkward connection to their mothers.

Across the participants, Group B had the largest representation, with 66% of the babies falling within this group. Group A and Group C had 20% and 14%, respectively. When behaviors in the lab were compared to the home environment, a fair degree of congruence was seen, indicating that the experiment was a fair approximation of what naturally occurs. Babies who had the smoothest attachment-exploration dynamic at home reacted warmly to reunions in the strange situation. At home, these babies use their mother as a base from which to explore the environment around them and are not overly concerned about everyday separations. In contrast, home environments where baby–mother interactions were disjointed create a degree of anxiety within the child that gets expressed as heightened proximity and contact seeking as well as a low threshold for separation. Home environments where there is clearly a lack of connection between mother and child manifests itself with the avoidance of interaction across situations and a high degree of independence. These children would absorb themselves in play to fill the void left behind by the lack of parental responsiveness.

The implications of Ainsworth's research extend far beyond the participants she studied. The type of attachment a child had with his or her caregiver, whether secure, inconsistent, or nonexistent, frames up a self-concept that is remarkably stable across a person's lifetime. Securely attached children believe that they have a home base to return to when times get tough or confusing. This is not the case for those children who cannot predict their parents' reaction; sometimes they will end up OK and at other times they will be on their own. Such inconsistency can cause frustration and anger. Those latch-key children with no established connections may feel unloved and rejected, leading to a tendency to avoid social interaction.

The behavioral patterns established in childhood play a part in defining the way we interact as adults and how we form a broad range of social relationships. An individual's history of building and sustaining relationships transforms into working models that define expectations and shape the behaviors exhibited to others. Secure adults find it easy to get close to others, are comfortable depending on others for support, happily provide support to others, and do not generally worry about being accepted or being alone. These adults generally report higher self-confidence and greater satisfaction with their relationships. In contrast, insecure adults who may have had inconsistent experiences in their past tend to report that they want to get close to others but often fail to do so. They may feel undervalued and seek out a greater degree of intimacy, approval, and responsiveness from those around them, becoming highly dependent on those who show support. These adults often report greater anxiety and self-doubt as a result of not perceiving that they have a home base.

Avoidant behavior takes two discreet forms for adults. Individuals can become dismissive of relationships, believing that independence and self-sufficiency are values to live by and thus avoid dependence on or to others. They generally seek less intimacy, hide inner feelings, and report that they are invulnerable to rejection. A second group of adults are more fearful of connection than dismissive. These individuals have mixed emotions about relationships. On one hand, they seek out connections with others, yet, on the other hand, they are fearful that they will be hurt if they rely on or trust others. Like their dismissive counterparts, these adults tend to hide their emotions (which are generally full of negative self-views) and avoid forming relationships.

Whether secure, resistant, or avoidant, how individuals think and feel about relationships will influence the connection they share with others both in and out of the workplace. Whether or not an employee will trust his or her peers, seek the support of a manager, show empathy to a direct report, or engage in collaborative work all stems from the working models established during childhood. This does not mean that individuals are stuck in a particular behavioral pattern but rather that they approach relationships from an established perspective that might require extra support or signs of trust to overcome. As the workplace evolves, with a continuous pattern of establishing and then breaking down relationships, secure individuals will likely navigate the modern workplace more successfully. Avoiding a new team or dismissing the need to establish rapport and collaborate are likely maladaptive ways of working in the gig economy. Secure colleagues can play a meaningful role in helping their resistant or avoidant workmates. Instead of writing them off as unfriendly or rude, simply recognizing that each person comes to work with a different set of assumptions about relationships can go a long way to building understanding, patience, and a more inclusive workplace.

In 15 Minutes

What if someone could tell you the day before your wedding the chances that your marriage would end in divorce? Is this information you would want to know? How certain would they have to be before you began reconsidering your options? Would it be better that, instead of divorce, they gave you an indication of how happy you would be? Scarily enough, there are a group of researchers who are able to predict the outcomes of marriage (whether ending in divorce, a fulfilling relationship, or mutual discontent) with greater than 80% accuracy from a mere 15 minutes of observation.

Welcome to the Love Lab, the nickname given to the laboratory of John Gottman at the University of Washington. His work on couples began in 1989, when he first began recruiting newlywed couples from the Puget Sound area in Washington. Gottman initially recruited by newspaper ads, looking for couples who had married for the first time in the last 6 months and were childless. Couples who responded to the ads were phone screened and then sent a questionnaire that captured demographic information and perceptions about their marriage, well-being, and health. From the 179 initial couples who passed the phone screen on eligibility, 130 newlyweds were chosen, representing the full range of marital satisfaction and an approximation of the ethnic mix living in the Seattle area at the time.

Every year, the marital status of the couples and their satisfaction was measured. After 6 years, the couples were invited to the laboratory for an in-depth look at their relationship. In that time, Gottman learned that 17 of 130 couples had divorced, with an average of 3 years before the divorces occurred. The remaining couples were to go under the microscope at the Love Lab, where each of their interactions was recorded and picked apart by a group of psychologists. Using split screens of footage taken of husbands interacting with their wives, the facial expressions, vocal tones, and speech were analyzed second by second and coded into 16 categories. Five positive responses were searched for (interest, validation, affection, humor, and joy), as were 10 negative responses (disgust, contempt, belligerence, domineering, anger, fear/tension, defensiveness, whining, sadness, and stonewalling) and a single neutral response category. Each couple was watched by two independent psychologists to ensure accuracy; these psychologists agreed with each other on average 90% of the time.

When the couples arrived at the Love Lab, each spouse was asked to complete a questionnaire that probed into potential areas of disagreement, such as the in-laws, finances, and intimacy. For each conflict area, the participant was asked to rate the severity of the disagreement on a scale from 0 to 100, with top scores indicating that the issue was very important. The experimenter reviewed the completed questionnaires and utilized their content to help the couple choose a topic to discuss openly for 15 minutes. During the interaction, a variety of measurements were taken. Beyond the video recording, physiological measures were taken by polygraph, and self-ratings were captured from participants who adjusted a dial about how positive or negative they were feeling at that particular moment during the experiment. At the completion of the 15-minute interaction, the participants were required to watch the video footage from the session and independently rate their own behavior and their spouse's reactions.

The experiments attacked the data by looking for predictive patterns in how the newlyweds played off each other. They were specifically looking for evidence to support a variety of different hypotheses about why relationships go wrong. Contrary to conventional wisdom about relationships, the amount of anger held by husband or wife did not predict either divorce rate or overall happiness. Despite its ugliness, flying off the handle with anger does not predict how successful a marriage will be and can in fact vary considerably from culture to culture. Instead, the accumulation of high-intensity negative emotions (such as belligerence, defensiveness, and contempt) eat away at marital stability, as can a combination of low-intensity negative emotions (like whining, sadness, disgust, fear, or stonewalling) if exhibited specifically by wives.

In the heat of the moment, Gottman was surprised by just how bad both husbands and wives were at listening to their partners. At the outset of the experiment, the researchers were keen to find instances where either the husband or wife showed signs of active listening, as defined by taking interest in the other's grievance and using affection, humor, or validation as a way to ease the tension. On average, the participants were dreadful at active listening, spending less than half of 1% of the entire interaction attempting to listen to their spouse and empathize with them. With such scant evidence, it was impossible for the researchers to know whether active listening would have been effective at resolving the marital conflict. Instead, Gottman found a sequence of events that could accurately predict the stability of relationships.

Once on a negative path, some couples fail to stop things from escalating out of control, leading to a complete meltdown in the marriage. In prior research, Gottman discovered that 96% of conversations that started negatively failed to turn around into something more positive. As such, the start-up of a disagreement is critical to predicting its result. If a complaint is softened or raised on neutral footing, there would be a much greater chance that the interaction would turn out OK. Confirming earlier observations, women play a vital role in how disagreements are vented, both in starting the conversation and setting the tone. If a wife consistently raises complaints, the couple would be at a heightened risk of divorce. Interestingly, husbands' complaints had little to no bearing on a couple's chances for divorce. Rather, it was how he responded to the wife's criticism that mattered. Men who perceive the complaint as an attack fail to deescalate the situation, adding fuel to the fire.

From there, the ball is back in the wife's court. If she allows negativity to build, the marriage will go from bad to worse. It is not the high-intensity emotions that matter, but rather the low-intensity ones like sadness or disgust. Interaction upon interaction, bad times begin to accumulate and throw a couple's chances of stability into the air. Gottman discovered that stable couples spent significantly less time mirroring each other's negativity, and the key to this rested firmly with the husband. Instead of reciprocating the negativity, men in stable relationships were able to self-sooth by letting the criticisms fall off their backs. Men who were unable to let go were more likely to find themselves in broken relationships.

Up until this point, the discussion has focused on whether couples remain together, rather than how happy they are within their relationships. Happy couples are said to show agreement and approval, engage in humor and laughing, and show fondness through physical contact and smiling. Distressed couples show these signs approximately 25% less than their more satisfied peers. When Gottman analyzed the pattern of behaviors exhibited by the couples participating in his study, a striking difference was found for the stable, happy couples as compared to either those who divorced or were unhappily married. Only in the happy couples did the process of de-escalation lead to positive feelings toward each other. Through the resolution of conflict, the couples regained their affection for each other. For the others, de-escalation put a pause on the negativity that continued to fester until a future flare-up.

Overall, Gottman found a pattern of behavior that was able to predict with 82.5% accuracy the couples who divorced. A dance was discovered that began with wives starting up conflict, which was either magnified or quelled by the husband's acceptance of his wife's influence. If the conflict was allowed to persist, unhappy or divorced women allowed the negativity to fester and eat away at their relationships. Men played a vital part, too, by de-escalating the conflict through self-soothing. Above and beyond the dance, whether or not the couple grew in affection after resolving the conflict determined the relative happiness of married couples. Adding this element to his model, Gottman was able to predict marital satisfaction with a near equal level of accuracy. As a side note, wives who effectively use humor also help create a happy and stable marriage.

Beyond the power of Gottman's model to predict the success of relationships, there are a few other notable findings that have ramifications for relationships in general, in and out of the workplace. First, the participants did not naturally use active listening to understand and react to each other, thus raising concern that the technique might backfire due to a natural lack of skill. Active listening works by confronting issues head-on but relies on the listener to identify the core issue and explore it objectively, without bias or judgment. Without practice or guidance, there is a chance that the technique will simply increase the tension and negativity of the moment, getting in the way of what would have otherwise been de-escalation. Instead of jumping into active listening without the proper support, it might be better to focus on techniques that attack the other elements of Gottman's model, such as raising personal awareness about how much criticism is being lobbed at others, opening up to influence, learning how to break down long-term negativity in the relationship (soon to be discussed), or self-soothing.

Another core finding was the downhill trajectory that failing relationships followed. Instead of bouncing back and forth between positive and negative states, failed relationships ate away at their initial high level of satisfaction, never to return to where they started. Troubled relationships did not operate like a bank account where deposits and withdrawals are made, but rather acted like a trust fund where cash is depleted from an inheritance over time. The pattern is different for successful relationships, which somehow end up better off after a resolved conflict, with both partners feeling more positive about themselves and each other. In a work context, creating relationships that grow stronger through conflict and adversity may be a stretch. However, correctly identifying those in a downward spiral might save both manager and employee from months or years of mutual frustration. Recognizing that a relationship will simply not resolve itself and taking action to separate (e.g., through reassignment) might be the best way for both parties to improve their satisfaction at work.

Last, recognizing that openness to influence is an issue of personal power provides a potential mechanism for stopping the decay in relationships. Instead of forcibly trying to change someone outright, an approach that softens the level of criticism and recognizes the vulnerability of the other person in accepting change will likely have better results. For those resistant to change, confrontation only ramps up their natural tendency to preserve personal control and autonomy. In the workplace, managers must be astute observers of employees, looking for insight as to whether their employees are open or resistant to feedback. If the latter, a skilled manager will find a way to improve performance in concert with preserving an employee's control over his or her work. For sensitive employees, preserving power is just as important as the desired change if the relationship is to last.

Despite Gottman's impressive findings, his research has not gone without criticism. Specifically, the predictive power of the experimental design to identify troubled relationships has been challenged. Instead of studying newlyweds right after marriage and tracking their stability and happiness over time, Gottman looked backward at the data, knowing how well the story ended for each of the couples. The pattern of happy and stable relationships was not so much a prediction of what would happen to couples but instead a diagnosis of what did happen in the relationships post hoc. A truer study would have been to set up the variables up front, classify the couples into one of three groups (divorced, happily married, and unhappily married), and study whether these predictions were right. As is, Gottman's research effectively tells us the backstory for the relationships he studied, but it takes a leap of faith to say that these same rules would apply for every other couple out there.

Some researchers are simply not satisfied to take this leap of faith and are probably right to assume that a true predictive model would not be as successful as what Gottman reports. Nevertheless, the research findings provide a glimpse into how relationship can go wrong and, even without replication, give us food for thought on the roles we each play when caught in a downward spiral.

A Magic Ratio and the Four Horsemen

When Gottman and his team watched couples interact in the Love Lab, he noticed that certain couples were plagued by an imbalance in how much positive affection they showed each other. When conflict surfaced, they got stuck in negativity and ultimately never found a way back to showing affection for each other. Across the total observed time, Gottman and his team found a "magic ratio" that, for every negative moment, healthy relationships would be counterbalanced with five positive moments. The ratio is very different for couples who ended up in divorce, whose ratio was reversed: roughly four negative interactions for every three positive interactions. The unbalanced nature of this ratio between positive to negative interactions is startling. Saying sorry or doing something nice for the other person does not go nearly far enough to undo the damage done by a single negative interaction.

Restoring the ratio does not need to wait but rather can be made up during the heat of the moment. Gottman states, "When the masters of marriage are talking about something important, they may be arguing, but they are also laughing and teasing and there are signs of affection because they have made emotional connections." As noted earlier, showing anger does not necessarily damage the relationship but rather counts as a negative interaction if accompanied by criticism, contempt, or defensiveness. Body language does count toward the ratio, with signs such as eye rolling conveying as much as some poorly chosen words. What is probably most indicative of whether an interaction will count as a positive or negative is how the conflict begins. When a moment of conflict arises, struggling couples tend to have a harsh start-up, where a disagreement begins with criticism or sarcasm. Once rolling, the chances that a disagreement will turn positive drop to just 4% if nothing happens in the first 3 minutes.

A poor ratio is characterized by four specific types of negative interactions. So bad and predictable were these traits that Gottman nicknamed them the "Four Horsemen," in reference to the Four Horsemen of the Apocalypse. They include criticism, contempt, defensiveness, and stonewalling, usually popping up in that specific order. Each of the Four Horsemen has the potential to flood the relationship with negativity, leaving one or both partners shell-shocked with emotion. Over time, the combination of harsh start-ups and the relentless negativity of the Four Horsemen pile up until the marriage falls apart.

As the first Horseman, criticism is characterized by a personal attack of an individual's character. It is different from a complaint, which focuses on the outward behavior of the person. For example, a husband could complain that his partner is not listening, which is different from saying that he thinks his partner is selfish for not listening. When criticizing, the emphasis changes to an abstraction about the other person's character, across situations and contexts. It does not take into account the reasons for the behavior and tends to assume that the trait is inherent and not likely to change. When a partner criticizes, it works to dismantle the person at the core, causing the other person to feel assaulted, rejected, and hurt. Moreover, criticism will likely close down the other individual, put him or her on the back foot, reduce problem-solving, and take away his or her ability to empathize.

The second Horseman of defensiveness comes right off the heels of criticism. When backed into a corner, people will pop into self-preservation mode, rejecting what they hear with "righteous indignation or innocent victimhood" to ward off personal attacks. They are looking for a way, any way, to get their partner to back off. Yet the tactic doesn't diffuse the conflict at all, but simply redirects the negativity back on the accuser, escalating the whole situation further. Moreover, acting defensively sends the message that the individual's complaint is not being taken seriously and that his or her opinion, even if unjust, doesn't matter. With defensiveness, the fire is left burning, with no solution to the conflict in sight.

Eventually the negativity builds to outright contempt for the other person, which is the third Horseman. Partners begin to feel that they are superior to their spouse, changing their word choice to show sarcasm and cynicism. Interactions might turn juvenile, with the use of name-calling, eye-rolling, sneering, or mockery. Humor might take a nasty turn, putting the other as the punchline of every joke. In sum, contempt occurs when couples are disgusted with each other and experimenting with just how mean they can be toward each other. With such raw emotion, it is no wonder that Gottman found contempt to be the number one predictor of divorce across his research. He found that when couples are in a state of contempt, each partner suffers physically, emotionally, and psychologically. They even have higher rates of infectious illnesses, like flu and colds. Contempt is fueled by long-running disagreements that cause consistent and frequent negative thoughts about each other. There is no way that contempt does anything but destroy the relationship, and, over time, it sets up the last of the four Horsemen.

Married couples get to a point where they just cannot take any more negativity and they withdraw from each other, as a form of stonewalling. Feeling overwhelmed, an individual closes out the other person to stop the flood of negative emotion, rather than confronting the issue. Someone engaged in stonewalling is characteristically unresponsive. He or she might act busy or engage in obsessive behavior, but does nothing to respond to or react to his or her partner. For the spouse, he or she will likely feel frustrated and angry that his or her complaints are being completely ignored. With enough negativity, the spouse will likely check out of the relationship, feeling absolutely spent (psychologically and emotionally).

The good news about Gottman's research is that knowing how the Four Horsemen operate creates the opportunity to stop and potentially reverse their effects. The first takeaway from Gottman's research is to not allow the conflict to spiral out of control. The Horsemen act in a cumulative fashion and set up the context for a marriage to hit free fall. When the first signs of criticism start showing their ugly heads, changing the dynamic and restoring the magic ratio must be a priority. As shown in his studies, the odds are against a couple once the negativity train has left the station.

To deal with the first Horseman of criticism, couples are encouraged to learn how to complain without blame. Specifically, each partner should feel comfortable sharing openly if he or she is feeling upset in the relationship, but hold back from blaming the other person as the sole source of frustration. Partners should attempt to raise issues objectively, using the first-person pronoun to describe what they are feeling and attempting to show the intention behind the complaint. For example, instead of saying something like "You always make me feel foolish in front of our friends," the alternative could work: "I felt uncomfortable just now, as I forgot their kids' names. Next time, please help me out." As the person being complained to, partners should also attempt to remain objective and actively listen to the other individual by asking questions, showing curiosity in what is driving the other person's emotions, nodding, and restating his or her concerns.

If things do escalate to personal attacks being lobbed at each other, there are ways to repair the situation and avoid the second Horseman of defensiveness. Recognizing the complaint for what it is and attempting to look at the situation from the other's perspective can help diffuse the situation. Showing empathy, even if you don't agree entirely with the other's perspective, can go a long way to building back a feeling of partnership, as will recognizing that feelings have been hurt. Where possible, accept responsibility for the situation and steer the conversation back toward areas of agreement. Creating a sense of teamwork by recognizing that both people are not having fun and building off easy fixes can create momentum toward resolving the really contentious issues.

Unlike the previous two Horsemen, undoing contempt requires much more preparation and cannot be easily fixed in the heat of the moment. The recommended way to fight contempt is to build a culture of appreciation and respect. Partners should intentionally show appreciation for each other, whether remembering positive memories or drawing attention to admirable traits, on a consistent and frequent basis. Such actions demonstrate that the other person matters and that his or her interests are prioritized above oneself. During conflict, small signs of affection can help demonstrate that although the current situation is tough, both partners are ultimately on the same team and will find a way through the hardship.

When signs of the fourth Horseman arise, partners must stop the situation from exploding into stonewalling. Both individuals have a responsibility to recognize when one party is feeling emotionally flooded and to call for a timeout, with the intent of letting emotions cool off before the couple attempts to discuss the topic again. During the timeout, it is imperative that the partners think of something other than the conflict, as thinking self-righteous thoughts can amplify the tension. Gottman experimentally showed the benefits of a break during conflict. After 15 minutes of heated debate, Gottman misled some of his participants by informing them that he needed to adjust his recording equipment. He instructed them not to interact, but to pick up a magazine and read until it was time to start again. After 30 minutes, Gottman reconvened the couples and found that much of the tension had gone away. The resulting conversations were noticeably more positive and productive.

Although Gottman's research concentrated on married couples, the implications extend across a wide variety of relationships. As applied to the workplace, the methods and techniques he discovered could apply equally well to peer or hierarchical (boss and direct report) relationships. The most direct implication is the tendency for negativity to escalate in a poisoned relationship, as well as a need to maintain the magic ratio of positive to negative interactions. Other universal messages include the ability to complain without blame, listen objectively, switch from judgment to empathy, accept responsibility when appropriate, acknowledge hurt emotions, and, when all else fails, take a break. With all the variety of relationships existing in the same workplace, creating a culture of appreciation and respect probably has the best chances of stopping the Horsemen in their tracks. Such techniques make up a good part of leadership training and handbooks, but, like Gottman's participants, actually demonstrating these techniques is different from knowing about them.

Over the course of his career, Gottman has turned his attention from understanding the pitfalls of relationships to doing something about them through counseling troubled couples who come to his Love Lab. He provides guidance and builds experience in techniques that couples can use when they hit a difficult patch. Maybe something similar is needed in the workplace, with techniques that accurately predict which relationships are headed off the rails and provide resources for understanding and intervention before the relationship spirals out of control. Dealing with troubled relationships early would do much to alleviate the cost of turnover and the collateral damage caused to employees working in dysfunctional teams.

3

Reward

Have you ever caught yourself putting the milk in the pantry and the cereal in the refrigerator? How about wearing a mismatched pair of socks, or putting two contacts in the same eye? For all the qualities of the human intellect and the trillions of synaptic connects that make reading this sentence possible, mistakes like these are a normal occurrence and together prove the point that we are not always consciously thinking about the world around us, let alone in control of our own actions. In many ways, consciousness is akin to carrying around a flashlight in a dark room. Only a fraction of the environment can be seen at any given time; we can wave the light around from place to place, but there is no way to illuminate the entire room. Making matters worse, we can get distracted and shine the light at a totally unhelpful location (this is the moment when Captain Crunch goes into the fridge and the milk into the pantry). Part of being human is to assume that we are in control of ourselves and able to make choices that affect our own well-being. We also hate being reminded that this is not entirely the case.

Despite our best efforts, it is easy to fall prey to impulse and temptation. The apple in our own personal Garden of Eden can be that chocolate sitting at the edge of the kitchen counter, the one extra lottery ticket bought at the corner gas station, or having the last dance at a particularly good party. We are quick to find excuses for our own actions, saying that the reward is justified or earned, but unfortunately we are not as quick to defend the actions of others, identifying their fall to temptation as a flaw in character. If we came clean and admitted that not everything we do is under our personal control or in full consciousness, would we be as quick to judge the actions of others? Would we still scorn the gambler who gave away his last paycheck or the obese man who just ordered the double cheeseburger?

In the early twentieth century, a group of psychologists sought to unearth the basic tenets of how humans interact with their environments. The more extreme of these Behavioralists argued that, contrary to popular wisdom, humans have very little control over their impulses and behaviors. Instead, we build up associations between signals in the environment, rewards, and

Punching the Clock. Joe Ungemah, Oxford University Press (2021). © Oxford University Press.
DOI: 10.1093/oso/9780190061241.003.0003.

punishments that together cause us to act, whether or not we are fully aware of it. Behavioralists argue that their rules apply for even the most complex human actions, from a highly coordinated physical activity like riding a bike to showing great emotional resilience during times of tragedy. In addition, their power is thought to be universal, extending across contexts from the family room to the workplace.

The Sound of a Bell

There are times in the course of scientific exploration when an accidental discovery does more for the advancement of knowledge than the original purpose of the experiment. The discovery of penicillin is one such case, occurring when Alexander Fleming went on vacation and left some dirty Petri dishes covered with staphylococci in his lab. Upon his return, Fleming noticed that a fungus had killed off the bacteria, a discovery that has aided the health of countless millions. On a much more practical note, Percy Spencer was an engineer working at Raytheon who happened to walk too close to a magnetron with a snack. The chocolate bar in his pocket melted; curious to see if other foods would do the same thing, Spencer brought other edibles into the office. He was delighted to see that an egg would explode if exposed too long to the magnetron. Satisfied he was on to something, Spencer went on to invent the first microwave.

Ivan Petrovich Pavlov never intended to become a psychologist, but rather was very content with his intended career as a physiologist. He was successful, too, having been awarded a Nobel Prize for science for his work on digestion, which spanned more than 25 years of active research. Pavlov was in the midst of a detailed investigation of the digestive properties of dogs when a string of nagging experimental findings caused his career to take a left turn into the then budding field of psychology. It was an uncomfortable transition for Pavlov, who wrote that "It is still open to discussion whether psychology is a natural science, or whether it can be regarded as a science at all." Potentially it was due to his hard stance on what is true science that his diligent experimental designs and findings live on to this day relatively unscathed.

Pavlov sought to understand the process of salivation, exploring how various stimuli affected the amount and timing of saliva flow. In the beginning of his studies, he focused on how various food and non-food objectives changed

how much saliva was produced, measuring it directly through a minor surgery on his canine subjects. An incision was made to the dog's cheek, such
that the salivary duct could be dissected and redirected to the outside of the
mouth. A small funnel and bulb were cemented to the skin, which in turn
were attached to a series of tubes that allowed for the accurate measurement
of the amount of saliva a dog produced.

Pavlov's dogs unfortunately lived a very lonely life, separated as much as
possible from the world in the pursuit of a controlled environment. Pavlov
recognized that there could be a near infinite number of stimuli that
could affect the dogs, from eye contact with the experimenter to a smell
of food floating in from another room. The dogs were thus placed into a
purpose-built institute in Petrograd that was equipped with an isolating
trench surrounding the building, crisscrossing corridors to minimize
noise, empty rooms between experimental labs, and barriers between the
experimenters and their subjects. Despite all of these precautions, Pavlov
was ultimately unsuccessful at controlling all the stimuli experienced by
the dogs.

Among his findings, Pavlov discovered that moist food did not produce
as much saliva as hard food. Not an earth-shattering result, but important
nonetheless for documenting that saliva is a reflexive response that varies
depending on the properties of a substance. Saliva changes the chemical
properties of a substance and, in the case of food, helps the dog to consume it
faster. Saliva is equally handy for non-food items, helping the dog to protect
its mouth and wash out foreign substances. Pavlov surmised that dogs who
salivate faster, either through direct contact with a substance or through the
prediction of its occurrence, have an evolutionary advantage over dogs who
are slow to react.

Pavlov pointed out that dogs do not actively control the amount of saliva
produced, but rather emphasized that the flow was a reaction to the environment. The same holds true for humans; we cannot control how much
saliva we produce, but rather we need some sort of stimuli to cause us to salivate, whether it is an actual pickle or the thought of eating something sour.
As the experiment progressed, Pavlov noticed that salivary glands are quite
smart, in the sense that saliva can be produced in anticipation of food, even
when no direct food is visible or in smelling distance. Despite the isolated
environment he had created, the dogs began to react to a range of stimuli.
For example, the footsteps of the experimenter would cause the dogs' salivary glands to kick into high gear. Unintentionally and to his initial chagrin,

Pavlov had discovered a scientific discovery that would outlive his Nobel Prize-winning work on digestion.

Pavlov could not resist exploring what he observed as the response could not be explained by physiology. The dogs were reacting regardless of whether or not real food existed. Pavlov theorized that the dogs were sensitive to signal stimuli that are initially neutral, but over time can be associated with something real that triggers a reflex. Through experience and learning, the signal stimuli (footsteps of the experimenter) can be associated with the real trigger (food) to cause a reflex (saliva) through a process that was termed *classical conditioning*. All living things are hardwired with unconditioned reflexes that occur outside of conscious control, from experiencing a startle following an unexpected bang from a falling object, to pupil dilation under dim light.

What Pavlov stumbled on was an unnatural reflex, one that could be conditioned to a wide range of stimuli. For example, in Pavlov's initial experiments, he would expose the dogs to the sound of a metronome when they were fed, measuring the rate of their salivary secretion. Over multiple trials, the sound of the metronome was all that was required to cause the dogs to salivate; they anticipated the food that usually accompanied the metronome's sound. Sadly and to their disappointment, sometimes they were denied the food that they got so excited about. To prove that there was nothing magical about the metronome, Pavlov experimented with a range of stimuli, from the odor of vanilla to a rotating disk. The effect was the same. After a handful of trials, the dogs began to have an automatic reflex in anticipation of being fed.

If you would like to try out classical conditioning yourself, grab a bell and head into a room with a mirror. Ensure that you choose a room where you have full control over how much light there is. Close the door, pull the blinds, and switch on the light. Next, ring the bell and immediately turn off the light. Wait for 15 seconds in complete darkness and then turn the light back on. Repeat this process 20 times, ringing the bell only just before switching off the light. On the 21st time, look closely in the mirror and ring the bell. Hopefully what you will see is your pupils dilating slightly, without any change in light level. What was once a neutral stimulus (the bell) has been paired with a conditioned reflex (your eyes dilating).

There is a different, more powerful form of conditioning that wields great power over human behavior. *Operant conditioning* is the scientific term that explains the relationship between actions and rewards, and nowhere are the laws governing it more evident than in a casino. For every coin dropped (or credit deposited) into a slot machine, the player has the opportunity to win. Sometimes the payoff is meager, with a few coins pumped out at the bottom of the tray (or, these days, credits added back onto a player's card with the sad artificial sound of coins dropping). Once in a while, sirens and lights announce the winning of a jackpot. More typically, nothing happens. Why do players feel compelled to feed money into a machine when the chances for joy are by no means guaranteed?

Payoffs follow four basic reinforcement schedules that vary in their power to shape an individual's behavior. The first distinction is based on whether rewards are dished out on a fixed or variable schedule, with the reward either guaranteed or left up to chance. The second distinction is based on whether the reward will occur over a specific interval of time or determined by a ratio of actions to rewards (e.g., pulling the handle of a slot machine). The resulting mix of these two distinctions creates four separate reinforcement schedules.

Continuing to use the slot machine as our example, a fixed interval would be demonstrated by a player pulling down on the lever, gaining a reward, waiting a specific amount of time, and then pulling down to receive another reward. This type of reinforcement would make for a very dull but at least predictable game. Almost equally dull, a fixed-ratio pattern could be established whereby the payoff is determined by a certain number of actions. This model is best illustrated by the punch card at the local coffee shop. If a customer receives 10 punches for the drinks they purchase, he or she in turn earns a free drink. The pattern is easy to understand and completely under the control of the consumer.

To create some interest, the game could change its reward pattern to a variable-interval pattern, meaning that the player would have no clue about how long to wait before pulling a lever. Maybe the reward would occur after a few minutes or, with luck, directly after the first pull. The player is able to anticipate the number of rewards over a given period, but the spread of the rewards over the time period remains a mystery. This pattern is akin to fishing on a lake. On any given Saturday, fishermen could anticipate a certain number of catches, yet they would not know if they are going be back home by dinner or lunchtime.

The most intense reinforcement schedule, variable-ratio, is exactly that used by real-life casinos. Unlike a variable-interval, the power is with the player to speed up the payoff. The player's actions (pulling the lever or playing an extra hand) have a direct impact on their reward. The more and faster they do it, the sooner the payoff is likely to occur. The catch is that gambling is not free, and, eventually, the player will run out of cash and be unable to chase the jackpot indefinitely. The old adage is correct: the house always wins.

Ratio schedules (either fixed or variable) place the power of reinforcement in the hands of the individual and therefore elicit greater response rates than interval schedules. Moreover, variable schedules are unpredictable by definition and therefore become addictive and resist extinction (where individuals give up doing the action associated with the reward). Gamblers come back to the casino after cashing their paycheck, while fishermen wait an extra hour on the lake to see if their luck changes. The power of variable-ratio payoffs is so strong that laboratory studies have shown that animals will continue an activity more than 10,000 times without a single payoff; they simply will not give up on the belief that a reward is coming.

Knowing that the power of reinforcement schedules is not equal, it is striking that the majority of workplace relationships follow only two reinforcement schedules. In a traditional employment relationship, pay is based on the amount of time contributed to the company and follows a fixed-interval schedule. The employee's output is only considered when it fails to meet an agreed standard. Alternatively, a fixed-ratio schedule characterizes the work of a freelancer, where the output is the basis for payment. As companies continue to contract more contingent workers as part of the gig economy, this distinction between reinforcement schedules should be strongly considered. The emphasis on output instead of time encourages the freelancer to adjust his or her quality to a minimal level of acceptable output, to get ready for the next reward. If the work is not clearly defined or communicated, there is a greater chance of disappointment with the end product, especially if the worker does not have as much affinity for the contracting organization as compared to a full-time employee. No such pressures exist for a traditional employee, who instead may suffer from not producing output in the first place.

Variable schedule reinforcements are rarely used in the workplace and are best represented by the spot-bonus, where a manager is given a pot of money to recognize staff as the opportunity arises. In many ways, the variable reward schedule may be an untapped way to encourage employees to contribute, collaborate, or try something new. For example, providing a variable-ratio reward for going to the company gym based on a random number of workouts completed could reinforce healthy behaviors to a greater extent than programs that provide partial reimbursement of gym fees. Giving employees the ability to opt-in to such a program should help settle any qualms that the strategy is underhanded in any way.

The Feeling of an Electric Shock

Rewards wield incredible power over behavior and, depending on the schedule of reinforcement, may be incredibly difficult to extinguish. We attempt, sometimes futilely, to adapt our behavior as a means of quickening the path between the trigger and reward. We may wander the floor of a casino looking for the right slot machine, try our luck by doubling our bet, or change strategies by sitting down for a game of blackjack, all in the pursuit of a jackpot. When none of these alternatives pays off, we'll attempt to learn from our experience and try something else, maybe going to the horse races instead.

B. F. Skinner was fascinated by how humans learn from experience, and, through this pursuit for knowledge, he became famous for his work and support of behaviorism. Boiling it down to the simplest of terms, an individual's behavior in a given situation will result in some form of consequence. When positive, reinforcement of the behavior occurs and the individual has learned to repeat his or her actions. When the results are negative, the individual has been punished for his or her actions and is likely to avoid doing whatever it was that caused the punishment.

This is not earth-shattering and tallies with everything we know about training dogs or rewarding our children for doing excellent schoolwork. What makes the topic interesting is when something goes awry in the links between situation, behavior, and consequence. Being one of the more stringent advocates for behavioralism, Skinner was keen to prove that a wide range of human actions could be explained by operant conditioning, including the development of superstitions. Like many other psychological phenomena, he believed that they could be boiled down to an automatic reaction to the environment.

Some of the best examples of superstitious behavior are demonstrated by the super humans among us. Turk Wendell, former pitcher for the Chicago Cubs and New York Mets, had the particularly hygienic habit of brushing his teeth between innings, while Wade Boggs, former third baseman for the Boston Red Socks, ate chicken before each game. The legendary Michael Jordan is said to have worn his North Carolina college shorts under his

Chicago Bulls uniform during every game (by the end of his career, his shorts must have been threadbare). In tennis, Serena Williams insists on bouncing the ball five times before her first serve, while Rafael Nadal requires that all his water bottles are lined up, with the labels facing the baseline.

One can only speculate where each of these routines got its start. The distance between Boggs's fondness for chicken is further away from the game than Williams's bouncing a ball before a serve, but each routine does its part to allay unwanted anxiety. Skinner sought to prove that the trigger for such behavior was a misplaced association between the superstitious behavior and the reinforcing consequence. Through complete happen-chance, every time Wade Boggs ate chicken early in his career, his sporting behavior was self-perceived as better than on his non–chicken eating days. With enough reinforcement, he was convinced not to tempt fate by ordering lamb or pork before the game.

In Skinner's experiments, animals were placed into a plain cage containing a food dish and a lever that would dispense a defined portion, as set by the experimenter. Specific to this study, Skinner rigged the dispenser to release a food disk automatically after a set period of time. His subjects, eight pigeons, had no real control over when the food would be released. To prepare them for the study, Skinner made the pigeons very hungry, depriving them of normal feeding for several days prior to the experiment. When placed in the cage, the pigeons were allowed to do whatever they liked and were automatically dished out food every 15 seconds. The pigeons were obviously overjoyed, until they were taken out of the cage. Thankfully, they were exposed to the feeding cage every day for the remainder of the experiment.

The pigeons adopted distinct behaviors in reaction to their good fortune. One pigeon decided that three counterclockwise turns was responsible for the food release, while another took up pecking movements toward the floor as a means of urging the food out. As a third example, a pigeon developed a tossing response that looked like it was lifting an invisible bar. Skinner was quick to note that none of these behaviors existed prior to the cage exposure, yet developed by pure chance in relation to the dispensing of food.

In the next phase of the experiment, Skinner lengthened the time between feedings to see what would happen. When the time period elongated to 1 minute, the pigeons stepped up their behaviors, making their head bobs, pecks, or leg movements more energetic and extreme in an apparent attempt to coax out more food. The final test was to see how long it would take to exhaust the behaviors in the absence of reinforcement. For the majority of pigeons, the behaviors gradually disappeared, yet for one particularly head-strong bird, the hopping ritual it developed persevered for more than 10,000 times before realizing that its beautiful dance was doing nothing to dispense food.

With this simple experiment, Skinner demonstrated how behavioral learning occurs. A situation calls for a behavioral reaction that, when paired with a successful consequence, is repeated. Superstitious behavior develops as a quirk in the system, with a misperception that the consequence is indeed related to the behavior associated with it. Superstar athletes know deep down that their pre-game routines are not normally related to performance, but, like it or not, the habits have become a way of life. If Wade Boggs decided to go vegan, his break with chicken could backfire with anxiety or self-doubt, spilling over into his game-day performance. Creating a new pattern of behavior may simply be too much work when compared to eating the same meal during the baseball season, especially if you like chicken.

So far, we have only considered the effects of *positive reinforcements* on learning and behavior. More sinister in nature, *negative reinforcements* or punishments work in the opposite direction, driving people away from repeating a specific behavior. More recent research has indicated that negative reinforcements may be the more powerful kind, with people adopting extreme superstitious or proactive behavior to avoid catastrophe rather than with the intent of gaining something new.

Much of what we know about learning has been at the expense of lab animals, and, in the studies described next, our canine companions underwent significant pain to advance our understanding of punishment. If there is an upside, their sacrifice has helped illuminate the psychological consequences of abuse. J. Bruce Overmier and Martin Seligman sought to understand how punishment in inescapable situations affected long-term learning and wellness. Their initial work was followed-up by Seligman and a new research partner, Steven Maier, providing a more detailed account of what has become known as *learned helplessness*.

Thirty dogs of mixed pedigree were enlisted to take part in a study. The dogs had not been experimented on before, weighed between 25 and 29 pounds, and were maintained in separate cages. During the experiment, the majority of dogs experienced two very different environments. The first involved a cloth hammock inside a white, sound-attenuating cubicle. The dogs were suspended in the hammock, with their feet held in place below them. The dog's head was secured with panels on either side, with a yoke running right below their neck. The floor beneath the dogs contained brass plate electrodes, through which a high voltage shock could be applied. To ensure the dogs received a full charge, the electrodes were pasted and taped to the dogs' hind feet.

Each harnessed dog was tormented with a series of 64 shocks, with a mere 90 second break between them. For half of the dogs (the escape condition), they were given a way to turn off the electricity. By pressing the panels on the side of their head, the dogs could successfully terminate the shock until the next wave. Not all the dogs in this condition learned that they had this power and unfortunately fared the same as the dogs in the yoked group, who had to endure a full 30 seconds of shock across all 64 waves.

After 24 hours, the dogs experienced their second environment, a shuttle box with two black compartments separated by a barrier. Each side of the box was illuminated by two 50-watt light bulbs that could be switched on and off by the experimenters. Each dog began on the same side of the barrier. When the lights went off, a timer began, and, after 10 seconds, a shock was administered to the dogs through the floor. If the dogs learned to the jump the barrier and enter the other compartment, they could escape the shock. Failure to learn the association between the lights, electric shock, and barrier would result in a full minute of electrocution. The dogs were given a break of approximately 90 seconds between trials and in total experienced 10 opportunities to learn how to escape the shock. If a dog failed to learn how to jump the barrier after five trials, the experimenter physically picked up the dog and moved it to the other side as a form of training.

A third group of dogs was assigned to a control condition. Although they experienced the shuttle box just described, they did not take part in the first phase of the experiment and, therefore, avoided time in the harness. These dogs provided a baseline for how fast barrier jumping could be learned without interference from a previous experience with electric shock.

When comparing the escape condition (the dogs who were able to stop the shocks in their harness) to the yoked condition (those with no control), the escape dogs learned to do a single press of the panel shortly after the shock began. The yoked dogs kept attempting to stop the shocks up until around the 30th trial, when they gave up pressing on the panel. When presented with the shuttle box, the dogs from the escape condition all learned that jumping the barrier was a successful way to avoid shocks. Moreover, they learned this trick rapidly, averaging just under three shocks that they had to fully endure. The results for the escape condition did not differ significantly from the control condition in the time it took to leap the barrier or the average number of failures to escape shock.

The yoke condition told a very different story. The dogs who were unable to escape shock in the first environment failed to jump the barrier 7 out of 10 times. Only 25% of dogs were able to repeat a successful escape, and, when they did, it took nearly twice as long as either the control or escape conditions. When the experiment was repeated 7 days later, the effects carried over, with 63% of the dogs failing to jump the barrier and escape the shocks. The experimenters surmised that the dogs in the yoked condition learned that escape was futile and therefore did not attempt to escape when presented with shock in a new environment. The dogs accepted the eventuality of their torment and simply endured being electrocuted.

Punishment, like reward, changes how individuals perceive the world around them, as well as shapes expectations about how much control they have over their own lives. To avoid pain (physical or otherwise), humans are keen to learn from mistakes and even take measures to plan around potential pitfalls or spend time observing others before acting. Yet sometimes this learning comes up flat, with a perception that punishment is unavoidable. Like the harnessed dogs, we can get stuck into thinking that acceptance of an intolerable situation is the only alternative. The ramifications of this research for people in abusive relationships is clear; however, learned helplessness has more subtle outlets across relationships, in and out of the workplace. Instead of challenging the status quo, quitting their jobs, or speaking up about injustice in the workplace, employees can fall victim to a belief that their lives will not change despite their best efforts. They become passive; not agreeing with what is going on around them, but likewise doing nothing to change the situation. They simply wait, hoping that the shocks will come to an end.

The Taste of a Marshmallow

Preschoolers are impulsive by nature. If left to their own devices, it is easy to imagine that a three-course meal made entirely of chocolate would be the norm, as would an endless stream of books before bedtime. Yet by the time children reach school age, they have mastered the basic elements of self-control. Even if their impulses get the better of them, at least these children know that delaying their gratification is possible and might lead to a more beneficial outcome. The development of self-control was put under the microscope by Walter Mischel and his colleagues at Stanford University, in probably one of the most adorable sets of studies ever conducted in the social sciences.

Four-year-old children were invited into the psychology lab, and, after a short acclimatization period, provided with a bell that, when rung, would summon the experimenter back into the room. Next, the child was presented with a game. A pair of treats was presented to the child, which were carefully chosen to be both desirable and age-appropriate. Although a range of items were used, from pretzels and cookies to small toys and tokens, the experiment is best known for its use of marshmallows. The child was given a choice: when the experimenter left the room, they could either wait until the experimenter returned to win two marshmallows or ring the bell to immediately receive one marshmallow. When the child showed that they understood the rules, the experimenter left the room and the game began.

In one condition, the marshmallows were on display for the children to look at, a single marshmallow on one side of a table and two on the other. In another condition, the marshmallows were covered before the experimenter left the room. Across these conditions, the children showed a great degree of variation in how they dealt with the situation. Some avoided directly staring at the marshmallows and instead looked at them from the corner of their eyes. Others rested their heads on their hands, talked quietly to themselves, sang, created games, or even pretended to be asleep. Most of these strategies were futile and eventually the children gave up and dug into the perfectly formed, fresh cloud of sugar.

From these initial experiments, the researchers discovered that the marshmallows put on display significantly decreased self-control, from 11 minutes on average with covered marshmallows to 6 minutes when the marshmallows were exposed. When it came to strategies to distract attention away from the treats, fun thoughts not involving marshmallows in any way helped the children cope, enabling the child to wait more than 10 minutes before ringing the bell, whether or not the marshmallow was staring them down.

Digging a little deeper, the experimenters sought to understand what types of thoughts were most effective at increasing a delay of gratification. In the next series of studies, children were not shown the actual marshmallows but provided with pictures of them. When the experiment was conducted this way, exposure to pictures of marshmallows actually lengthened the time children were willing to wait. The delay jumped to 18 minutes. As such, cognitively thinking about their choices was determined to be different than choosing between tangible rewards that were immediately available. In person, the marshmallows aroused the children's senses and the temptation became overwhelming, while the pictures were informative in nature and allowed for contemplation.

The next group of children was not shown pictures but instead asked to think specifically about the quality of the food they were about to eat. When asked to think about taste or texture, such thoughts created temptation and resulted in a mere 5 minutes of wait time. In contrast, thinking abstractly about the shape of the food did not arouse the children, allowing them to wait 13 minutes before ringing the bell for their snack. The longest wait times occurred when the children were asked to focus on arousing food qualities that were unrelated to their target treat. For example, children asked to think about the crunchy saltiness of pretzels waited the longest to receive their marshmallow at 17 minutes on average.

Four-year-olds are not great at self-control and often undermine their own efforts. When given the choice to expose or cover the marshmallow, they preferred to look at the marshmallow, explaining that "it made them feel good." By 5 years of age, children generally learn that hiding the marshmallow is a good tactic. They also learn how to create self-distraction, singing songs or repeating the mantra that a better reward will be theirs if they wait, stating things like "do not ring the bell. Ringing the bell will mean that the teacher comes in and I will only get one."

What made the research so compelling and memorable was the follow-up work done by the experimenters. Ten years later, the experimenters revisited the children and looked at individual differences in how they grew up and developed. Children who were better at self-control as 4-year-olds developed into more cognitively and socially competent teens. They were described by parents as more able to deal with personal set-backs, stress, and frustration. More shocking, differences between the children's ability to delay gratification predicted up to 30% of their future standardized test scores (as measured by the SAT). The experimenters were careful not to make any type of causal assumption from their research. Children who delay gratification might be able to apply these skills throughout their lives, or, alternatively, the environment in which they matured might encourage similar behaviors across situations and contexts.

Whether learned or not, the ability to turn off the automatic link between signal and reward is a powerful tool for people to use across their lives. For example, delayed gratification allows students to invest time in the pursuit of a career. Taking a job directly after graduating high school might be tempting, but richer rewards are more likely to occur by pursuing a college or advanced degree. Equally, slogging away at an entry-level job unrelated to your dream occupation can make sense if it leads to recognition or promotion. Outside of the workplace, deciding to buy a used rather than new car or renting an economy apartment might be the practical choice if saving up for a deposit on a first home.

In many cultures, there is a stigma against people who live beyond their means. This disdain for a lavish life might not be entirely fair, as individuals are seldom 100% in control of their impulses, as demonstrated by the 4-year-olds at Stanford University. Temptation is shaped by how explicitly a reward is dangled in front of us, as well as how we are encouraged to think about it. Thinking about the pleasure of the experience is very different from a clinical description of it. Advertisers know this and ensure that we are exposed to products in a way that will elicit all the right reactions. In addition, people are not equal in their ability to delay gratification in exchange for potentially larger rewards. Some individuals remove themselves from temptation, change their mental mindset, or simply sing a song in the pursuit of a better reward.

Taken together with the foundational work by Skinner and Pavlov, the powers of punishment and reward hold significant control over our impulses and behaviors, often occurring outside of conscious recognition that our environment is getting the better of us. Humans will adopt superstitions in an attempt to control their environment, place major bets or act with relentless effort when exposed to variable-ratio reward schedules, and potentially give up entirely when taught that their actions have no consequence over their situation.

These same tendencies are played on by companies in how they reward and incentivize employees. Take an employee who is making a decision about whether to put in extra hours over the weekend to increase his or her chances of earning a bonus. He or she will weigh up the immediate gratification of enjoying a relaxing weekend against the potential to go on a more lavish and potentially more relaxing vacation later in the year with the help of his or her bonus check. The bonus itself is set up on a reinforcement schedule, with pay occurring either directly after a specified target is achieved or at a specific time. Also driving the employee's decision is his or her personal history of attaining bonuses in the past. If past targets were unachievable, a pattern of learned helplessness might set in, in which all actions toward making the bonus are considered pointless and avoided.

Employers, without necessarily recognizing the power of behavioralism, have put in motion some of the most fundamental drivers of human behavior. Freelancers working in the gig economy don't escape these behavioral pressures, but instead take cues about where they are most likely to be successful in building their experience and business. Beyond practices for pay and performance, line managers hold great sway over their employees' behavior. If feedback about work is late or not linked appropriately to the desired behavior, its meaning will be lost. Equally, repeated contempt and disapproval of work can lead an employee to feel powerless over his or her work output. Instead of quitting the job, such an employee might stay in the organization until forced to go, like the dogs in Skinner's cages. On the positive side, showcasing rewards or the potential benefits of doing a good job might play on the child in all of us who cannot resist a marshmallow or two.

4
Choice

The mid-1990s was the heyday of the big box store. Littered across the country, massive parking lots connected pseudo-warehouses full of consumer goods with the goal of enticing consumers to stop in and get a bargain. Each big box store had its twist, some positioning themselves as exclusive clubs, while others attempted to be a one-stop shop. Within the established genre of consumer electronics stores like Best Buy, Comp USA, and Fry's, a new concept was launched and promised to be bigger and better than the rest. Incredible Universe sought to transform the typical shopping experience into a theme park attraction; a place to go whether you were interested in buying something or not. With 185,000 square feet of sales floor and 85,000 items in its typical store, the company boasted in its tag-line, "If it's not in the Universe, it doesn't exist!!!!!" So bold was the tag-line that it needed five exclamation points.

To be fair, the stores were huge and offered more choice than any of their rivals. The concept was an unlikely joint venture between Tandy Corporation and Trans World Entertainment. In each of its 17 locations, the terminology familiar to theme parks was applied to the store and its employees alike. Departments were referred to as "scenes" and employees were "cast members" who wore "costumes" rather than uniforms. In the middle of the store, a rotunda was built with a large stage used for sales presentations, product demonstrations, celebrity visits, and the occasional musician. If not watching a show or listening to a presentation, shoppers were encouraged to browse products across the full range of consumer electronics, from software and music through computers and accessories. In-store studios provided the space for demonstrations of the more specialist audio-visual equipment, while the larger stores provided fast-food outlets and daycare facilities.

Walking into the TV department was an experience. Well over a hundred screens glistened on display, providing a wow factor that the other retailers couldn't replicate. There existed a product for everyone and that is what the company banked on. Screen size, resolution, sound capability, and features like picture-in-picture differentiated the range, and, with so much choice, the

Punching the Clock. Joe Ungemah, Oxford University Press (2021). © Oxford University Press.
DOI: 10.1093/oso/9780190061241.003.0004.

company believed it could seize the market by being the most obvious place to buy electronics.

This dream never materialized, and, within a few short years, the company went under. Of the 17 stores it operated, only 6 were consistently profitable. Offering choice resulted in the need for a huge retail footprint, which in turn cost more to operate than its competitors. The owners knew the model would have its operational challenges but made the assumption that its market share would more than make up for the difference. Adding salt to the wound, when Incredible Universe attempted to liquidate its properties, they discovered a total lack of buyers. The stores were simply too big and specialized to be repurposed into something else, leaving Tandy to sell the properties at a fraction of their perceived value. Of the few success stories, one property was redeveloped into the southwest campus of Houston Community College.

As a concept, the mix of electronics and entertainment might have been a good one. The 1990s saw a blossoming of technology that was exciting, which translated into real consumer appetite to learn about the latest gadgets. What Incredible Universe got wrong was how this interest would translate into buying behavior. When faced with more than a hundred choices in TVs, shoppers who were initially eager to learn about a product found themselves overloaded with features and options. It was easy to become paralyzed by the range of makers, sizes, and models. Instead of engaging with the sales staff to discuss their options, shoppers decided to simply walk out of the store and buy nothing. When they did buy a TV, customers chose to shop at the competition where they found a more relaxed environment and a range of available models that they could more easily wrap their arms around. The ironic thing is that buyers were more confident in their decision and placed in a better mood than if they persisted to buy from Incredible Universe.

When Choice Is the Problem

In an article by *Fast Company*, writer Jane Porter speaks about her frustration in finding a toilet brush on Amazon. With a quick search, she found 1,161 toilet brushes on offer, and, after sinking 1 hour of time scanning webpages and reviews, she gave up and went to the local dollar store. At the time of writing and in the two and half years since she wrote the article, Amazon has grown its portfolio of toilet brushes to 2,919. What is most surprising are the top-end options, with 326 models each costing more than $200. The most expensive toilet brush was selling for $990, on sale from $1,544.40. Jane's dollar store option has just become that much more appealing.

The toilet brush example is our new reality. Choice and information abounds in almost every decision we make, which has caused concern among social scientists. Too many choices, especially on those topics where we have very little interest, can exhaust cognitive resources away from the topics and issues that matter most. A greater number of options requires more time to scan alternatives. This in turn decreases the amount of certainty that a good decision will be made and results in a greater chance of personal regret afterward for making the wrong choice, assuming that a choice is actually made. The time and effort wasted on making a choice negatively impacts our mood and often results in decision avoidance. Like shopping at Incredible Universe, when the decision-making process asks too much of us, it is easier to simply tune out and do nothing. The effects of decision-making on our mood are most pointed when a decision is important and unavoidable, as when arranging for a mortgage on a new house or enrolling in 401k programs.

One of the best illustrations of the effect of choice on decision-making was created by Sheena Iyengar, a professor of business at Columbia University. In 1995, she set up a booth at a gourmet food market in California offering samples of Wilkin and Sons jams. Every few hours, she switched from offering 24 varieties of jam to just 6. When a customer approached, they were offered a taste and a coupon for $1 off a jar of jam. Despite the fact that customers tasted on average two varieties irrespective of the presentation, the buying behavior differed depending on how many jars of jam were on offer. Of the total number of patrons who walked by the booth, 60% were drawn to the large assortment and stopped for a taste, as compared to 40% stopping by the smaller assortment. When it came to buying, the normal logic failed and choice was no longer a good thing, with only 3% buying from the large assortment compared to 30% buying from the small assortment. Customers who had less to choose from bought more consistently.

To conclude that too much choice is the problem may simplify the situation. Our reactions to choice depend on the type of information we are provided, how much experience or confidence we have in the topic, and how much importance we ascribe to the situation. If we know we like strawberry-kiwi jam and know a bit about the company that makes it, we might be able to navigate the large assortment and make a painless buying decision. The real issue is information overload and whether decisions are made overly difficult for the people making them.

Other factors play into just how bad information overload can be. Some individuals are more prone to avoiding the possible options, preferring instead quick and efficient decision-making. For anyone who has taken a Myers Briggs Personality Type assessment, individuals who have a "J" preference look for closure to situations, as opposed to those with a "P" preference who edge toward keeping options open until the very last minute. Beyond personality, an individual's emotional and physical state can affect decision-making. Being sick, low on sleep, or preoccupied with other worries can all affect the amount of cognitive resources available for decision-making. Psychologists came up with the personification of the *cognitive miser* to explain what goes on in our heads when berated with multiple demands. Like the stingy Scrooge sitting behind his desk hoarding the coals for the fire, cognitive resources are doled out sparingly to only the most pressing needs. Cognitive resources are precious, finite things that should not be taken for granted.

This is why impulse goods are placed by the cash register and special deals are offered at the online checkout. Having spent your cognitive resources on the main reasons for shopping, retailers hope to capitalize on their shoppers' fatigue, bypassing a rational assessment of whether the customer truly needs that extra pack of lip balm. Beyond causing impulse purchases, depleted cognitive resources cause individuals to focus on one or two defining characteristics, like price or size, rather than weighing up the total offering. The more obvious the characteristic, the easier it is for individuals to spot and focus on it, to the chagrin of entrepreneurs who seek to make a fortune on objectively better but more complex alternative products or services. The key is to get prospective buyers to invest more time and energy in the buying process by increasing their involvement in making a sound decision.

As a twist on Incredible Universe's story, companies and governments alike have experimented with pushing work onto their customers as a way of saving cost. Instead of having sales reps listen to needs, customers are often presented with a series of questions or forms at the first point of contact. Although potentially more efficient for the seller, a tradeoff has been made on the amount of cognitive resources left over for the customer. For example, when booking a hotel room, the first couple of steps might involve signing in, updating the personal profile associated with the account, typing in location and dates, and considering potential hotels on a map. By the time the customer is presented with 10 different options for room type, varying in view, number of reward points earned, payment type, bed type, feather free and firmness of pillows, and square footage, the customer may have already tuned out and will simply click on the cheapest option. The chances for the up-sell went far away after the first couple of clicks. Worse still, the customer may carry some resentment about the process in general and feel less confident that they made the right hotel choice. It is no wonder that retailers like Amazon have pioneered one-click shopping; they understand the tradeoffs between efficiency and cognitive load, betting instead on the return customer.

Choice, Control, and Plant Sitting

Central to the notion of personal choice is whether someone has control over his or her social and physical environments. On the far end of the spectrum, prisoners in solitary confinement or hospital patients experiencing medically induced paralysis know what it is like to succumb to the will of others. On the other side of the spectrum are the day-to-day altercations involving bosses who take on an authoritarian tone, parents revoking rights to the iPad, and neighbors making a point about where the property line is. No matter what the cause, a loss of control feels dehumanizing and can wreak havoc on our anxiety levels.

Yet the extent of personal control ebbs and flows naturally over one's lifetime. Until they learn otherwise, children are at the mercy of their parents' will. When we age, the pendulum turns and often it is the parents who are at the mercy of their children. With age, the ability to look after ourselves physically, emotionally, and/or cognitively can decline with tough choices to make about where to live and how get around town. We all hope to be part of the one-third of society that ages gracefully and who do not experience any major limitations until extreme old age. The reality is that the fear and experience of broken hips, Alzheimer's, and loneliness keep many from enjoying their golden years. Being sent to an old age home is the worst nightmare for a great proportion of Baby Boomers, and whole industries are built on selling preventative measures that promise seniors that they can live out their lives happy and in control.

The power of personal control was eloquently demonstrated in a field experiment by Ellen Langer and Judith Rodin, who partnered with a well-known and reputable nursing home in Connecticut that offered the full range of medical and recreational services for its residents. By working closely with the nursing home administrator, 91 residents, aged between 65 and 90 years, were identified to take part in a study that investigated the impact of personal control across a wide range of measures for well-being. Using the floor plan to their advantage, the participants were sorted into two groups based on which floor they lived on.

One group of residents was encouraged to think about and take control of their lives. The experiment began with a gathering of residents in the lounge and an announcement by the nursing home administrator, who stated "I was surprised to learn that many of you don't know about the things that are available to you and more important, that many of you don't realize the influence you have over your own lives here. Take a minute to think of the decisions you can and should be making." The administrator continued by pointing out that the residents could influence who they interacted with and when, the arrangement of their rooms, and how socially active they wanted to be. He continued by talking about the complaints process, "If you are unsatisfied with anything here, you have the influence to change it. It is your responsibility to make your complaints known."

Each of the residents was then given the opportunity to take a houseplant back to their rooms. To follow through on the theme of control, the residents had the option to reject the gift (although none did) or choose which type of plant they wanted. The administrator said, "The plants are yours to keep and take care of as you'd like." The gathering closed with the announcement that movie night was happening in a fortnight and that the participants had the choice whether to attend, and to determine if they preferred Thursday or Friday night to see the film.

The second group of residents were encouraged not to think about personal control but rather to consider how much the staff do on their behalf. After beginning in a similar way, the announcement by the administrator took a different course, "I was surprised to learn that many of you don't know about the things that are available to you; that many of you don't realize all you're allowed to do here. For example, you're permitted to visit people on other floors. . . . We feel that it's our responsibility to make this a home you can be proud of and happy in, and we want to do all we can to help you." The emphasis was firmly set on the nursing staff making decisions and taking actions on behalf of the residents, with or without their input. Although complaints and suggestions were encouraged, it was clear from what the administrator said that the staff were in control of the home.

Just like the other group, houseplants were handed out to the residents; however, these participants did not have the ability to refuse the gift nor were they given a choice in what type of plant they preferred. They were also told that the nurses were responsible for the plant and that they were not required to help care for it. Regarding the movie, the participants were assigned a spot on either Thursday or Friday night, with the assumption that they would go at their assigned time.

The researchers were keen to explore whether the manipulation of the administrator's message and freedom of choice would impact the residents' perceived and observed wellness over the following 3 weeks. To gather evidence, Langer and Rodin used a range of measures. First, they looked at self-report by residents about how much personal control and happiness they felt before and after the announcement and plant sitting. Second, they asked two nurses to evaluate each of the residents in a similar fashion, looking at how happy, alert, dependent, sociable, and active they were prior to and after the experiment. Last, they looked at the behavioral measures like movie attendance, participation in a spontaneous jellybeans-in-a-jar competition, and even how much they rolled around the hallways in their wheelchairs.

Giving residents the opportunity to make decisions and care for their plants had profound ramifications on their well-being. For those who were given more control, 48% reported feeling happier than they were prior to the experiment, compared to just 25% of the comparison group. More shocking was the results from the nurses, who were kept completely in the dark about the experiment. The residents who were provided more control were judged to have improved over the 3-week period in 93% of the cases, whereas 71% of the comparison group declined in health over the same period. The residents who were given and had control over decisions, as well as responsibility for caring for the plant, spent more time visiting other residents, talking to staff, and inviting family and friends to visit. They also spent less time in passive activities and were quick to take up the opportunity to attend movie night.

There is a postscript to this story. The researchers decided to go back to the nursing home 18 months after their intervention to see what, if anything, had changed. For those residents who were still at the home, Langer and Rodin asked nurses and doctors to evaluate the health of the residents and offered an opportunity for them to attend a special talk on psychology to measure their level of cognitive engagement. When comparing participants from the original study who were given more control against those whose freedom was restricted, a stark difference was found. Participants who were given control were rated as 34% healthier than their peers. More startling, the relative health of these participants had actually increased over the 18-month period, as compared to their peers who experienced a slight decline in health. To further prove the point, the researchers looked at the death rate among residents and found that 15% of residents who were given control of their environment died between the original study and the follow-up, whereas 30% of the comparison group had passed away during this same time period.

The study and its follow-up contributed in a novel way to amass evidence demonstrating the impact of personal control on well-being, anxiety, confidence, and risk taking. Having an opportunity to weigh up personal preferences and make a decision has dramatic and long-lasting effects on an individual, leaving little doubt why taking away freedom of choice is a primary form of punishment. Unintentionally, some of the very organizations that attempt to help and heal (such as hospitals and nursing homes) can mimic imprisonment by reducing mobility and expression of free will. There are many roads to becoming institutionalized; the efficient and safe operation of a facility must be placed in balance with the needs of its residents.

At the workplace, providing employees with freedom in how they work can reap rewards in staff engagement if not overall organizational productivity. Google took this advice to heart in setting aside one day a week where employees had full control over whatever they worked on as long as it contributed to the organization's mission. The gig economy amps up this practice, providing a wealth of opportunity for entrepreneurially minded talent to take control of their decisions. Even the layouts of contemporary workplaces play a part, where workers "hotel" and book an available workspace according to the type of the work being done, desk configuration, or social group. If the process is fast and easy to navigate, choice in environment likely overpowers the extra cognitive load needed to make a decision about where to work. On the flipside, managers typically take away control and increase the level of oversight when performance wanes, resorting to performance improvement plans for traditional employees and strict adherence to contractual terms for freelancers, to the detriment of worker engagement. Personal control may be at the heart of what is already well-known for those studying the workplace, specifically that autonomous work where employees can build mastery in their profession drives motivation.

A Perfect Storm

"It's fire . . . and it's crashing. It's crashing terrible. Oh, my. Get out of the way, please. It's burning and bursting into flames and the . . . this is the worst of the worst catastrophes in the world. . . . It's smoke, and it's in flames now and the frame is crashing to the ground, not quite to the mooring mast. Oh, the humanity," were the words uttered by radio reporter Herbert Morrison on May 6, 1937. Eighty years ago, Morrison witnessed the first major transport disaster captured on film, specifically the failed landing of the *Hindenburg* at Lakehurst, New Jersey. Those images burned into the collective consciousness and brought the era of the airship to an abrupt end, with the Hindenburg's sister ship, *Graf Zeppelin 2*, making its last voyage along the British coast later that year.

There was no hint of disaster when the *Hindenburg* set out on its voyage across the Atlantic 3 days earlier from Frankfurt, Germany. Thirty-six passengers joined another 61 crew members on board the world's largest dirigible airship. By any account, the *Hindenburg* was huge. At 804 feet long and 15 stories high, the airship was nearly the size of the *RMS Titanic* and floated a few hundred feet above the ground. Not only was it a spectacle to see from the ground, the view from inside was reported as extraordinary. The ride was smooth and peaceful, allowing passengers to watch the world go by. If passengers got bored, the cabin was adorned with a baby grand piano for entertainment.

The *Hindenburg* was a well-tested ship, having flown 62 prior flights without incident. Thirty-four of these trips crossed the Atlantic, with Brazil as the favored port. Long-distance travel is exactly what the *Hindenburg* was designed to do. In 1937, airplanes did not yet have the stamina to cross an ocean, while dirigibles cut the time from 5 days at sea by steamship to under 3 days by air. Passengers made up the elite of society; if the *Hindenburg* had survived its journey, it was to carry a group of dignitaries back to Europe for the coronation of King George VI.

All was going to plan during its final flight until the *Hindenburg* made landfall outside of Boston. Journeying down the coast toward New York City, weather conditions deteriorated and delayed the intended late-morning landing at Lakehurst. Captain Max Pruss made a last-minute decision to take the airship back out to sea by flying over Manhattan and the Empire State Building, creating a stir among the spectators below. Having decided that the worst of the weather was behind him, the captain made the run for Lakehurst at 6:22 PM, and, by 7 PM, the airship was on its final approach for landing.

When airships arrived at Lakehurst, ropes were thrown down, touched against the ground to discharge electricity, then brought through a rig and into a winch, a procedure known as a *flying moor*. As the *Hindenburg* approached Lakehurst and began to drop altitude, the winds shifted severely, causing the captain to make two extreme left turns into the wind in order to maintain direction and propeller thrust. It was during these maneuvers that a steering cable at the back of the airship was theorized to have broken free, potentially causing the sparks that ignited the fire that would later engulf the *Hindenburg*. At 295 feet, the ropes were thrown down and tied to the winches. Thirty-four seconds later and the *Hindenburg* was no more, killing 35 of the 97 people on board, in addition to one person from the ground crew.

Unfortunately, camera crews did not capture the moment when the *Hindenburg* caught fire, but observers reported that flames began at the stern of the ship. As the tail began to drift toward the ground, the flames moved through the 16 separate hydrogen-holding cells, reaching the nose-cone just as the craft hit the ground. Werner Doehner, the last remaining survivor of the crash, described the moment when disaster was eminent, "Suddenly the air was on fire." Werner's mother was quick to react, throwing him and his brother through a window before the airship hit the ground. His mother survived, but Werner lost his father and sister to the disaster. Werner's father left his family to take some photos from a different vantage point in the ship moments before the crash. His sister sustained fatal burns after deciding to search for her father, having initially survived the craft's impact with the ground.

What caused the disaster has been coined a "perfect storm" of mishaps. As mentioned, a loose cable might have played a role in sparking the fire. Another hypothesis points to the type of material used to coat the inside wall of the canvas body. The specific type of paint was a mix of iron oxide and aluminum-impregnated cellulose, which maintain their highly flammable nature even after drying. Addison Bain, a former rocket scientist at NASA, took up the study of *Hindenburg* as a pet project and uncovered written warnings from the Zeppelin company that raised concerns about the paint igniting with an electrostatic discharge.

Static electricity was definitely in the air the day the *Hindenburg* went down. The dirigible built up a considerable amount of charge in its prolonged wait over Lakehurst, as a result of flying among thunderstorms and attempting to land under rainy conditions. When the ropes were lowered, they became wet and, instead of dissipating the charge, may have acted like conductors and sent a charge up to the waiting hole in the hydrogen cell. With a puncture in the canvas and sparks to ignite it, the use of hydrogen instead of helium sealed the fate of the *Hindenburg*, with fire moving readily from cell to cell and eventually encompassing the whole of the ship.

Beyond the physical elements of a broken cable, ignitable paint, use of hydrogen, and rainy conditions, poor judgment by the captain may also have contributed. Although the *Hindenburg* was late, the craft had plenty of fuel left on board and an alternative location could have been chosen. Alternatively, the captain could have waited until the rain had completely passed before landing. This would have allowed a low-altitude landing, in which the airship would cruise gently to the earth and be dragged by the ground crew to the mooring mast, foregoing the need for a winch. Instead, the captain opted for the riskier high-altitude landing, reacting to the pressure to turn the ship around quickly for the trip back to Europe and the coronation of George VI. His choice kept the escaping hydrogen close to the ship as it hovered above the mast waiting to be pulled down. Zeppelin as a company had a hand to play in the accident, too, by not doing more to eradicate the risk of the flammable paint and the decision to use pure hydrogen, rather than a mix of gases to keep the airship aloft.

Like many other catastrophes, from Three Mile Island to the Challenger Space Shuttle, no single factor was to blame for the *Hindenburg* disaster. Rather, a number of contributing factors piled up until reaching a tipping point that ended up in disaster. The initial problem in any catastrophic event can be very minor, such as the poor weather encountered by the *Hindenburg*, but it compounds itself very quickly with other factors, like a headstrong captain who does not look for alternative airstrips or choose to wait patiently for a better time to land. Situations that spiral out of control from an initially small and solvable situation have been termed the "butterfly effect," a metaphor in which a butterfly flapping its wings is said to put in motion a series of events that cause a tornado on the other side of the planet.

Humans are not great at recognizing the complex and multifaceted environment in which they live. Instead, we prefer straightforward and unidimensional relationships between cause and effect. In studying how humans perceive the world around them, psychologists uncovered a number of biases that play out in our everyday interactions. Specifically, individuals will look at a situation and quickly determine whether they have the ability to control it or not. If they determine that the situation is within their personal control, such a decision will shape their future actions. For example, a person shooting a basket at the local carnival will likely play again if she feels that her chances of winning a prize is based on skill, especially if she considers herself a great ball player. Equally, if she feels that the game was rigged with a small basket or an overly inflated ball that would likely bounce too strongly off the backboard, she would decide not to play for a second time.

Julian Rotter was an early pioneer in the study of perceptions of cause and effect (termed *attributions*). What interested Rotter was whether individuals differed in how they generally thought about the world around them, favoring either internal (skill and behavior) or external (luck, chance, fate, or situational) dispositions, as well as their effects on learning. He recognized that assigning causation is not a binary choice, but rather can vary by degree. On balance, if an individual perceives a positive situation as within his or her personal control, then Rotter argued that he or she would likely continue doing the same behavior as long as it continued to pay off. He tested this assumption across a variety of experimental games, from gambling to fine-motor puzzles and even one allegedly identifying talents for extrasensory perception (ESP). Sometimes he would tell his participants that the game was due to skill or luck, while in other experiments, he would let his participants decide how a game was won.

Rotter discovered that individuals have a bias to overestimate their personal control when they won the game. Termed the *fundamental attribution error*, humans tend to ascribe winning to their own skills and effort. The contrary holds true: when faced with a loss, humans tend to look for a scapegoat, blaming the situation on bad luck or on an unfair situation. When told that a task is largely out of their control, people will tend to either close down and tune out or adopt superstitious behaviors, creating elaborate techniques that provide an illusion of control.

Attributions also play into how we describe the success and failures of others and similarly follow a distinctive pattern. When we observe someone's failure, we tend to make an internal attribution, blaming their lack of skill or effort. However, when we see someone succeed, we tend to downplay his or her achievement by making an external attribution, believing that chance or fate played a significant role, potentially as a way of maintaining our own self-confidence. Although these patterns are consistent across people and situations, Rotter discovered that people vary in how much emphasis they place on either internal or external attributions. Some people will tend to look for and place greater importance on their own personal control, with some notable benefits. Rotter argues that such people will be more alert to their environment, learn more about what works, take steps to act on this knowledge, place greater emphasis on continuous skill improvement, and resist pressures to change. Yet these gains in personal drive may come at the expense of recognizing the struggle of others and how the environment might need to change in order to create a level playing field.

Control is a tenuous thing. On one hand, the benefits of personal control can improve health, learning, and productivity, as witnessed both within laboratory experiments and in the field with the nursing home residents. Surprisingly, a little bit of personal control seems to go a long way, such as having the power to look after another living thing or choosing whether or not to attend a recreational event. It is no wonder that taking away such freedom is the most popular form of punishment in society. Yet having too much control can be debilitating, taxing cognitive resources unnecessarily and creating undue anxiety. Taking choice out of the equation may actually be the right strategy, especially when there is no real need to become highly involved in the decision.

With the explosion of choice in contemporary society, as well as a misguided belief that choice is universally a good thing, it is no wonder that psychologists recommend that people regulate their attention and involvement in making decisions. Their advice comes in three parts. First, bucket the decision as either important or unimportant to gauge how much energy should be spent on it. If the situation warrants a deeper consideration, scan for information to a point, without overdoing it. For example, buying a home is much more important than buying a blender and therefore should get more cognitive energy. Second, consciously restrict your options to a few really interesting ones. Too many choices often result in no decision whatsoever. Third, sleep on it. Important decisions require our full attention and therefore should be given the cognitive space for processing and the time to warm emotionally to the end result.

In the workplace, leaders have the potential to shape the organizational culture to reap the benefits of worker autonomy. Leaders have a choice in management philosophy to decide how much independence and authority they would like to provide their workers. In some ways, employee-owned companies or co-ops put this mentality out front, where each employee has a stake in how the company is managed and operated. Leaders also play a role in taking away administrative or routine decisions where there is minimal value for employee involvement. Finding one-click solutions across work processes can free up time and energy for the problems that employees should be dedicating their time on. It is no wonder that employees and managers gripe about internal IT systems, where they are asked to select from drop-down menu after drop-down menu when logging anything from customer contact information to rating the performance of a direct report. Such an overload of administrative burden plays a part in driving away talent in a search for greater freedom as freelancers or to work within small business. Even in areas like Total Rewards, endless options in employee benefits are less desirable than a few really different choices.

When something goes amazingly right or catastrophically wrong, leaders can help get at the heart of the matter. Humans are fantastic at categorizing causation as either internally (personal disposition) or externally (environmental or luck) driven, when the reality is much more complex. Not only is causation usually somewhere between internal and external, but it is also multifaceted. Before blaming an employee for a failed product launch or rewarding the salesperson for blowing up their targets, considering what factors (and usually there are a handful) contributed to the situation creates a fairer and smarter business model. The top salesperson may have demonstrated great hustle, but equally could have been given the best portfolio to work on or was in the right place at the right time. The way companies reward staff often suffers from the same attribution biases, establishing incentives that by default point to the individual rather than recognizing the contribution of others or the external environment. Employee-owned businesses or co-ops may buck this trend but may also potentially go overboard in emphasizing team contribution.

Getting the balance right in how much personal control employees should have is no easy task, and, as the economic environment changes, taking away an employee's rope is tempting. Employee autonomy is so much harder to support when a company is struggling, but perhaps it is needed the most during such times. Without feeling in control, employee productivity and engagement wane, making the chances for business recovery that much harder. For really tough decisions, employees need the tools and space to understand their environments and create a shortlist of compelling ideas and the time to land solidly on a decision. At the same time, they need to be freed from all the noise of irrelevant decisions faced during the average workday. Deciding which option in a drop-down list to categorize a customer opportunity is not the same as deciding how best to close the actual deal, yet the time and effort invested can often be the same.

5

Confidence

"If it bleeds, it leads" is as true today with online media as it was during the heyday of the newspaper age. At the top of the list alongside murder, wars, and natural disasters are airplane crashes. Maybe it is their relative infrequency that draws our attention or possibly the situation itself, where everyday people are held hostage to the event and are helpless to control a disaster. No matter the cause, so strong is the emotional appeal of a plane crash that our interest is piqued even for near misses, where nothing really noteworthy occurred. Statistically speaking, the chances of being caught up in an airplane crash are extremely rare, somewhere in the neighborhood of 1 in 5 million. That said, it is compelling to think about what would happen if caught up in an emergency situation and, more specifically, what would increase the chances of surviving.

On January 15, 2009, the passengers and crew of US Airways Flight 1549 were caught up in one of the most remarkable crashes of the past decade. Flight 1549 was scheduled to depart LaGuardia in New York City and fly to Charlotte, North Carolina. After a few delays, the plane pushed back from the gate at 3:26 PM local time. On board the Airbus A320 were a total of 155 passengers and crew. The plane was in a good state of repair and nothing could have predicted the series of events that were about to transpire. After being airborne for just 1 minute and having attained an altitude of only 2,750 feet, the plane suffered from a double bird-strike causing a complete lack of power to both engines. Two minutes later, the plane had crashed back to earth.

Reacting to the bird strike, Captain Chesley Sullenberger radioed air traffic control to request a return to the airport before realizing that this was unrealistic. The pilot made a split-second choice to avoid built-up areas and ditch the plane in the Hudson River, announcing over the intercom to brace for hard impact. Stunned witnesses who flanked the Hudson from high-rise buildings described the crash landing as controlled rather than erratic, as if it was landing on a normal airstrip. The plane created huge plumes of water and came to a halt somewhere around West 48th Street, midway between

Punching the Clock. Joe Ungemah, Oxford University Press (2021). © Oxford University Press.
DOI: 10.1093/oso/9780190061241.003.0005.

Manhattan and Weehawken, New Jersey. The aircraft did not sink initially, but began to float, twist, and drift downstream. This provided much-needed time for the victims onboard to disembark the plane.

The emergency doors opened and passengers made their way to an assemblage of ferries, rescue craft, tugboats, and Coast Guard ships that began to converge at the crash site. The responders had to move fast; the water temperature was a frigid 35 degrees Fahrenheit and the plane had begun to take on water. Standing on the wings, the victims were partly submerged in the water and faced the risk of hypothermia. Wet-suited police divers dropped down from helicopters to usher passengers onto boats, while measures were taken to stop the plane from drifting and prop it up as long as possible. After approximately 1 hour, the entire plane was emptied (including at least one baby, both pilots, and three flight attendants) and the victims were on their way to nearby hospitals. Before exiting the plane, Captain Sullenberger walked the aisle twice to ensure that all his passengers and crew had safely left the airplane. Only then did he allow himself to be rescued.

The passengers and crew had just experienced a very narrow escape, and, although no one perished, the victims came away battered and bruised. Paramedics treated a total of 78 patients, mostly for minor injuries, including one unfortunate individual who fractured both legs. What could have ended in a total disaster was termed a "Miracle on the Hudson" by New York Governor David Paterson due to the quick thinking and sure-handedness of the pilot. He stated, "We've had a miracle on 34th Street. I believe now we've had a miracle on the Hudson. This pilot, somehow, without any engines, was somehow able to land this plane." The pilot had given each passenger and crew member the chance of survival, which was guaranteed as soon as they stepped onboard the rescue boats. Tom Fox, president of New York Water Taxi, said it best, "The pilot must have been both talented and charmed."

At the time of the crash, Chesley B. "Sully" Sullenberger III was 57 years old and had been flying with US Airways for 29 years. He had just pulled off a remarkable feat of flying, involving both fast decision-making about where to crash and the ability to pull off a complex maneuver. Shortly after arriving at the New York Waterway terminal on Pier 79, Captain Sullenberger was described as composed and unflustered, his navy-blue pilot's uniform barely wrinkled and his tie still straight. The New York Deputy Secretary for Public Safety recounted his interaction with the pilot, "He said to me, in the most unaffected, humble way, he says, 'That's what we're trained to do.' No boasting, no emotion, no nothing." A passenger, Nick Gamache, echoed these sentiments, describing the pilot as "the picture of calm." Although largely untested until that cold January day, Captain Sullenberger was right: the heroism he demonstrated was a career in the making.

Beyond having more than 30 years of flying experience as both a commercial pilot and Air Force fighter pilot, Captain Sullenberger was heavily steeped in safety. He had experience partnering with federal aviation officials investigating crashes and improving evacuation techniques. His appreciation for safety was evidenced by his walking the defunct craft to ensure a complete evacuation. Complementing his experience was a high level of aviation skill. Hidden deep down on his resume, Captain Sullenberger was awarded the Outstanding Cadet in Airmanship Award from the Air Force Academy, which is given to the top flier from each graduating class. Earlier still, he was also chosen for the cadet glider program from among a select group of about a dozen students, which provided an opportunity to learn a different type of flying. By the end of the year, he was an instructor on the program.

There is something else to Captain Sullenberger's make-up. Jake Brown, a neighbor to the family in Danville, California, was not surprised by the pilot's actions, stating, "He is someone who walks into a room and you know he is in charge." Other accounts of Sullenberger from his academy years confirm his high level of confidence and poise. Eric Vogel, a member of Captain Sullenberger's squadron and pilot with Southwest Airlines, described him as "unflappable."

Even in the midst of the emergency, Sullenberger's communication and tone of voice showed composure. During the interchange between air traffic controllers and the crew of Flight 1549, the only sign of fluster is when the plane's call sign was momentarily forgotten. Normally, the role of radio communication lies with the first officer, but in this instance, the first officer was struggling to restart the engines. It was left to Captain Sullenberger to both fly the plane and communicate with the controllers. In his first report of the emergency, he stated, ". . . hit birds, we lost thrust in both engines; we're turning back towards La Guardia." The tone and content would not be considered unusual for communications between pilots and controllers. In response to the controller asking if he could make it back, he stated, "Unable. . . . I am not sure if we can make any runway." When asked about Teterboro, New Jersey, the pilot responded, "We can't do it. We're gonna be in the Hudson." At this point, he was a few hundred feet off the ground and had not once described his situation as an emergency. The controller, Patrick Harten, in disbelief, later described his reaction, "I believed at that moment I was going to be the last person to talk to anyone on that plane alive. . . . I asked him to repeat himself even though I heard him just fine. I simply could not wrap my mind around those words."

This composure is not because Captain Sullenberger failed to understand the gravity of his situation. In an interview with the TV program *60 Minutes*, Captain Sullenberger described the event, "It was the worst sickening, pit-of-your-stomach, falling-through-the-floor feeling I've ever felt in my life. I knew immediately it was very bad." Yet he did not allow these feelings to overwhelm him into inaction or panic but rather to allow his training and talent to break free. There was absolutely no sign of choking under the pressure.

A recent study led by Samuel Vine at the University of Exeter sheds light on why Captain Sullenberger succeeded in a situation where other capable pilots would likely fail. The research team was interested in exploring how perceptions of stress relate to performance as well as to an individual's ability to focus attention on the task. Taking their cue from real life, the researchers created a replica of the conditions facing Flight 1549, an engine failure shortly after take-off, in a high-fidelity simulator. A group of professional pilots were put under the microscope to assess how effectively they would deal with the situation. Hard data about the pilots' actions were recorded via the simulation, while a professional flight instructor provided subjective feedback about their performance.

It was hypothesized that the way pilots thought about their situation would affect their ability to deal successfully with the emergency. Specifically, if the pilot decided that he or she had the capability to deal sufficiently with the demands of the situation, he or she would consider it to be a challenge rather than a threat. In addition, the researchers believed that how resilient the pilots were to feeling anxious would predict their ability to keep focused on the job. Under high levels of anxiety, the balance between goal-directed behavior (e.g., landing the plane) and a stimulus-driven reaction (e.g., paying attention to a flashing light) becomes off-kilter. Pilots susceptible to anxiety (viewing the emergency as a threat) were hypothesized to become distracted and lose the ability to plan and control their behaviors. They would choke.

The results of the simulator were clear. Pilots who reported that they had ample capability to deal with the emergency, regarding it more as a challenge than a threat, demonstrated a higher level of performance in what was captured both by the simulator (metrics such as speed and heading deviation) and evaluations by the flight instructor. Moreover, pilots who considered the emergency as a threat were more nervous and showed less ability to focus on how to effectively land the plane. Anxious pilots looked around more, became erratic in what they paid attention to, and were overwhelmed by information that was not immediately important to the goal of landing the plane.

The strength of the findings is truly amazing. Perceiving the situation as a threat or challenge predicted 61% of the flight instructor's evaluation, 33% of the heading deviation, and 21% of the speed deviation. In comparison, the years of the pilot's flying experience accounted for 12% of the instructor's evaluation, 15% of the heading deviation, and 30% of the speed deviation. In other words, how pilots thought about the emergency had a greater influence on the outcome than the amount of their flying experience. Coming in at a distant third, the age of the pilot accounted for between 2% and 5% of the pilot's performance on these three measures. As predicted, perceiving the situation as a threat accounted for as much as 68% of the pilot's ability to focus on controlling the intricacies of the plane's maneuvers.

Captain Sullenberger exemplifies the traits unearthed by the research team. Consistent with the opinions of his friends and neighbors, he exudes confidence in his ability to fly and, therefore, would no doubt think of the emergency situation more like a challenge than a threat. As shown through his interactions with the controller and eye-witness accounts of the crash, he was absolutely focused on the task and made split-second decisions that allowed for the best possible outcome given the situation that he faced. To top it all off, Captain Sullenberger had racked up a wealth of experience that was highly aligned with the scenario, specifically his academy years flying gliders and his safety work in evacuations. Captain Sullenberger was right to have confidence in his abilities and, thankfully, he put them all to good use on that frigid day in January. If he was any less confident in his ability, the outcome may have been very different.

Betting the Bank

There are times when confidence, especially when misplaced and unrelated to true capability, leads to spectacular failure. Such is the story of Nick Leeson, whose dramatic rise and fall from fortune landed him a place in *Time Magazine*'s Top 25 Crimes of Century. Yet, unlike other criminals on the list, such as the Unabomber or Jeffrey Dahmer, Nick is relatively unknown, especially outside of the United Kingdom. The type of damage done by Nick is not in the same category as murder, but it nonetheless wreaked havoc on the lives of those who worked alongside him at Barings Bank.

Nick came from humble beginnings. He was born on February 25, 1967, and started his life in the Watford, UK, council estate, the son of a plasterer. Nothing in his early education would indicate the type of high-powered financial jobs he was to hold as a young professional. Nick failed his final math exam and left school with only a handful of qualifications. Nonetheless, Nick landed a job in the City, working as a clerk in one of the most esteemed financial institutions, the Royal Bank of Coutts and Company. After a string of successful jobs in financial services, including 2 years at Morgan Stanley, he joined Barings Bank in 1989 and was soon promoted to the trading floor. Nick's reputation grew rapidly, and he soon found himself in a powerful position managing a new operation trading futures on the Singapore Monetary Exchange. By placing trades on the future direction of the Nikkei Index, Nick made millions for Barings and became a trusted name. For his part, Nick was earning close to £150,000, taking luxury vacations, and living in highly desirable apartment with his wife Lisa.

Barings Bank was founded in 1762, initially as a merchant house for wool traders, but it soon expanded its services to a wide range of customers. With this move, it became Britain's oldest merchant bank. Among its most highly known achievements was the funding of the Louisiana Purchase in 1803, where the United States acquired a significant portion of land from France and, in so doing, doubled its size. Later that century, Barings expanded its commercial activities, such as floating the Guinness Brewery in 1886. Despite nearly going bust in 1890, when Argentina appeared close to defaulting on its debts to the bank, Barings survived and began acquiring securities businesses. The bank built its reputation as one of the most prestigious in the banking sector. The bank didn't have a logo, but instead had a crest; Her Majesty the Queen was a key customer. All the while, the bank was controlled by the Barings family.

Nick's job at the bank was to trade in derivatives, betting on how well the Nikkei 225 Index would fair in the future. Nick excelled at his job. In 1993 alone, he made £10 million for the bank, representing 10% of the total profit for the bank that year. In his autobiography, Nick described his time at the bank, "We were all driven to make profits, profits, and more profits. . . . I was the rising star." According to Jason Rodrigues writing for *The Guardian*, his colleagues agreed: "Some colleagues said he was 'brilliant' and the 'most confident trader in town.' Others said he was a 'high-flyer who liked to dabble in dare-devil trades.'" Unknown to the leadership team in London, the seeds for Leeson's downfall were already sowed. An inexperienced team member had made a mistake that caused a loss of £20,000 for the bank. Nick's reaction was telling; he decided to hide what had occurred by creating a false client account under the code 88888. When Nick's luck began to take a turn for the worse, he began to hide his own losses in the same account. This was not helped by the fact that Nick oversaw both the trading floor and transaction settlement operations, something that would not be allowed today.

A spiral of unfortunate events began to occur, and Nick found himself on the losing side of the bets he made about the Japanese economy. Fueling Nick's spiral were the rules governing market trading at the time, which stipulated that only a small percentage of the trade value was required at the time of purchase. By the end of 1994, Nick was hiding £208 million of losses in account 88888. This sum amounted to almost half of the capital held by Barings. His bosses in London were unaware of the losses, believing Nick's explanation that the hole in the accounts represented debts owed by Baring's clients. Believing that the business was performing well, they trebled Nick's bonus, rewarding him with a £450,000 paycheck.

Rather than face reality and the scorn of his bosses, Nick dug in deeper. He made the bet that the Nikkei Index would not fall below 19,000 points, which was a reasonable assumption given that the Japanese economy was rebounding from a 30-month recession. What Nick was not able to predict was the devastating earthquake that hit the Japanese city of Kobe on January 17, 1995. The market plunged by 7% and, with it, Nick's hope to escape the hole he had dug for himself.

With the market below 19,000 points, Nick asked for and was granted $1 billion to continue trading in the hope of a post-quake rebound. The financial exposure for the bank was huge and getting worse. Instead of hedging the exposure, Nick continued to buy futures, mounting to more than 20,000 contracts worth about $180,000 each. He alone was trying to move the market back to the magical 19,000-point mark. The market failed to respond, and, in the end, Nick had amassed $1.3 billion in losses, three-quarters of which occurred in his last-ditch efforts. The scale of the losses could no longer be disguised, and, in February 1995, Barings conducted a spot audit of Nick's operations. Taking in the full extent of the situation, Peter Baring met the deputy governor for the Bank of England to inform him that the bank had gone bust. A week later, Barings was purchased by the Dutch bank

ING for just £1. Many of Nick's 1,200 fellow employees lost their jobs and the bank's investors were seething.

The collapse sent shockwaves through the financial services industry in London. The situation exposed that the Bank of England did not have sufficient oversight of Barings and therefore was unable to take preventive action. In his report to the Commons, the chancellor, Kenneth Clarke, iterated that Baring's fall "came from unauthorized and concealed trading positions" and "serious problems of controls and management failings within the Barings group." Two years after Barings' collapse, the Bank of England was stripped of some of its powers, and the Financial Services Authority was established to police the banking sector. The event also confirmed the need to separate the front from the back office, as well as the role of risk control within investment banks.

Realizing the trouble he was in, Nick went on the run with his wife, first to Borneo and then to Frankfurt, Germany. On his final day in the Barings office, he scribbled a note that simply said, "I'm sorry." He was found, arrested, and eventually extradited to Singapore after being held for close to 9 months in a German prison. Landing at Changi Airport in Singapore, Nick wore gym gear and a reversed baseball cap. He looked relaxed and composed despite facing charges of forgery and fraud. Nick pleaded guilty to his charges, and, in an attempt for leniency, his lawyer related the personal hardship Nick experienced with a recent miscarriage and his personal financial ruin. Unmoved, the judge sentenced him to 6 ½ years in prison. Nick did not appeal the decision, but in the end only served 4 years in jail. Two-thirds of the way through his sentence, he was diagnosed with colon cancer and was released for recovery.

The trip back to London was nothing short of a celebration, with Nick indulging in champagne and smoked salmon with a group of British journalists. Despite his recklessness and illicit behavior, Nick financially ended up on top, making £200,000 for a combined book deal and newspaper serialization about his story. He also garnered a share of the £7 million profit from *Rogue Trader*, the 1999 film based on his book, starring Ewan McGregor and Anna Friel. Although sensationalized, the description of the movie captures the gist of Nick's story.

Ewan McGregor brings a dynamic screen presence to this riveting motion picture about how greed, excess, and high-stakes gambling brought down one of Britain's oldest and most successful financial institutions. When he

is sent to Singapore by the 200-year-old Barings Bank, futures trader Nick
Leeson (McGregor) dreams of making a killing in the stock market. But
even though his firm believes Nick is the most successful trader they've ever
employed, he secretly begins to steal vast amounts of their own money to
cover his risky financial wagering. With debts to match his desperation for
a way out, Nick risks everything in a frantic bid to beat the system and win
back the money!

Nick's marriage did not fare as well. Despite Lisa's initial support and frequent prison visits, their marriage could not survive the revelation that Nick
had indulged in hiring Geisha girls when he was living the high life.

Nick stated that, early in his jail sentence, he exercised vigorously and became spiritual. This deteriorated with the combination of his divorce from
Lisa, surgery and chemotherapy to treat his cancer, and the general drudgery
of being locked up in a small cell 23 hours out of the day. Nick proved resilient, rebounding both professionally and in personal health. He attained
a psychology degree from Middlesex University, remarried, and became a
father to a baby boy in 2004. Surprisingly, he also became an active speaker
on topics of risk management, compliance, and corporate responsibility. In
2005, Nick was appointed Commercial Manager of Galway United Football
Club, which led first to a promotion to General Manager and eventually CEO
with the club.

Across the articles written about him, as well as his personal accounts, it
is unclear just how much personal responsibility Nick accepts about what
occurred. On his personal website, Nick writes, "Rogue trading is probably
a daily occurrence amongst the financial markets. Not enough focus goes on
those risk management areas, those compliance areas, those settlement areas,
that can ultimately save them money." The talks he gives to corporations and
as a motivational speaker focus on either what companies can do to avoid the
next rogue trader or how individuals can recover from adversity. What goes
unsaid is how much personal responsibility he accepts for the downfall of
Barings or, specifically, why he was the one who broke the bank.

The Harder They Fall

Confidence in one's ability can enable individuals to do truly great and he-
roic things. Such was the case of Captain Sullenberger, whose personal

confidence came together with his expert flying skills to pull off a successful landing on the Hudson River. What Captain Sullenberger showed us is that confidence is not enough; individuals need to the ability to master their own fate. This lesson was clearly visible in the tale of Nick Leeson. Despite having all the confidence in the world, Nick's delusion that he was a master trader with absolute control of the market did not pan out. Nick's ability to control his environment was out of step with his confidence. Instead of admitting defeat when the situation turned south, he decided to double-down on his strategy, setting in motion one of the most significant crimes of the century.

Nick's tenacity is intriguing. Given a similar challenge to one's ego, others might have accepted defeat or used the feedback as a point of reflection and a reason to change. Instead, Nick failed to accept the feedback, believing that he could recoup the losses he amassed. At the core of it, Nick's ego and reputation were on the line. Nick was known as a financial wiz on derivatives, a financial product that was neither widely known about nor understood. Admitting defeat would dent his perfect record and status in the company, raising doubt that his prior success might have been due to luck rather than inherent skill. Instead of walking away with a bruised ego, Nick opted for handcuffs.

Individual differences in dealing with ego threat are not uncommon and play out across social contexts, from politics to industry. Of the more visible variety, professional sports provides the rare opportunity to track what happens to performance following ego threat. Every year, a headline appears of a star athlete who has fallen from grace in a spectacularly bad way. Names like Tiger Woods and Lance Armstrong come to mind, with sports enthusiasts scratching their heads about how such incredibly talented individuals could go wrong. When the cracks first begin to show, well-known athletes turn to drugs to enhance performance, act out in strange ways, or simply fizzle out to the bottom of the leader board.

Recent research by Jennifer Carson Marr and Stefan Thau has confirmed what has been often suspected among athletes: the higher the athlete's status, the harder the fall when his or her ego is threatened. Of the different sports to study, professional baseball is rich in data and therefore fertile ground for psychologists. The research team investigated professional baseball players who had undergone final-offer salary arbitration between 1974 and 2011, investigating whether status loss experienced in the arbitration process would impact performance during the following season. The type of arbitrations studied are the last-ditch efforts by the league to resolve salary disputes between clubs and players. Both the player and the club submit a salary figure to a third-party arbitrator who is given the task to accept the number provided by either the player or club. With no compromise position available, there is a clear winner and loser to the arbitration, which itself is highly visible to those following the game.

In general, players and clubs wish to avoid the arbitration process as much as possible because bad blood can build up between the parties. In arbitration, clubs are required to justify their salary position, poking holes in the players' talents, contributions to the club, and off-field support, all of which also damage the reputation of the team. When the arbitration goes against the player, it is a clear message that the player is not as good as he thinks. Yet how the arbitrator got to his or her position is masked in subjectivity, especially as the arbitrator is not required to submit written documentation. Factors such as comparable salaries, long-term player trends in performance and team contribution, and past compensation all enter into the equation. In addition, the arbitrator is under tight time pressure to make a judgment call, given only 24 hours to make a final decision.

Across the years studied, 186 players underwent arbitration and met the researchers' criteria for having full, clean performance data. To establish a baseline for each player's status before arbitration, a combination of All-Star Game selections and major awards (Silver Slugger, Gold Glove, Rookie of the Year, and Most Valuable Player) were considered. Post arbitration performance was measured by looking at on-base percentage (the number of times a player reaches a base independent of how he got there, divided by the number of times he was at bat) and slugging percentage (how many bases the player attained at bat, which is considered a measure of hit quality). Beyond these measures, the researchers explored a range of other variables that might affect performance, including individual and team performance prior to arbitration, player age, and injuries.

When all the numbers were crunched, the researchers found that high-status players were as likely as low-status players to lose in salary arbitration, yet the effects of this choice were very different. Beyond the overall trends of individual and team performance, a noticeable and significant pattern emerged. Players who had the highest pre-arbitration status (having more All-Star Game selections and given major awards) experienced a major slump in performance following an arbitration loss. The same was not true for low-status players; the arbitration decision had no effect on their performance and they continued to play baseball as if nothing had occurred.

With a knock to their ego, high-status players might have been expected to improve their game as a way of proving what they were worth and that they were in fact All-Stars. Rather, the players appear to have responded by doubting their own worth and ability, taking the arbitrator's decision to heart. It is a great demonstration of a well-known phenomenon of choking under pressure, where negative feedback impedes performance, especially on complex or novel tasks, by encouraging distracting thoughts. Under ego threat, players have a tendency to pay attention to the wrong things and second-guess their ability. Those with the highest status experience the greatest threat (the feedback received is considerably different from the self-perception that they have become accustomed to) and therefore are thought to succumb to a downward spiral more easily. In the case of a star baseball player who has recently lost his arbitration, he might feel distracted and question his own abilities when at bat rather than paying attention to the speed and direction of the pitch.

In more typical workplaces, challenges to an individual's status may occur on a fairly frequent basis. Companies come together in mergers and acquisitions, causing a realignment in titles, levels, or pay. Sales territories change, promotions are decided, and individuals are pulled from projects prematurely based on customer or peer feedback. The opportunities for negative feedback and ego threat are boundless, and what this research demonstrates is that those individuals with the greatest track record (the equivalent of being selected for the All-Star Game or being recognized as the Rookie of the Year) are at the greatest risk of choking and falling into a downward spiral. This is particularly alarming for the Captain Sullenbergers of the world who back up their confidence with a great degree of talent. These are the individuals that every organization wishes to retain and therefore extra care should be taken to lessen the blow of unwarranted negative feedback.

As at no other time, the average employee is immersed in feedback. Customer statistics are captured on a minute-by-minute basis, satisfaction surveys are the norm, and development experts all push for greater self-awareness and an open feedback culture. Contingent workers in the gig economy are not immune from this trend, as contract performance is tightly monitored. A freelancer's track record is also well known, with five-star reviews tagged to work products. There is a general assumption that the more feedback the better, without considering what happens to the confidence of those receiving the feedback. If an individual has relatively low status in their profession or lacks the ability to justify their status, the benefits might outweigh the costs. Yet, for those individuals with the best track records and proven ability, significantly negative feedback might jeopardize future performance to the extent that their initial greatness is unlikely to resurface. A self-fulfilling prophecy is started where negative feedback is proved with future poor performance. As such, organizations might want to pause before encouraging a free-for-all on feedback.

Yet negative feedback is often unavoidable. Careers do go sideways, and projects will fail even for the most seasoned employee. How organizations and managers deal with adverse situations may play a large part in restoring the confidence of the most talented employees. Focusing on the constructive elements of failure, viewing it as a challenge to overcome rather than a test of personal capability, and being sensitive to how status changes can impact the psyche of employees can all go a long way toward minimizing the chances of choking. Reminding them how they got selected to the equivalent of the All-Star Game can build up resilience to self-threat by undoing the recency effect, where focus is drawn to whatever just occurred.

What is made clear by this combination of stories is that individuals need support when experiencing significant ego threat. Without intervention, star players become mediocre, while those with reckless personalities and a lack of ability go rouge. Recognizing and reacting to ego threats on behalf of direct reports should be on the mind of any leader whose organization is undergoing change, as well as those who are required to deliver bad news. Meanwhile, preserving talented employees' confidence and providing them new opportunities to thrive can allow them to be selected to the equivalent of the All-Star Game for a second time.

6

Power

During the long days of summer, on a typical Sunday morning in Palo Alto, California, a police car pulled up to the curb in front a house in a quiet residential section of the city. The officer jumped out of the car, walked to the front door of an unassuming house, and quietly proceeded to arrest a young man. Unknown to his neighbors, the man was being charged with burglary. As per normal procedures, the suspect was searched, handcuffed, read his rights, and loaded into the squad car. At the station, the suspect was formally booked, fingerprinted, and placed into a holding cell. The arrest went as well as could be expected, and the officer was soon off to arrest another suspect. It was a busy day for the police as the suspect was one of nine others included for mass arrest that morning for similar violations. Five young men were charged with burglary and another four for armed robbery.

After a short wait, the nine prisoners were transferred individually to the Stanford County Jail for further processing and to be held until trial. Atypical for police procedures, each prisoner was blind-folded prior to transport to the jail. Upon arrival, they were searched a second time, stripped naked, and deloused with spray to limit the spread of lice and other disease. They were issued a uniform, which was nothing more than a smock and sandals with no underclothes, and a prison ID number. A chain was attached to each man's ankle, and they were instructed to wear a nylon stocking cap to maintain hygiene while in custody. They were placed into cells and left to consider the seriousness of the charges held against them.

Common among the prisoners was their absolute innocence in committing the alleged charges. They were guilty of no more than responding to a local newspaper ad calling for volunteers to take part in a psychological experiment. The nine men arrested were the lucky applicants from a pool of 70 individuals who responded to the advertisement. The men chosen for the study passed a series of assessments, including psychological and medical screenings and a review of their criminal history and drug use. The successful volunteers were chosen to represent an average group of healthy, intelligent,

Punching the Clock. Joe Ungemah, Oxford University Press (2021). © Oxford University Press.
DOI: 10.1093/oso/9780190061241.003.0006.

and middle-class males who were thought capable of enduring the stress of being placed in a prison environment.

The prisoners were not the only participants in the experiment. Nine other men were chosen by the flip of a coin to become prison guards. They were to run the day-to-day operations of the prison. New to their positions, they were provided no specific training on how to do their jobs, but rather were given free rein to do what they believed was necessary to maintain order and gain the respect of the prisoners. The guards were issued uniforms of their own comprised of khaki clothes, a whistle, billy club, and mirrored sunglasses, which allowed the guards a certain amount of anonymity and the concealment of emotion.

Overlooking the prison was Warden David Jaffe, an undergraduate from Stanford University, and the Prison Superintendent, Dr. Philip Zimbardo. The experiment was Zimbardo's brainchild to explore the effects of roles, labels, and social expectations in prison environments. In constructing his prison, Zimbardo went to great lengths to create an environment where the variables affecting real prisoners could play themselves out and be observed. He partnered with a former prisoner to construct the simulated jail, as well as conducted interviews with ex-convicts and correctional officers.

The basement of Stanford's Psychology Department became the Stanford County Jail (explaining why the prisoners were blindfolded during transfer). A long corridor became the yard, which was the only area where prisoners could walk, eat, or exercise outside their cells. Prison cells were created from individual laboratories by installing doors with steel bars and cell numbers. A small closet opposite the cells became the hole, which was to be used for solitary confinement. At only 2 feet wide and 2 feet deep, the room was just big enough to stand in. The prison had no windows or clocks to mark the passage of time. An intercom system allowed public announcements to prisoners, as well as a means to record conversations and gather data.

Zimbardo did his best to simulate a prison environment with the resources he had. Equally, the treatment of prisoners on their arrival to the prison mirrored real life, without being 100% accurate. In reality, prison uniforms are not smocks, and wearing underwear is highly encouraged if not mandatory. Zimbardo intended the uniforms to humiliate the prisoners and make them feel emasculated. The chain on the foot was intended to remind volunteers of their oppression and that escape was unlikely. ID numbers created anonymity; from booking onward, the volunteers were called by their

ID numbers only. Last, the stocking cap was used to simulate the shaving of prisoners' heads, which minimizes individuality and exerts control over the prisoners.

Upon arrival, Zimbardo greeted each prisoner by stating, "As you probably know, I'm your warden. All of you have shown that you are unable to function outside in the real world for one reason or the another—that somehow you lack the responsibility of good citizens of this great country. We of this prison, your correctional staff, are going to help you learn what your responsibilities as citizens of this country are." From there, prisoners were given a set of 17 rules to abide by, which were reinforced and repeated often. Guards were instructed to read the list twice and on the second reading to state, "Prisoners are part of a correctional community. In order to keep the community running smoothly, prisoners must obey the following rules." Notable rules that maintained the illusion of a real institution included "Prisoners must address each other by number only," "Prisoners must always address the guards as Mr. Correctional Officer," and "Prisoners must never refer to their condition as an experiment or a simulation. They are prisoners until paroled."

Among the rules were a set of privileges or deterrents that the guards could use to reward or punish prisoners as they saw fit. These rules included, "Smoking is a privilege. Smoking will be allowed after meals or at the discretion of the guards," "Mail is a privilege. All mail flowing in and out of the prison will be inspected and censored," and "Visitors are a privilege. Prisoners who are allowed a visitor must meet him at the door of the yard. The visit will be supervised by a guard. The guard may terminate the visit at his discretion." As will be discussed shortly, the use of privileges became a central means for guards to take control of the situation and exert their authority.

The first hours of the experiment were dominated by guards and prisoners deciding how they should react to their new environment and roles. At first, the prisoners showed signs that they were not taking the experiment seriously. Picking up on this sentiment, the guards decided to assert their authority. At 2:30 in the morning, the first of many prisoner counts occurred. Guards blew strongly into their whistles, waking the prisoners from a dead sleep and requiring them to call out their numbers. If disobedience was witnessed during one of these counts or otherwise, the guards imposed physical punishments on the prisoners. For example, a prisoner might be required to do push-ups while being stepped on by a guard or, alternatively, with another prisoner sitting on his back.

Not all the prisoners accepted the guards' authority. On the morning of the second day, a prison rebellion broke out. Prisoners took off their caps, removed their numbers, and barricaded themselves in their rooms, using their beds for leverage. Acting with anger and frustration, the night guards stayed on shift to join the day guards, while the on-call guards were also brought into the prison. Improvising with the fire extinguishers found in the building, the nine guards forced prisoners away from the doors with a chilling stream of carbon dioxide. Cell by cell, the guards retook the prison and re-established order. They stripped the prisoners naked, removed the beds from the rooms, and placed the assumed ringleader into the closet that served as solitary confinement. From then onward, prisoner harassment and intimidation was a daily affair.

To bolster their control under normal conditions, with a prisoner-to-guard ratio of 3:1, the guards set up a privilege cell, where prisoners received special treatment. The three prisoners least involved in the rebellion were given their clothes and bed back, provided an opportunity to bathe, and allowed to eat while the others were denied food or drink. From the look of things, it appeared that the guards were attempting to reward obedient behavior and punish all those who challenged their authority. Yet, after a few hours, the guards switched up the mix by placing some of the most disobedient prisoners into the privilege cell. This switch caused a great deal of confusion among prisoners, and, ultimately, they began to distrust each other for their individual relationships with the guards. Why and how prisoners received special treatment was no longer public knowledge. Through such tactics, the guards succeeding in not only turning the prisoners against each other, but also in creating more solidarity among themselves.

The laboratory became more and more like a prison by the hour. All aspects of the prisoner's day were controlled by the whim of the guards. A simple request to walk down the yard to the toilet became a privilege often denied, with the result that many prisoners resorted to using a bucket kept in their cells for that purpose. Emptying the buckets also became a privilege, and it was not long until the prison began to reek of excrement. The guards held grudges and treated prisoner 5401 especially badly for his role in the rebellion. Knowing that he was a heavy smoker, they played with his dependency and controlled when he had access to his cigarettes. Other tactics included tedious tasks, like moving cartons back and forth between closets. The guards even dragged the prisoners' blankets through a patch of thorns to create work for the prisoners to pick them off prior to lights out.

The power of their actions began to have the desired effect, and, less than 36 hours after the opening of the prison, the guards had to release their first prisoner. Prisoner 8612 began showing signs of emotional distress that included uncontrollable crying, erratic thinking, and anger. Instead of immediately recognizing these signs as indicators of true distress, the research team asked the participant to think things over before quitting and promptly returned him to his cell. During the next count, Prisoner 8612 told the other prisoners, "You can't leave. You can't quit," before breaking down in a bout of uncontrolled rage.

Eventually Prisoner 8612 was released; however, the effect he had on the prison was felt for days to come. Guards overheard a rumor among the inmates that Prisoner 8612 was intending to return to the prison with a group of his friends to break the others free. Instead of acting as objective scientists, Zimbardo and his research team became concerned about the security of their prison and took immediate measures to foil the plot. First, they introduced a confederate into the prison, placing him into Prisoner 8612's original cell, to gain information on the escape plan. Second, Zimbardo approached the Palo Alto Police Department to arrange for the prisoners to be transferred to a real jail. Zimbardo was disgusted that his request was denied due to a lack of insurance by the county. Fully immersed in his fictional world, Zimbardo struggled to understand the lack of support between the correctional facilities.

Moving quickly to Plan B, Zimbardo instructed the guards to dismantle the jail, call in reinforcements, place bags over the prisoners' heads, chain them together, and transport them to a storage room located on the fifth floor. Zimbardo would wait for the escape party to arrive, tell them that the experiment was over, and ask the conspirators to leave. After they left, Zimbardo would double the security of the prison to ensure that no further breakouts would be possible. Nothing materialized that night, and Zimbardo found himself waiting alone, fully immersed in his role of prison superintendent.

Visitation was offered to parents and friends of the prisoners. To keep up appearances that all was right with the experiment, the prisoners were washed, shaved, and groomed. The cells were swept out and prisoners fed a larger meal than normal to improve their spirits. Music was played over the intercom and an attractive cheerleader was even hired as the receptionist for the day. To control the visitation experience further, each visitor was required to register, wait 30 minutes before seeing their loved one, and were permitted only 10 minutes to interact under the constant surveillance of a guard. Fiction began to bleed into reality when parents arrived. Before entering the visitation area, they were required to meet with the warden to discuss the criminal case against their sons. After witnessing signs of emotional and physical stress, the parents failed to challenge the efficacy of the experiment, but rather made appeals to improve conditions. They, too, had succumbed to the simulation.

Parents and friends were not the only visitors to the jail. Zimbardo invited a Catholic priest who had previously served as a prison chaplain to observe the experiment. He proceeded to interview each prisoner individually, whereupon half of the prisoners introduced themselves by number. After some initial discussion, the priest asked, "Son, what are you doing to get out of here?" He then suggested that the prisoners seek legal counsel and offered to contact their parents to make arrangements. Several inmates took him up on the offer. The situation got so far out of hand that one set of parents had contacted their cousin, who was a public defender. The lawyer came to the prison, interviewed each of the inmates, and talked through options to raise bail.

One prisoner refused to meet with the priest. Prisoner 819 was in a bad state. Feeling sick and refusing food, he requested to see a doctor rather than the priest. When persuaded to come out of his cell, the prisoner began to cry hysterically. Zimbardo removed him from the prison and allowed him to rest in a nearby room. While resting, Prisoner 819 began to hear a noise from the yard. The other prisoners were chanting, "Prisoner 819 is a bad prisoner. Because of what Prisoner 819 did, my cell is a mess, Mr. Correctional Officer," which was repeated a dozen times. This made matters worse for Prisoner 819, who was now crying uncontrollably. He began to waiver in his desire to leave the prison, now feeling a need to improve his reputation among the other inmates. It was only when Zimbardo snapped out of his role as Prison Superintendent and reiterated that it was an experiment and not a real prison that Prisoner 819 gained the courage to leave the prison.

With prisoner numbers falling, a new participant was called in and admitted to the prison. Unlike the others who had become accustomed to the torment of the guards, Prisoner 416 was taken by surprise by the situation. When told by the other inmates that quitting was impossible, Prisoner 416 began a hunger strike to force his release. The guards reacted and broke their own rules about how long a prisoner could be left in solitary confinement, placing Prisoner 416 in the hole for 3 hours. Whereas his bold actions would have been celebrated earlier in the experiment, the other inmates branded

Prisoner 416 a troublemaker. Taking advantage of the situation, the guards asked the other prisoners whether they would trade in their blankets for the release of Prisoner 416 from solitary confinement. Instead, they opted to keep him there for the night.

A parole board was created to hear the plights of the prisoners, comprised of departmental secretaries and graduate students who were unknown to the participants. One by one, each prisoner appeared before the board to argue for his release. When asked whether they would forfeit the money earned to take part in the experiment, most prisoners said yes. What sparked Zimbardo's interest is that this same result could have occurred at any time by simply quitting the experiment. Yet, without fail, the prisoners returned to their cells, not realizing their freedom and succumbing to the power of the situation.

After only 6 days of a planned 2-week experiment, Zimbardo called an end to the experiment. By reviewing video footage of the prison, the guards were escalating their harassment at night, causing a very real liability for long-term physical and emotional harm. The implications of this deterioration in prisoner treatment was brought home for Zimbardo when Dr. Christina Maslach, a fellow psychologist and his future wife, visited the prison to conduct interviews with the participants. Having witnessed the prisoners being paraded to the toilet chained together with bags over their heads, she strongly voiced her outrage to Zimbardo, arguing that he had become indifferent to the suffering of the participants by playing the role of Prison Superintendent. Her concern was real. Even with extensive counseling after the experiment, the participants felt that they had experienced something profound. Two months after the experiment, Prisoner 416 spoke about his experience.

> I began to feel that I was losing my identity . . . because it was a prison to me; it still is a prison to me. I don't regard it as an experiment or a simulation because it was a prison run by psychologists instead of run by the state. I began to feel that identity, the person that I was that had decided to go to prison was distant from me—was remote until finally I wasn't that, I was 416. I was really my number.

The Role Makes the Man

Among the guards, some took a great deal of pleasure from the power that they wielded. The most brutal was nicknamed "John Wayne," so-called for his macho demeanor and candor at forcing prisoners to obey. Even among the more level-headed guards, none wished to end the experiment prematurely, and all guards came to work on time, worked their full shifts, and put in extra hours without demanding paid overtime. Inspiration for how they treated the prisoners came from popular media about what it meant to be a guard. At the time, real guard training was scant, with new guards left to learn the job from the "old bulls" who had already mastered how to do it. For example, the orientation manual for San Quentin stated, "the only way to know San Quentin is through experience and time. Some of us take more time and must go through more experiences than others to accomplish this; some really never do get there."

Emulating the real world, Zimbardo's guards made choices to act according to what they believed was right and expected in their powerful roles. Changes in behavior occurred quickly and were profound. One of the guards reflected,

> I was surprised at myself. . . . I made them call each other names and clean toilets out with their bare hands. I practically considered the prisoners cattle, and I kept thinking: "I have to watch out for them in case they try something."

Another guard spoke about the transformation in his emotions and actions

> During the inspection, I went to cell 2 to mess up a bed which the prisoner had made and he grabbed me, screaming that he had just made it, and he wasn't going to let me mess it up. He grabbed my throat, and although he was laughing I was pretty scared. . . . I lashed out with my stick and hit him in the chin (although not very hard), and when I freed myself I became angry. I wanted to get back in the cell and have a go with him, since he attacked me when I was not ready.

Participants who would normally be described as healthy, normal, and educated young men had resorted to violence fueled by anger due to the roles and environment that had arbitrarily been assigned to them.

Just as there were differences among guards, so, too, did the prisoners differ in their coping strategies. Initially, many of the prisoners reacted to their situation by directly challenging the guards. After the failed rebellion, such attacks were less common. Others coped by becoming model prisoners, agreeing to all demands of the guards in the hope of preferential treatment.

A third group didn't react well to the experiment at all, breaking down emotionally and, in one instance, developing a psychosomatic rash over his entire body. Analysis of the audio recordings revealed a lack of solidarity among the prisoners, with 85% of comments found to be uncomplimentary and deprecating about each other. Unlike the guards who gained in group cohesion during the course of the experiment, the prisoners became more like an assemblage of individuals than a solitary group.

When later asked about the purpose of the experiment and to reflect on its core findings, Zimbardo draws attention to the way that social norms are played out based on roles, labels, and social expectations. In the experiment, the guards and prisoners took their roles so seriously that the line between simulation and reality became blurred, to the point that the experiment had to be called off less than halfway through its intended run. Believing that the experimental design would make for great television, the BBC decided to replicate the experiment and air it during the Spring of 2002. Just like the original, the TV version came to a premature end due to a deterioration of prisoner treatment. Participants were warned that they would be exposed to exercise, tasks, hardship, hunger, solitude, and anger; however, the extent of the abuse was unanticipated, causing severe stress and anxiety.

In 1973, Zimbardo asked the American Psychological Association to review the ethics of the experiment and, surprising to some, the organization ruled that all existing ethical guidelines were followed. Just like many other studies of the time, the level of scrutiny today would likely never allow for such an experiment to be conducted at an institution for higher education. For his part, Zimbardo is honest in his personal regrets about how the experiment was conducted, "I was guilty of the sin of omission—the evil of inaction—of not providing adequate oversight and surveillance when it was required . . . the findings came at the expense of human suffering. I am sorry for that and to this day apologize for contributing to this inhumanity."

Yet the experiment did occur and we have gained insight into how human behavior is transformed by positions of power and influence. The applications of this insight extend beyond the walls of a prison to any position that allows for the control of other human beings, as in politics or commerce. When given a position of power, behavioral scripts are formed by referencing examples of people who have held similar positions, whether they are from an individual's personal network or in the popular media. Some of these reference points can be described as benevolent, while others take on more of an authoritarian and ruthless tone. For example, in Charles Dickens's *A*

Christmas Carol, Scrooge worked for the benevolent Mr. Fezziwig in his youth. Instead of following the example set before him, Scrooge turned into a miser, keeping the poor Bob Cratchit under his watchful eye. How and why Scrooge deviated from his original reference point is anyone's guess.

Others in authority provide a model for actions, demeanor, and approach that is tested out by those new to their position of power. For example, if a manager finds it difficult to approach an employee who is demonstrating poor performance, they might adopt an authoritarian tone and push harder for results as a starting point. This is especially true if he or she lacked a role model who used more encouraging tactics to find out the root cause for the employee's behavior. The strength of the behavioral script builds with each perceived success or role model exhibiting like-minded behavior. It is not hard to see how a particularly hierarchical or authoritarian culture emerges as the script of each leader plays off and feeds the scripts of others. Just like the guards in the experiment, managers grow in their solidarity, believing that their approach to management is the only right and proper way to run an organization. With the role of a consistent and well-experienced manager under threat in the gig economy, there is a potential for an increase in stereotypically authoritarian behavior. Opportunities to observe positive role models who take the time to understand employee needs and desires may become a rarity.

The difference between exerting authority and bullying is sometimes a fine line. In the prison experiment, signs of harassment leading to real physical and emotional harm were clearly evident. Such behaviors do occur in the real world, where one party has power and control over another, in contexts ranging from domestic abuse to military occupations. The natural tendency to demonstrate power through action is so prevalent that safeguards are put in place to keep it at bay. Companies go through great lengths to establish policies, grievance processes, employee help lines, and training to ensure that damages caused by bullying are not only corrected, but prevented from occurring in the first place. Yet such programs are dealing with only the most visible forms of abuse and do little to counteract the deep-seated psychological processes that govern behavior.

When the Effects of Power Are Hidden

The 2016 Academy Awards could be described as anything but ordinary. Beginning with the announcements of the nominees and building up through the month of January, the Academy became the center of intense scrutiny for lacking to recognize the work of females and minorities. Rebranded as "OscarsSoWhite," a tipping point was reached about the dominance of white nominees that was building up for half a decade. The list of 2016 nominees included not a single black or minority actor for any of the four Oscar acting categories (Best Actor, Best Supporting Actor, Best Actress, Best Supporting Actress). In pure numbers, that represents 20 nominees without representation. Worse still, this was the second year in a row where a lack of diversity was evident across categories. Outcry was raised over the dismissal of *Straight Outta Compton* for best picture and a notably strong performance by Will Smith in *Concussion*. The situation was made more awkward by the fact that prominent black comedian Chris Rock was chosen in part by the Academy to help make the event more inclusive, but the comedian faced pressure from his peers to step down from his commitment.

Notable talent began to boycott the event, including Spike Lee and Jada Pinkett Smith, timing their decision with the celebration of the Martin Luther King Day. Reaction to the boycott among the Academy was mixed. Some members showed solidarity with the boycott. One anonymous member commented "They're not embarrassed today, they're disgusted." Another stated, "The irony is, if Hollywood is not open to diversity, then we're in real trouble as a country, because Hollywood is supposed to be liberal and open." Other members questioned whether a boycott was the right approach. Colin McFarlane was quoted as saying, "You've got to be at the party to change the conversation, but I completely understand the frustration—black actors are being written out of history." And others showed no support for the cause. Charlotte Rampling, who was nominated for Best Actress for her role in *45 Years*, was quoted as stating, "We can never know. . . . But maybe it's because no black actors merited being nominated."

The nomination process can be considered a classic example of indirect discrimination. Specifically, the makeup of the Academy itself is likely to blame for the lack of recognition. To become an Academy member, individuals are required to be employed in the film industry and generally fall within 17 branches covering actors, writers, directors, and producers. Two other categories were created to cover individuals who fell outside of these branches and were called members-at-large or associates. Each branch had its own requirements for membership. For actors, this included three theatrical film credits that were of "a caliber that reflect the high standards of the Academy," with one appearance occurring in the past 5 years. In contrast, directors required a minimum of two directional credits, one of which should be within the past 10 years. In order to become a member, an individual required sponsorship from two existing Academy members from the same branch (e.g., actors sponsoring actors). The only loophole to the sponsorship rule was if someone received a nomination for an Academy Award. Both nominees and sponsored candidates were reviewed by the branch committees, who made a recommendation to the board of governors. The board ultimately had the authority to grant membership, which was good for life.

The profile of the academy was anything but diverse. Of the 6,300 members, approximately 94% were Caucasian and 77% were male. Black members made up only 2% of the membership, with Latinos making up an additional 2%. The median age of the members was 62, with people younger than 50 comprising only 14% of the Academy. Depending on the branch or category, these statistics were skewed even further into a predominantly mature, white, male demographic.

Some experts point out that the Academy Awards is simply the most visible aspect of a much larger diversity and inclusion problem plaguing Hollywood. A report by the University of Southern California studied 414 films and TV series that included 11,300 speaking roles, finding that 33% were female, 28% were ethnically diverse, and 2% were clearly LGBT. Hidden in these statistics was a finding that approximately 50% of movies and TV series did not feature a single Asian or Asian American character, while 20% did not include a single black character. The gap was more extreme behind the scenes, with females representing only 15.2% of directors, 28.9% of writers, and 22.6% series creators. Specific to film and not TV, only 3.4% of movies were directed by women, which is a key statistic considering the prominence that directors play in the industry.

It is no wonder that the Academy is so skewed in its membership, considering the lack of inclusion plaguing Hollywood. The hurdles to become a member only make matters worse, prolonging a change in the membership base and potentially putting off candidates by the stringent way that sponsorship is managed. In an already difficult industry to crack, the rules governing membership have locked the doors even tighter. With pressures mounting, Academy president Cheryl Boone Isaacs announced that the rules governing membership would be overhauled in the coming years. She pledged that the Academy would strip voting rights from anyone not active in the film industry during the past decade. Only its longest serving members and those who were previously nominated for an Oscar would be spared removal. In addition, three new seats were added to the board of governors, which alone approves who becomes part of the Academy, while a recruitment drive would target more diverse members. The hope was that, by 2020, the Academy will have doubled its female and ethnic minority numbers.

The plan did not receive universal acceptance. For example, actor Stephen Furst spoke publicly about his disagreement with the change in rules. Furst asserts that the membership was not to blame for the lack of representation among nominees. Rather, he blames the Academy for failing to monitor the way new movies were watched. Furst states, "One of the many reasons for the lack of diversity in nominees this year is that many members vote without watching all the films." Furst believes that the Academy should focus on ensuring that a certain percentage of films are watched by each member, instead of removing inactive members. He argues that neither he nor any other members were racist or did not appreciate the art of minorities. Moreover, he clearly affirms his support of inclusion by stating, "diversity in film is important, and having that diversity represented in the Oscar nominees is important."

Stephen Furst's reaction provides a mechanism to talk about the differences between direct and indirect discrimination. Furst's assertion that members are not making prejudiced decisions against female and minority talent maybe absolutely true. To do so would be a form of direct discrimination and is likely not driving the crisis in nominations. The alternative perspective that members are not truly watching a fair proportion of movies constitutes a form of indirect discrimination and is more likely contributing to the trend. Without considering the alternatives, members are nominating known peers or movies that they believe they would enjoy based on preconceived notions about the talent involved or the talent's previous involvement in earlier films. Mixed with a very real issue that Hollywood lacks diversity and therefore puts forward a narrowed field of talent results in a massively skewed list of nominees. This line of reasoning does not dismiss that some direct discrimination is occurring, but rather asserts that the primary driver behind the controversy is the close-knit nature of the Academy.

Making bold moves to change the membership will likely impact the list of nominees in future years. Different expectations about talent working in the industry and increased openness to less-established talent (especially if the percentage of watched films is low) will result in a more balanced list of nominees, which in turn will feed into the Academy's makeup (seeing that nominees face fewer hurdles to membership and will retain that status for life). However, the effects of such moves will likely be stunted by the diversity and inclusion problems facing Hollywood in general. Without the studios taking similar steps, the absolute number of alternatives will remain narrow (remember that only 3.4% of movies were directed by women).

Four years later and tangible progress of minority representation in Oscar nominations was scant. Despite a larger field of non-white stars initially tipped as contenders, just one out of the 20 major acting nominations was a person of color (one more than in 2016), specifically Cynthia Erivo for her role in *Harriet*. Missing from the list were strong performances by Awkwafina in *The Farewell*, Jennifer Lopez in *Hustlers*, Lupita Nyong'o in *Us*, and Jamie Foxx in *Just Mercy*. Bong Joon-ho, creator of *Parasite*, was the sole non-white nominee and eventual winner for Best Director. The Academy's lauded changes in membership did result in better representation, moving the needle from 8% to 16% for people of color and from 25% to 32% for women, while the field itself broadened for films released in 2019. Out of the top 100 grossing films, 31 had a minority star or co-star (a 14% increase from 2018 and a full 138% increase from 2007). This progress just did not translate into Oscar nominations. Academy Award nominee Joaquin Phoenix sums it up, "I think that we send a very clear message to people of color that you're not welcome here. I don't think anybody wants a handout of preferential treatment, although that's what we give ourselves every year. I think people want to be appreciated and respected for their work."

For now, the power appears to remain in the hands of the mature white male in what has been termed one of the most liberal industries. Even if the privileged elite of Hollywood do not actively assert their authority, like the guards in Zimbardo's experiment, a machine has been put in motion that preserves the status quo. Inaction may be a better way to express much of Hollywood's approach to date, preserving the power differential and turning a blind eye toward calls for change. It is no wonder that the Academy, similar to commercial entities in general, turn to formalized diversity and inclusion plans and policies, especially when pressures mount from the outside.

Diversity and inclusion initiatives are the flip side of the same coin as anti-bullying and anti-harassment policies; both sets of rules are established to safeguard subordinates against the improper use of power. The signs of direct discrimination, in the forms of physical or emotional harm, are easier to identify and address. The bully's actions are observable and can be assessed against a code of conduct for ethical and fair treatment. In contrast, indirect discrimination is systemic in nature and harder to detect, although it often affects a wider group of people by limiting their opportunity, freedom, and choice. Those in power are not necessarily making discriminatory decisions, but rather they ignore what is going on around them or take actions that maintain the status quo. Host Chris Rock alluded to this difference between direct and indirect discrimination during his opening speech for the 2016 Oscars.

> Everyone wants to know is Hollywood racist? You have to go at it the right way. Is it burning-cross racist? Fetch-me-some-lemonade racist? No. It's a different kind of racist. Is Hollywood racist? You're damn right it's racist, but it's sorority racist. It's like: We like you Rhonda, but you're not a Kappa.

It is difficult to quantify which form of discrimination is more harmful. Direct discrimination is about the here and now, whereas indirect discrimination can rob the future.

The Stanford Prison Experiment uncovered that roles, labels, and social expectations provide behavioral scripts that are easily followed and create a ready-made way for individuals to understand their environment. The 2016 Oscar controversy demonstrates that, once established, power differentials are self-sustaining. Together they show that relying on the elite to change the status quo without a nudge may sit outside of human nature. We accept the roles and positions we are given, believing that power differentials are both right and justified. Over time, such assumptions plant the seeds for eventual change, when the logic for an unfair distribution of power is challenged by those who believe in a different social reality. The question is whether policies and practices targeting bullying and inclusiveness are effective at preventing power differentials from running their natural course.

7

Helping

During the spring of 1964, one of the most notorious events occurred in the history of psychology. A 28-year-old woman named Kitty Genovese returned to her apartment after closing the bar that she managed in Manhattan, New York. As she parked her car and approached her apartment building in a middle-class neighborhood in Queens, she was approached by Winston Moseley, who quickly proceeded to sexually assault and viciously attack her with a knife. Kitty was stabbed multiple times and screamed out in extreme pain. Acknowledging that her screams could be heard, one of her neighbors did eventually yell down to "leave that girl alone," which caused Winston to stop and begin to walk away. Kitty got up and started wobbling her way back to her building. Winston returned, found Kitty in the stairwell and continued to stab her. When the police were called a full 35 minutes later, Kitty was in poor shape and Winston was long gone. Kitty died a short time later.

So what makes this incident stand out from any of the 636 other tragic murders that occurred in 1964 and after? Early reports identified that there were no less than 38 witnesses to this event, all of whom failed to come to the aid of the victim. The *New York Times* article published on March 27, under the headline "37 Who Saw Murder Didn't Call the Police: Apathy at Stabbing of Queens Woman Shocks Inspector," reported

> For more than half an hour, thirty-eight respectable, law-abiding citizens in Queens watched a killer stalk and stab a woman in three separate attacks in Kew Gardens. Twice, the sound of their voices and the sudden glow of their bedroom lights interrupted him and frightened him off. Each time he returned, sought her out and stabbed her again. Not one person telephoned the police during the assault; one witness called after the woman was dead.

Other accounts went further and reported that a couple moved their chairs next to the window in order to watch the drama unfold as a form of perverse entertainment.

Punching the Clock. Joe Ungemah, Oxford University Press (2021). © Oxford University Press.
DOI: 10.1093/oso/9780190061241.003.0007.

Why no one came to help Kitty in her time of need struck a nerve with the American public. If a brave individual came to her rescue, Kitty's life very well might have been saved. Even a little persistence in reaching the police would have been more than what transpired that night. Although New York was not necessarily the safest of places in the 1960s, the apparent lack of caring on the part of Kitty's neighbors was hard to comprehend, and people reached out for an answer. Theories abounded, from blaming the alienation that resulted from living in a major city, to the specific reputation of Kitty's neighborhood for anti-social behavior. In a more recent article, Rachel Manning, Mark Levine, and Alan Collins point out that early descriptions of the event exaggerated matters, creating a parable that easily grasped the public's attention. By describing the witnesses as neighbors who were at their windows in direct view of the assault, fascinated by what they saw and yet paralyzed to act, the story grabbed attention and played on the reader's imagination. Entirely accurate or not, the story was memorable for what it unearthed about the human psyche.

Fast-forward to May 2015 and an unremarkable corner of London. The Number 212 double-decker bus was about to turn right on its route toward Chingford. At that moment, Anthony Shields crossed the street behind the bus, riding a unicycle. This would have been even stranger if Anthony wasn't a circus performer. He rode up alongside the bus and stopped on the in-lane side of the bus, just behind the window, hidden from the driver's view. Witness Zoheb Ishfaq, described Anthony wobbling a bit just before he heard a pop, causing him to exclaim, "Where's the unicyclist gone?" The answer: Under the front tire.

The driver of the bus, confused as to what had happened, began to edge the bus forward, which was disastrous for Anthony. Alex Sophocieous, an estate agent who witnessed the event, ran to the bus and slammed on the windscreen to make the bus driver stop, unfortunately causing him to reverse a little, back over Anthony's leg. Attention quickly turned from the bus driver to the wheel that pinned Anthony to the ground. A common recognition emerged among the witnesses that something needed to be done. Without a word being exchanged, somewhere between three and five individuals attempted to lift the 12-ton bus. Futile in their first attempt, Zoheb relates that the action was more like an invitation for others to come and help.

Soon, the team had amassed to 40 or 50 members as people came from restaurants and stores that surrounded the intersection. Those working on the wheel were joined by a crowd, and, in short order, the entire bus had hands on it. Witnesses related that little coordination occurred and the majority of communication was unspoken, although some remember a few directions being given, such as "heave" or "come on." The efforts of the crowd were thwarted by the fact that passengers were still on the bus, somehow unaware of what was transpiring outside. With all passengers now off the bus, a tipping point was reached and the crowd was able to lift the bus enough for Anthony to escape.

The ordeal was over in just a few minutes. Despite the success, very little elation was heard as witnesses observed that Anthony was in bad shape and needed immediate medical attention. The ambulance arrived and Anthony was whisked away to hospital. The crowd dispersed and life around that corner of London began to return to normal. But it did leave a mark on its witnesses. Zoheb commented,

> As horrific as this situation was, I've never seen such instant co-operation based on a mutual good. I've lived here my whole life, my mum's born and bred here, too, and it comes across as quite a cold, careless city. I've seen things happen and people don't pay attention. It's like everyone's too scared to defend someone or to help and that always angered me. That was part of the shock factor. I expected people trying to help but would assume that people just said let's wait for the ambulance to get here and follow the usual protocol.

Instead, the crowd did come to the rescue and the incident went viral. Examples like this are not unheard of. In August 2014, a man was freed from a train in Perth, Australia, when his leg became lodged in the gap between the carriage and platform, requiring a crowd of people to rock the carriage and free the pinned leg. Yet both examples stand in direct contrast to the tragedy of Kitty Genovese and other instances of inaction, such as the case of a Chinese toddler struck by a car in 2011, an accident that was ignored by passers-by. The evocative nature of all these occurrences (both good and bad) spurred a spate of research that got at the heart of what causes individuals to help.

Teasing Out Why People Help (or Not)

To uncover the psychological processes that drive helping behavior, researchers had to create a believable situation where individuals could be carefully observed. In a seminal series of experiments, John Darley and Bibb Latane took on the task of explaining why bystanders to an emergency situation could stand by and do nothing despite obvious humanitarian social norms that should have encouraged intervention. They considered individuals in such situations as in conflict between satisfying social norms on one hand and fears about the repercussions on the other. For example, intervening with Kitty's murder could have placed the bystander in harm's way or, in the least, meant a commitment in time and energy into a police investigation. The problem with this particular tragedy is that plenty could have been done from the bystanders' apartments, from drawing others' attention to the assault to phoning the police. The pressure to come to the rescue should have overpowered the pressure to idly stand by, yet it is the opposite that occurred.

Darley and Latane suspected that the presence of other bystanders played a crucial role in inhibiting action. Specifically, the bystanders to Kitty's murder could see lights in the apartments and knew that others were witnessing the same tragedy. Without communicating or knowing how others were reacting, individual bystanders might have hesitated to gain further information about what was happening or may have assumed that somebody else was already helping. Alternatively, they might have decided to do nothing, relying on others to learn what was going on and to intervene if necessary. With so many other onlookers, personal responsibility diminished and no single individual could be blamed for inaction. The researchers coined the phrase *diffusion of responsibility* as a way of capturing this hypothesis.

To test it out, the researchers created an emergency situation in the laboratory, one where they could measure the speed and frequency of helping behavior. Participants in their experiment responded to an invitation to discuss personal problems that are typically experienced by college students in a high-pressure, urban environment. To preserve their anonymity and allow for a more honest discussion, participants were given their own room equipped with a communication system connected to other participants. The reality was that the isolation and control of communication was the primary way for the researchers to control the environment. Also, there was only one real participant taking part in the experiment at any given time.

To help create the illusion of multiple people taking part in the experiment, participants were ushered through a corridor lined with doors that seemingly led into rooms with other participants. Upon entering their assigned room, participants were seated at a table and given headphones and access to a microphone. Instructions were read over an intercom as one way of removing the obvious presence of an authority figure. Since an experimenter was absent and all reactions recorded later by questionnaire, the participants were instructed to follow a protocol during the conversation. Each participant was to talk in turn and present their own personal reflections of life as a college student. They would then have the opportunity to comment on each other's issues (again by taking turns), followed by an open discussion.

A mechanical switching device was to regulate the discussion, limiting each person to 2 minutes. When the microphone was on, all others would be muted and therefore only one person could be heard at a given time. This design allowed for a similar experience across participants, especially as no real discussion was occurring. All the other participants were recorded and played back in the same order. Moreover, the one-way nature of the switching device did not allow for the possibility of any real type of communication.

The first voice heard by the participants was soon to be the victim in the experiment. He related that he found college life difficult and, with obvious embarrassment, indicated that he sometimes had seizures when studying or taking exams. After he talked, a set of other voices were heard in turn relating their own personal challenges in attending college. The real participant went last.

On the next round, the victim's voice was heard again, but something was different. He became increasing loud and incoherent, stating

> "I-er-um-I think I-I need-re-if-if could er-er-somebody er-er-er-er-er-er-er give me a little-er-give me a little help here because-er-I-er-I'm-er-er-h-h-having a-a-a real problem-er-right now and I-er-if somebody could help me out it would-it would-er-er s-s-sure be-sure be good . . . because-er-there-er-er-a cause I-er-I-uh-I've got a-a one of the-er-sei-er-er-things coming on and-and-and I could really-er-use some help so if somebody would-er-give me a little h-help-uh-er-er-er-er-er c-could somebody-er-er-help-er-uh-uh-uh (choking sounds). . . . I'm gonna die-er-er-I'm . . . gonna die-er-help-er-er-seizure-er- (chokes, then quiet)."

After approximately 2 minutes, the victim's voice was cut off, keeping consistent with the allotted time determined by the experimental procedure.

From the moment the victim's voice was heard, a timer began to measure the speed of the participant's response. Time stopped when the participants left their rooms to seek out the help of the experimental assistant, who greeted them at the start of the experiment and remained at the end of the hallway.

If the participants did not exit their rooms after 6 minutes, the experiment was terminated automatically. All of this was consistent across participants except for a couple of things. Some participants believed they were in a conversation with just the victim (small group), while others thought they were in a three-person group (the victim, themselves, and another person) or a six-person group (large group). A second variable was also introduced in the three-person group, specifically whether the other bystander was a male, female, or a premedical student who occasionally worked at a hospital.

All participants in the small, two-person group came to the aid of the victim and did so quite quickly, with 85% responding while the victim was audibly having the fit. In comparison, only 62% of participants in the large, six-person group ever reported the emergency. Their speed was also slower, with only 31% doing so while the victim could be heard having the fit. Across all groups, no participant took action after 3 minutes had passed. If they had failed to act by 3 minutes, it was reasonable to assume they never would. As predicted, the size of the group influenced both the responsiveness and the speed of response to an emergency. Interestingly, having a medically trained person on hand in the three-person group did little to alter the participant's reaction to the emergency.

Participant responses, recorded via the microphone in the room, were telling. They varied from "My God, he's having a fit" to "It's just my kind of luck, something has to happen to me" and "Oh God, what should I do?" Such comments were consistent across helpers and non-helpers. So, too, was the concern shown over the welfare of the victim. When the experimenter came into the room to stop the experiment for those who failed to help, participants asked "Is he being taken care of?" and "He's all right, isn't he?" Far from being indifferent to the victim's pleas, the participants showed concern for the victim and were noticeably upset, yet they still failed to respond. Darley and Latane concluded that these participants were stuck in a state of indecision about what to do and therefore did nothing. They were stuck between the pressure to help and the potential for embarrassment or blame for ruining the experiment. With fewer bystanders on hand, the pressure to help overpowered the potential ramifications of stopping the experiment.

These results were consistent across male and female participants, while personality differences played no part on responsiveness. Contrary to popular thought, failure to intervene does not indicate that someone is a psychopath or jaded by a dehumanized and alienated world. Rather, the experiment suggests that we are all capable of inaction depending on the situation presented to us. Only one factor emerged as related to helping behavior, specifically the size of the community where the participant was raised. Participants from a small community helped out more than their urban peers.

The experiment just described accounts for one specific type of situation whereby bystanders lack the opportunity to communicate and interact with each other. The conditions created in the laboratory may have replicated the night of Kitty's murder but do not cover the full range of possible emergencies. To explore other types of situations, Latane and Darley set up a second experiment, this time creating an illusion of a fire. Participants were invited to take part in an interview to discuss the same issue as before, specifically life as a college student in an urban environment. They were greeted and brought to a waiting room to complete a questionnaire. When they completed the second page of the questionnaire, the experimenters began puffing white smoke into the waiting room through a small vent in the wall. After 5 minutes, the smoke was thick enough to obscure vision. In typical *Law and Order* interrogation room style, the participants were observed through one-way glass.

As before, the researchers had no real interest in hearing about life as a college student but instead wanted to know whether the participants would act to resolve the emergency. Three conditions were created to tease out how social influence would change the participants' actions. In the baseline condition, the participant was on his own (all participants were male in the study being described) filling out the questionnaire. When smoke began billowing out of the vent, the typical response was for him to investigate the situation by sniffing the smoke, waving a hand through it, and testing its temperature. The participants would generally hesitate slightly before walking out of the room and reporting the smoke. Without panic, they stated "There's something strange going on in there, there seems to be some sort of smoke coming through the wall." On average, the smoke was reported within 2 minutes of first noticing it and a full 75% of participants acted to resolve the emergency within the allotted time of 6 minutes.

In the second condition, the participant was not alone in the waiting room but sat next to two other people (confederates of the experimenters). The confederates limited their interactions with the participant prior to the smoke and appeared heavily engaged in filling out their questionnaires. When smoke began, they stared at it briefly, made no comment, shrugged their shoulders, and simply carried on working. If engaged by the participant in conversation, they showed indifference and simply responded, "I dunno." In this situation, only 10% of participants took action. The remainder sat there with the confederates, coughing, rubbing eyes, and attempting to futilely wave away the smoke.

In the third condition, the group of three were all true participants in the experiment and were free to interact in any way they saw fit. Theoretically, since there were three times the number of people to report the same emergency event, the response rate should have been higher than when participants were alone. Instead, the participants were much slower and reluctant to act. Unlike the lone participants, with 63% reacting within the first 5 seconds, only 26% of participants in the group condition did so in the same time period. It took an extra 15–20 seconds for them to catch up in just noticing what was going on. In terms of taking action, only 38% of the group condition had an individual report the smoke. Moreover, the delay in this action was noticeable, with only one group taking action within 4 minutes (when the room became noticeably unpleasant).

Unlike the other experiment, a diffusion of responsibility does not explain the study's findings because the motivation for self-preservation should have been constant across all conditions. Rather, Latane and Darley suggest that social influence acted earlier in the participant's thinking by changing perceptions about whether an emergency was actually occurring. The key to this argument was found in the post-emergency interview, when each participant sat across from the experimenter and was asked if he "had any difficulty while filling out the questionnaire." At this point, participants who reported the fire would describe it as "strange" or "like something was wrong." This was different from participants who failed to act, who instead interpreted the smoke as a nondangerous event. Common explanations included steam, air-conditioning vapors, or smog. Two participants, who probably should have been experimented on further, independently thought it was "truth gas" to encourage more honest questionnaire responses. Both individuals apparently were OK with this notion. Instead of feeling conflicted about what to do, participants in groups largely decided that no fire was occurring and therefore, nothing needed to be done. Taking no action was a reasonable response given this conclusion.

This experimental finding helped define a series of steps that could predict whether an individual is likely to come to the aid of others.

1. *An individual must notice the event.* This can be easier said than done when a person is in a hurry or focused on something else.

2. *He or she must interpret the event as a situation where help is needed.* Action is less likely to occur if the request is ambiguous or can be interpreted in alternative ways.

3. *He or she must decide that it is his or her responsibility to act.* If alone, the responsibility is clear, but in groups with no direct communication, the situation is fuzzier.

4. *The individual decides to take action.* If a person feels that he or she lacks the knowledge or confidence to act, hesitation can creep in.

5. *The intention to act becomes reality.* Just because an individual intends to help others does not mean they actually follow-through and do something.

Only if all these steps are fulfilled will the individual intervene and help others.

To help encourage individuals to act, recipients can influence the psychological processes governing diffusion of responsibility and social influence. Where possible, recipients can make appeals that clearly communicate help is needed (removing the need for interpretation of the event) as well as remove potential distractions or competing demands. Second, the recipient should call out the responsibility of the other person to act, potentially by dictating the way that is most likely to resolve the current situation. Third, recipients can remind others about their group identity and where collective action successfully worked in the past. Pushing for quick action is a priority because hesitation tends to spiral out of control until such a point that no action occurs.

Not an Emergency, but Still Important

The emergencies simulated in these types of experiments are thankfully quite rare. It is estimated that the average person experiences fewer than half a dozen crises in his or her lifetime. The bad news is that since they are so infrequent, an individual will most likely be poorly equipped to handle them. In contrast, requests for help and assistance in the workplace occur on a daily basis. Everything from holding a door open as a coworker carries a coffee, laptop, or biking gear into the office, to frantic e-mails asking the IT department to recover lost data—we ask a lot of our colleagues. All too often, we are disappointed by their lack of sympathy and support.

When considering the research by Latane and Darley, there might be little basis for this disappointment, and blame may actually fall on the person asking for help. Simply the request for help might not have encouraged others to act. Our colleagues probably did not decide against helping us but rather failed to decide anything, letting the poorly formed request for help slide into oblivion. It would be an interesting thought experiment to consider how many requests for help, either explicitly stated or inferred, are ignored in a given week. My guess is that in any large organization, the number is significant. The real question is whether people focused on making the right requests and gave their time to issues that were truly in the best interest of the company or customer. From a selfish perspective, there are lessons to be learned on how to improve the chances that your request will get the attention it deserves.

Beyond having a strong reputation as someone who helps others and therefore is deserving of support, the situation surrounding the request can have a big impact on any subsequent action by coworkers. The difference between Kitty's murder and Anthony's survival was in part influenced by how apparent the need for help was for the bystanders. Anthony was clearly in need to those who witnessed the accident, while Kitty's observers had to physically move themselves to the window to see what was going on, especially considering it was the middle of the night. Even then, the situation may not have been clear because the murder could have been assumed to be a quarrel rather than a more serious event. In contrast, there was no doubt that Anthony was under the bus.

In the relatively benign workplace environment, holding a door open for a colleague whose arms are full is more evocative than a more typical request for help, such as a request to send old documents via e-mail. Virtual interaction, which is the norm in the modern workplace, does not communicate needs in the same way as physical encounters. This is illustrated most by those uncomfortable silences on conference calls where no one is willing to commit to helping. The personal distance between the people on the phone heightens the chances for miscommunication that there is a need, as well as creates assumptions that others are willing and able to help. The longer the uncomfortable silence goes on, the lower the chances that a voluntary offer of help will surface.

As the world moves to more virtual working in the gig economy, where employees can work from anywhere and at any time, the importance of overcoming the inertia to help is increasingly important. Requesters for help cannot rely on nonverbal cues or indirect social pressures to stir action. Moreover, the response might not be immediate if colleagues are working across time zones. Having the ability to be a bystander and seeing others chipping in, as when Anthony was pulled from under the bus, encourages participation and focuses attention on the situation, an occurrence that is devoid in virtual working.

In the workplace of the future, requesters must become much more purposeful in how they communicate needs, while distractions must be minimized to the greatest extent possible. How often are we guilty of checking phones or e-mail when we should be paying attention to a live or phone-based conversation? Not only do our actions convey that the speaker is unimportant, but the distraction also could lead to a call for help being ignored. Having a "no distraction policy," where employees must switch off their phones, is one way to force consideration of others' needs. One major investment bank had a policy in place that employees were required to turn off their phones and shut down their computers whenever engaging in a meeting, so that they could give undivided attention to the other person. The reality was that, in a given hour, their traders were subjected to hundreds of emails and a half dozen phone messages. So high was their normal level of distraction that they would have no time for anything else.

Creating a social norm like this is heavily influenced by leaders. Having a boss who sits in the back of the room checking his or her phone conveys to the group that the in-person meeting is unimportant. If a social norm against distraction cannot be created, the simple act of involving others in a continuous dialogue limits how much time their attention can wander. Asking questions when presenting a topic or assigning roles to members of the team during meetings can bring focus to the issues at hand.

Beyond limiting distraction, the message itself can be altered to ensure that others interpret it correctly as a call for help. In the gig economy, workers will be swapping teams and roles more frequently, which works against having a clear picture of others' talents and needs. Making explicit exactly what is required and who is responsible can cut through this gap in understanding and circumvent the diffusion of responsibility. Equivalent to Kitty yelling for a specific neighbor to call the police, an explicit request takes away any need for interpretation as well as puts an individual on the hook for responding. Across workplace environments, asking a colleague by name for a specific action is far better than a general call out for help with little guidance about what exactly is needed. Unfortunately, it is far easier to do the opposite: e-mailing a company distribution list or posting a generic request on a social networking site is far easier than a tailored message with actions clearly articulated or, better yet, picking up the phone. The effort put into a request is paid back in the amount of help provided.

Added to this, making the request public creates social pressure that action will truly occur. Reminiscent of a teacher calling on a day-dreaming student in class, such directness in public calls incites action. Not only will the person be working against societal norms if they refuse to help, but they will likely be working against pressures for group cohesion and identity. By not acting, they are calling themselves out as non-members of the collective and, by doing so, may be foregoing their own requests for help in the future. The requester should ask for immediate commitment, as any option to weigh pros and cons opens the door to hesitation and to the possibility that no help will be forthcoming.

One of the buzz words circulating in the business press is the need for greater *collaboration* on behalf of the whole company. Pundits are advocating that the only way to push performance is to leverage the whole organization by identifying and then leveraging social networks. Yet, as observed by Latane and Darley, help is not guaranteed even in the most dire of circumstances due to the diffusion of responsibility and social influence. In many ways, a more distributed workforce, connected by technology and with limited time to interact for the sake interacting, works against helping behavior. Seeing that technology is here to stay, the responsibility is on the requester to combat distraction, make requests as clear as possible, assign personal responsibility, and pull on positive social pressures that encourage action. This is a tall order and there is no doubt why a generic corporate e-mail is a typical approach when help is needed. We should just not be surprised when nobody comes forward to help.

8

Intent

Delivering on commitments is generally considered a good thing. When politicians break campaign promises, voters feel betrayed and can seek revenge on the candidates and the political party they represent during the next election. Even with the best explanation about why a policy is no longer feasible or providing a better alternative does not satisfy the break in trust built up with the electorate. Voters have expectations that their leaders will follow through, or least fight for, the topics that they campaigned about. As a very different example, parolees who break the terms of their release undo all the good behavior that they built up just prior to parole. Their actions take away the goodwill restored between them and society and work to confirm the stereotype that prisoners cannot be trusted despite having the best of intentions for a reformed life.

Society is founded on a set of norms that, in their absence, would result in a failure for people to coordinate in a meaningful way. It is hard to imagine a world where every encounter between two individuals requires a negotiation about what the appropriate behavior should be. For example, the act of buying food at the grocery store is based on a range of social conventions. We take it for granted that issues like the commodity being traded (the cash in your pocket) has been agreed before we enter the shop. Trading a few dollars is much easier that attempting to trade livestock, textiles, or whatever else we happen to have on any given day. Even the way money changes hands has been worked out for us. We have the expectation that once the agreed sum is paid, we will be allowed to leave the store with our groceries with no further fuss. A recent trend by some grocery store chains to ask for a person's spare change for charity breaks the agreed script, causing people to pause from the near automatic way in which they shop.

Our habits are based on convention, and, when broken, we can feel out of sorts. Still on the theme of grocery shopping, going to a store in a country accustomed to negotiation is a different experience than that in the United States, where the price listed on the shelf is expected to be paid in full. Questions about how much to offer, what is an appropriate counteroffer, and

Punching the Clock. Joe Ungemah, Oxford University Press (2021). © Oxford University Press.
DOI: 10.1093/oso/9780190061241.003.0008.

when to walk away do not enter into the equation (except when buying a car, which somehow escaped this social convention). First-time buyers in a negotiation environment exert more energy in the interaction and try to figure out what is expected of them. The habits they have built up over time will be at best unhelpful, if not detrimental in the new context.

Showing intent, in the form of a promise, allows others to set expectations and plan. It works to reinforce social norms by showing courtesy for the other individual and indicating the ways that two individuals will interact. A sale price is a promise that groceries will cost less when we check out at the register. Alternatively, agreeing to meet up for a date at a specific time and location allows for two people to have fun. Keeping promises is generally a good thing, yet there are times when breaking a promise can be the right thing to do. A convincing conversation might break the chain between intention and action, forcing an individual to reconsider their established position. More interestingly from a psychological perspective, a person's actions can simply run away without any conscious control.

A Road Trip up the Pacific Highway

In 1930, a young Chinese couple embarked on an epic trip up and down the Pacific Highway and across the United States. New to the country, the couple was described as personable, articulate, and charming, able to build rapport quickly with the people they encountered. Over the course of 2 years, the couple crisscrossed the United States twice, traveling close to 10,000 miles, staying at 66 different hotels and inns, and eating at 184 different restaurants and cafes. It is safe to say the couple got their full sampling of Americana.

The couple were not alone in their journey. They were joined by Richard LaPiere from Stanford University, who was secretly studying the couple without their knowledge. As creepy as this might sound, LaPiere was not lurking in the corner and did not initially set out to conduct a psychological study on his friends. Rather, it was a chance observation that occurred early in his relationship with them. LaPiere had recently conducted a study investigating the attitudes of hoteliers toward African Americans, comparing questionnaire results to the actual policies stated by owners on whether they would accept potential patrons. When LaPiere observed his friends check in at a hotel that he knew from his previous study was rather bigoted, he spotted an opportunity to explore the relationship between attitudes and action.

LaPiere was familiar with the latest research on American social attitudes toward the Chinese, specifically that social distance would be an anticipated reaction by the average American. When the party of three came to the reception desk of a hotel with a bigoted reputation, LaPiere noticed an ever so slightly raised eyebrow when the clerk accepted them as guests. His curiosity got the better of him, and, 2 weeks later, LaPiere phoned the hotel and asked whether the property would accept "an important Chinese gentleman." The answer was a firm "no." LaPiere had stumbled into a career-defining moment and decided to take full advantage of a perfect field experiment.

To ensure that the field study was as controlled as possible, LaPiere did not inform his friends of the study until their travels had ended. In fact, the results were not published until 1934; in a footnote, LaPiere explained that he delayed publication in consideration of the couple's emotions. We might infer that his friends were not entirely happy that LaPiere's had studied them without their knowledge for 2 years. In hindsight, LaPiere's aloof behavior at check-in became clear. Instead of helping the couple out, he busied himself with the car or luggage, purposely putting himself in the background to observe the first encounter. LaPiere self-disclosed his behavior as "crab-wise," receiving much more scorn and scrutiny by hotel clerks than the Chinese couple who preceded him to check-in.

Across the encounters, LaPiere observed gracious behavior at all but one establishment. In fact, he noted that 72 of the 184 restaurant encounters went above and beyond the service that would normally be expected. The one situation where the couple was refused service occurred in a small Californian town, at a low-end auto-camp. In LaPiere's words,

> we drove in a very dilapidated car piled with camp equipment. It was early evening, the light so dim that the proprietor found it somewhat difficult to decide the genus voyageur to which we belonged. I left the car and spoke to him. He hesitated, wavered, said he was not sure that he had two cabins, meanwhile edging towards our car. The realization that the two occupants were Orientals turned the balance or, more likely, gave him the excuse he was looking for. "No," he said, "I don't like Japs!"

This was the sole refusal in 251 encounters and in many ways broke the established research paradigm, where LaPiere let the couple initiate the conversation.

Across their journeys, LaPiere observed that other cues were more influential on the interaction than the physical appearance of the couple. Specifically, the quality and condition of the clothing they wore, the appearance of baggage, and level of cleanliness were more meaningful. He also concluded that curiosity might have actually increased the attention and responsiveness of staff in light of the fact that significant Chinese populations were isolated to the Pacific Coast, Chicago, and New York in the 1930s.

The kicker in LaPiere's study was that the actions of hoteliers and restaurant owners diverged significantly from their intentions. Six months after their encounter with the Chinese couple (a time period that LaPiere hoped would fade their memories), LaPiere sent a questionnaire to the establishments. The questionnaire asked bluntly, "Will you accept members of the Chinese race as guests in your establishment?" A slightly longer questionnaire was sent to half the recipients, asking for their policies regarding a range of nationalities. A total of 128 replies were received and, without fail, 91% of restaurants and 92% of hotels stated that they would reject Chinese patrons. The remainder provided a conditional response, stated that it depended on the circumstance. Only one person said "Yes," the owner of a small auto-camp who included a letter about how she had a delightful experience with a young Chinese couple the summer before (LaPiere's friends were indeed personable).

It is rare for a study to have results so clearly differentiated, and, despite all the factors that could have tarnished the data in one way or the other, the pattern cannot be denied. LaPiere had found a gap between what individuals said they would do and their actions when faced with the actual situation. Born out of this unlikely study is an abundance of research on attitudes and their links to behavior. In general, the likelihood that individuals will follow through on their attitudes is determined by the strength and stability of the attitude, its relevance and salience to the situation, and whether there are situational pressures to act in a different way. For the Chinese couple, hoteliers and restauranteurs probably did not encounter many Chinese people in the past and therefore their attitudes were not well established. The couple themselves probably did not fit the stereotype they had of Chinese people, thus challenging the relevance and salience of the attitude. Last, the pressure to serve customers likely outweighed their intent to discriminate. Too much was stacked up against the attitude for it to be translated into action.

Fast-forward to 2016 and a modern version of LaPiere's study played out in the short-term rental marketplace, Airbnb. Founded in 2008, the site lists more than 2 million rooms worldwide, serving more than 40 million guests in 90 countries. Although offering a similar booking service to sites like Expedia or Priceline, Airbnb specializes in connecting potential patrons to hosts offering rooms that would sit outside what would normally be consider a hotel or an inn. Rooms can be anywhere in a house, from the basement to the attic, ranging in size from a glorified closet to a master suite in an authentic castle. As properties go, almost anything is possible, and, as a result, there is a different level of scrutiny about what hosts can and cannot do.

In January 2016, a damning study was released investigating claims of discrimination occurring on the site. Researchers from Harvard Business School deliberately set up a situation to catch hosts in the act of discriminating against potential lodgers. Reminiscent of LaPiere's epic car trip 80 years before them, the researchers enquired about whether hosts would accept African Americans at their properties. The researchers created 20 user profiles on Airbnb that were identical except for the name of the customer. Five typical white male names were used and compared to five white female names, five black male names, and five black female names. They were interested to know whether Tamika would receive more positive responses than Kristin or whether Brad would fare better than Rasheed. In all, enquiries were made to 6,400 listings across five cities (Baltimore, Dallas, Los Angeles, St. Louis, and Washington DC). Responses from hosts were tracked for 30 days and categorized into whether they provided a firm "yes," a firm "no," a request for further information, or no response.

What they found is startling. Despite the intent of Airbnb to create trust within their marketplace by reducing anonymity in transactions, the opposite appears to have occurred. African American names were accepted approximately 16% less than identical guests tagged with distinctively white names. The pattern held whether the host was black or white, female or male, and experienced or first-time lister. Moreover, the discrimination occurred alike for expensive and cheap properties, in diverse and homogeneous neighborhoods, and where the host lived side by side with their lodgers or offsite. The gap disappeared in one particular instance. Specifically, if the host accepted an African American lodger in the recent past, as measured by looking at the 10 most recent reviews for each property, the gap disappeared. At least in the short term, a positive experience seems to have changed the default position of treating black individuals more skeptically than their white peers. This, too, harks back to LaPiere and the "yes" letter from the small auto-camp owner, who enjoyed her interaction with the Chinese couple.

The racial discrimination experienced online sometimes spills over into the real world. Two lodgers, Ronnia Cherry and Stefan Grant, were taken off guard when the police knocked at the door of their Airbnb rental with their guns drawn. The neighbors phoned the police, believing that thieves had broken into the property. Only with considerable effort did Ronnia and Stefan convince the police otherwise. Pressure mounted on Airbnb to act. A social media campaign #AirbnbWhileBlack told the stories of discrimination from users of the site, while a lawsuit was filed by Gregory Selden who claimed that his civil rights were violated by an Airbnb host. The quote from the host was telling, stating "it just didn't feel right. It was a gut feeling. . . . I have hosted African Americans before. That gave him no ground to prove that I'm rejecting him based on his race. He is trying to victimize himself." These words contradict the fact that Selden submitted online two other white profiles (one that was near identical to him in every way except race) as an experiment and both were accepted.

After an initial sluggish response, Airbnb ratcheted up its messaging that the company does not stand for discrimination and reviewed ways to eliminate bias. Brian Chesky, CEO of Airbnb, identified racial discrimination as "the greatest challenge we face as a company. It cuts to the core of who we are and the values we stand for." The company began requiring hosts to commit to a nondiscrimination policy that stated, "I agree to treat everyone in the Airbnb community—regardless of their race, religion, national origin, ethnicity, disability, sex, gender identity, sexual orientation, or age—with respect, and without judgement or bias. Discrimination prevents hosts, guests, and their families from feeling included and welcomed, and we have no tolerance for it." Hosts who are found to violate this commitment are banned from the platform. In support of the policy, the company provided unconscious bias training for hosts, developers, and customer service agents with the hope of promoting wide-scale behavioral change. A more structured approach to tackling unconscious bias was also undertaken by expanding the company's Instant Booking service, which eliminated the review process from a booking. Although a move in the right direction, early signs of this change were not encouraging: only 3% of patrons opted for Instant Booking, with African Americans disproportionately reluctant to use the service.

One might argue that society has made great strides since the 1930s, from near universal rejection of the Chinese couple to a 16% gap between black and white lodgers in the Airbnb study. Yet this comparison only tells half the story, as all but one of LaPiere's hoteliers and restaurant owners made a complete reversal on their intentions. In contrast, Airbnb hosts do not have the opportunity to come face to face with their potential tenants. They are locked into their opinion as soon as they hit the Reject button, and, over time, sites like Airbnb might make matters worse. Hosts with deep-seated anxieties are under no pressure to change their opinions, and, with few positive experiences to draw upon, their prejudicial attitudes may actually strengthen over time. Efforts by Airbnb to tighten its anti-discrimination policy and provide training might work well to encourage intent to accept minority lodgers but can still fall flat on behavioral change unless positive real-life experiences start occurring.

Deep-Seated Beliefs

Underlying an individual's outward behavior is a swirl of opinions, attitudes, and judgments that somehow come together and manifest as words or actions. This cognitive processing can be deliberate, taking the time needed for an individual to build up confidence in his or her stance, or it can be near instantaneous, relying on automatic reactions to the situation at hand. Occasionally, the cognitive swirl is allowed to go on indefinitely, with no decipherable opinion or action surfacing. What cognitive psychology tells us is that the pathway between thought and action becomes cemented over time, gaining in strength and clarity with every encounter. Even the anticipation of a future encounter can sharpen the link.

The connection between thought and action is akin to the people paths that emerge over time in parks and college greens. Picture a well-tended lawn with a stone path that runs on its borders (and even a sign that says "Keep Off the Grass"). Running late or simply being lazy, a student decides to walk across the lawn. No harm done, other than a few smashed blades of grass. Yet, as others follow suit, a noticeable path emerges. The grass is no longer green and has instead been trampled into the dirt. The new path is not perfect, taking a slight twist or turn, but it is now established and a permanent feature of the park. The gardener might as well give up and pave the path because the people themselves have decided where they want to walk.

The people path is representative of the cognitive script formed between thoughts and action, with some emotion sprinkled in. Strong associations between thoughts, emotions, and actions get reinforced over time, and, with each passing event, the chance of a change in mindset gets that much harder.

Yet politicians and economists are intent on finding ways to disrupt the cycle, knowing that what has worked before may no longer be the best or most socially accepted approach. From reducing fossil fuel dependency to raising acceptance of a marginalized social group, scientists are attempting to train old dogs to perform new tricks.

Of the many hot topics from the past decade, the rights of the LGBT community have recently taken center stage. On the frontline are activists who go door to door in an attempt to persuade voters to grant rights that have traditionally been reserved for the mainstream. Their job is not an easy one and puts the activists into direct confrontation with people who may hold very firm feelings contradictory to their own. The activists' goal is to use every tactic possible to nudge opinion closer to their political position and, with it, votes on Election Day.

Benoit Denizet-Lewis, writing for the *New York Times Magazine*, profiled one such activist from Los Angeles named Dave Fleischer. A typical interaction on one of Dave's routes starts with him asking a simple question about whether the person would be opposed to or in favor of "including gay and transgender people in no discrimination laws," requesting that they give a rating of their support on a 10-point scale. Wary of a generic antidiscriminatory declaration, where people go easy on themselves to appear accepting, Fleischer pushes the conversation further. He asks a pointed question: whether or not the individual personally knows of any transgender people, which is atypical. He then plays an impassioned video of a Baptist minister raising alarm over the risks posed by transgender people if they use bathrooms of their preferred gender. Fleischer asks his opening question again and often witnesses a change to a more discriminatory, yet more authentic response.

Up until a few years ago, the accepted approach among canvassers would be to use a great deal of data alongside a heartfelt plea to change opinion. That was until a PhD student from UCLA named Michael LaCour co-authored an article in *Science Magazine* with a well-established political science professor from Columbia named Donald Green. LaCour wrote up a major field study he conducted on how best to change political opinion. His research involved dispatching an army of canvassers to discuss the topic of gay marriage at the homes of potential voters in California. During the course of the conversation, the canvasser disclosed that he or she was homosexual and recounted emotional stories about being gay and the discrimination that he or she personally experienced. LaCour reported impressive changes in political opinion following the brief encounter with the canvasser, with long-lasting effects measured months afterward.

The study was indeed noteworthy. Although previously shown as effective, the benefits of canvassing are not typically long-lasting. Long-held political beliefs snap back into place without further encouragement and reinforcement. LaCour's approach, which made the interaction personal and emotional, created promise for combating prejudice. Unfortunately, LaCour's research was also a complete fabrication.

David Broockman was in the third year of his doctoral studies at UC Berkeley when he came across LaCour's research. The pair met during a conference and Broockman was inspired to replicate what LaCour had accomplished. Broockman got to task and began to plan out his own study using the personal canvassing style that LaCour had mastered. Right at the start, he ran into a major problem: the study was simply not feasible and, by association, neither was that supposedly carried out by LaCour. Research methodology aside, there was simply no way to pay the canvassers for their time. LaCour's data sample was more than 10,000 respondents, who were each paid $100 for their participation. The total bill tallies to more than $1 million, a sum completely out of reach for any graduate student. Convinced that he was missing something, Broockman contacted a number of the companies who organize canvassing, including the one reportedly used by LaCour. Not only did the companies confirm the expected fee, but many reported that the logistics of the study itself were simply too hard to fulfill.

Canvassing was not originally the primary focus for Broockman. Instead, he was captivated by the prospect of authentic interpersonal exchanges having the power to change opinion. Canvassing was just one potential mechanism to convey a message, with the particular strength of ensuring a captive audience when a person answers the door. Teaming up with fellow graduate student Joshua Kalla, the pair decided to have a look into LaCour's raw data to see how the model played out. What became immediately apparent was that the data were too perfect. For example, a feelings thermometer was used to pinpoint an individual's feelings for gay people both at the time of canvassing and a few months later. Instead of jumping around a bit and falling on a normal distribution, the ratings were surprisingly consistent between measurements. Random noise in a large sample is expected for any number of reasons, but was simply absent in LaCour's data.

Broockman brought his concerns to a confidant who worked as a professor at Stanford's business school. He was advised to tread carefully and not go public with the data irregularities. He was advised that there was no apparent upside to breaking the story and that, instead, Broockman had the potential to jeopardize his own career and reputation. Taking the advice, Broockman anonymously posted his suspicions on the message board PSR, described as a "cesspool" for all things academic. Even PSR deleted Broockman's post, insinuating that an attack on LaCour's research was inappropriate since the work had been published in a highly rated journal and co-authored by an established expert in the field.

Meanwhile, Broockman and Kalla continued to build their reputations and were soon recruited by the Leadership LAB (the same organization that hired Dave Fleischer in California) to conduct a project in Miami to investigate techniques to change opinion about transgender equality. The project opened a Pandora's box into all things wrong with LaCour's study. Specifically, Broockman and Kalla had difficulty getting a response rate anywhere close to LaCour's. Of the 13,878 invitations sent to the Miami sample, only 1% agreed to take part in comparison to LaCour's 12% participation. Seeing that they were offering the same amount of money per participant, the researchers began questioning what they were doing wrong. After posing the question directly to LaCour and receiving no real response, the pair contacted one of his research partners. This individual forwarded an e-mail chain from LaCour with a named employee, Jason Peterson, from the company that had helped in the original research.

When Broockman and Kalla called the company, they were informed that a Jason Peterson was never employed with the company at any time. In disbelief, they wrote the company to confirm what they heard. Jason Petersen was indeed a person of fiction. Additionally, the company reiterated its original message to Broockman, received over a year and half earlier, that the type of research requested by Broockman (a replication of the study conducted by LaCour) was ill-advised and could not be completed by the company. Concern about the legitimacy of LaCour's research just reached a new level. What they found by accident was much more than data manipulation.

Knowing that there existed a great stigma against whistleblowers in academia, Broockman and Kalla went searching for a smoking gun that would solidify the case that LaCour had fabricated his research. Such a fabrication not only would put LaCour's academic career on the line, but would blemish the reputations of both *Science Magazine* and Professor Green who coauthored the paper. Working on the assumption that LaCour's dataset was in fact real, the researchers went on a hunt for research that used similar scales. After a few statistical tests, they found that the 2012 Cooperative Campaign Analysis Project, a well-known dataset specific to political science, was the origin of LaCour's data. With their smoking gun in hand, the researchers presented the irregularities to LaCour's coauthor, Professor Green, who was taken aback by LaCour's actions. He had partnered in good faith with LaCour, assuming all was ethical and right in the way the research was conducted.

Within days of their discovery, a retraction of the *Science Magazine* article was requested by Professor Green, and the whole scandal became public a day later. A 27-page report was drafted to detail all the irregularities of LaCour's research, putting the evidence squarely in the public domain. For their part, Princeton University responded definitively by rescinding its job offer to LaCour. The ironic thing about this whole story is that LaCour's approach had merit, and there was no need to cook the books.

Returning to Dave Fleischer, he is tasked with getting an authentic change in opinion by encouraging participants to open their hearts to all sorts of people. Fleischer deliberately shifts the conversation to tap a participant's empathy and allow an emotional connection with transgender people. According to Fleischer, cerebral arguments are not effective when confronting participants, nor are broad appeals for fairness. Going down a different path, Fleischer asks openly if the participant has ever thought about transgender people in a meaningful way. He then pulls a picture out from his pocket of his friend Jackson, who grew up as a girl but transitioned to live as a man in his 20s. Fleischer talks about the happiness in Jackson's life now that he is living the way that he desires (in comparison to the very sad fact that more than 40% of transgender people have contemplated committing suicide).

Fleischer then pivots the conversation to the participant's experience with discrimination and when he or she was treated unfairly in the past. Fleischer also recounts his own experiences with discrimination to create a safe environment and to encourage empathy. By the end of the interaction, participants have the opportunity to think about transgender people differently, considering how restricting rights would likely feel if the shoe was placed on the other foot.

Broockman and Kalla's research of this highly personal approach found that a real and persistent change in opinion is indeed possible through canvassing. The pair was engaged by the Leadership LAB due to a fear of backlash in Miami against a recent ordinance to prohibit discrimination based on gender. Responders were assigned to either a treatment or placebo group, whereby the canvassing conversation either concentrated on transgender issues or on recycling. In the end, 56 canvassers, many of whom were transgender, took part in 501 conversations. Before the conversations, the participants received a survey about a wide range of social and political questions, with target questions included about attitudes toward transgender individuals. The participants were asked to complete four follow-up questionnaires over the course of a 3-month period. To allay fears that the data would be rigged for a second time, researchers at UC Berkeley were asked to verify that the data were truly collected. They were.

Broockman and Kalla found that the treatment group was markedly more accepting of transgender people, and this effect persisted for at least 3 months. For 1 in 10 people, the canvassing technique virtually erased transgender prejudice, and, unlike LaCour, who alleged that the identity of the canvasser mattered, Broockman and Kalla discovered that the effect existed whether or not the canvasser was transgender. It was the quality of the approach and message that mattered. The combination of asking participants to take a broader perspective and then having them engage in active processing set in motion a change of opinion. What is yet to be resolved is whether the technique universally works or is limited to relatively new political issues. The 15-minute canvassing interaction might not be potent enough to overcome a deeply rooted opinion; changing such opinions might require repeated messages or a combination of approaches to effectively unwind bias.

Going Off Script

In many ways, we depend on the layers of social norms and expectations about how we are to interact together. We follow scripts of behavior, established through experience, that get reinforced with each additional interaction. We teach our children to wait their turn, show good manners, and assert themselves when necessary. It would be hard to imagine a world that failed to impart this knowledge. Once in a blue moon, a story emerges of a wild child who was somehow lost from society and grew up alone in the wilderness. Over the past century, feral children have been said to have been raised by wolves, monkeys, and even ostriches, and, almost universally, they never truly reintegrate into society. Beyond the obvious developmental challenges of missing key learning milestones, they have lost their social compass of what others expect of them and, in turn, of what they should be expecting of others.

Despite all their worth in facilitating social interactions, there are times when a disruption in an established script is the best possible outcome. Just because a script is well-rehearsed does not mean that it is best possible way to treat others. The script may be outdated, having lost pace with social convention. For example, how many people still struggle with how to tip in an economy growing ever more reliant on apps to pay for services, like Uber or LevelUp, across a wider range of service options. Alternatively, the script might not really apply to the social context or has unintended consequences that can do more harm than good. It is this latter problem and the recognition of potential conflict that caused discomfort for the unwitting participants in LaPiere's study.

Thankfully for the hoteliers and restaurant owners encountered by LaPiere, their initial attitudes to refuse service to the Chinese couple reversed at the last moment, when they met the couple face-to-face and succumbed to social pressures for acceptance. In the Internet age, with a lower dependency on personal interaction and a greater ability to remain anonymous, discrimination is much easier and results in far fewer negative consequences. In part, this is why Airbnb has been plagued with controversy. Initially washing their hands of responsibility for their landlords' actions, the company has begun to recognize that an ethical line has been crossed and that they have the power to rectify it. By deliberatively altering the script of how people should transact on the website, Airbnb can enforce greater equality among their landlords. The parallels between Airbnb and technologies for connecting freelancers to employers are readily apparent. Making contractual decisions at an arm's length only heightens the chances for discrimination and works to limit offers to known suppliers or move funding to a personal network.

Though not an obvious path to scientific discovery, LaCour's devious behavior led to an alternative way to change the script by working on the beliefs that underlie action. Broockman and Kalla worked hard to find definitive evidence that the type of conversation held between participants and a canvasser had the power to change attitudes toward social groups. Specifically, engaging in a deep conversation about a target individual (in this case, a member of the LGBT community), encouraging them to make a personal connection and evoke empathy for the other's perspective, was proved effective for long-term changes in attitude.

What remains unclear is whether these effects are equally strong for deep-rooted beliefs, where an individual has thought long and hard about a social group. Transgender issues are a relatively new topic in the public discourse, and, as such, the participants may have had generic or light opinions about people belonging to this group. Potentially, they might never have come into contact with a transgender individual. It would follow that more deep-rooted opinions would require repeated expose to overcome the cognitive scripts already in place. Also, the conversations with the canvassers occurred in person, taking advantage of the social pressures to listen to the message and engage in thoughtful discussion. The canvassers had the ability to read the participants' nonverbal signals and adjust their approach to force a deeper consideration of the issue. Addressing the topic by phone, where social pressures are moderated, would likely not show as much promise.

The techniques profiled for political canvassing have applicability across social contexts, including the workplace. Engaging employees to think differently about their colleagues, whether unionized, Millennial, or from accounting, can pave the way to better interactions and dispel prejudice. Putting history aside, jumping into the others' shoes and exerting cognitive effort to challenge preexisting beliefs can help rebalance relationships and open new lines of dialogue. By starting anew, different scripts for behavior can be set in motion. For example, assuming that all Millennials require a great deal of direction in their jobs discounts individual variability in how employees go about work. Relying on broad generational characteristics, despite a manager's best intentions, to guide behavior may backfire and leave the employee feeling that his or her skills are not valued or appreciated.

Yet changing the attitude underlying the action does not always lead to success. Old habits are hard to break, especially when there are competing pressures in favor of the established way of thinking and feeling about the social order. Cognitive scripts get stronger with each interaction, and, when under pressure, they become the default way to interact with other people. This is evident when times get tough. Employees going through organizational change or resizing will likely resort to blaming their coworkers, reopening old divisions that were hidden during times of prosperity. They will point fingers at those who took away their bonus or job despite encouragement by leaders to think as one company. Without constant, persuasive reinforcement or a deliberate break in the link, behavior has the tendency to follow the established script. Just like a people path in the local park, it is hard to travel the less obvious or direct route.

9

Obedience

Teacher: "I can't stand it. I'm not going to kill that man in there. You hear
    him hollering?"
Experimenter: "As I told you before, the shocks may be painful, but. . . ."
Teacher: "But he's hollering. He can't stand it. What's going to happen
    to him?"
Experimenter: "The experiment requires that you continue, Teacher."
Teacher: "Aaah, but, I'm not going to get that man sick in there, know what
    I mean?"
Experimenter: "Whether the learner likes it or not, we must go on."

And so it went on the campus of Yale University in the early 1960s. At the age
of 28, Stanley Milgram began a series of experiments that would characterize
his approach to psychology and dominate his future career, as well as forever change how people think about obedience and the role we all play when
acting under orders. Milgram was set on exposing how subtle external social
forces could influence behavior and drive us to do things that would otherwise be considered unthinkable.

Obedience can at times be considered a virtue. We ask our children to
follow our directions, from staying out of traffic to trying out a new exotic
food. We give awards for perfect school attendance and badges for mastering
survival skills. It is hard to think of a society that would operate successfully
if everyone was allowed to go their own way without a central source of coordination. Yet there exists a tenuous balance between providing well-balanced
guidance that is in the best interest of humanity and orders that promote
vested interests, break societal values, or disadvantage others. At the time of
writing, this tension is playing out in the public sphere, with many communities questioning the fairness of their local police who are accused of using
excessive force in disadvantaged communities.

Punching the Clock. Joe Ungemah, Oxford University Press (2021). © Oxford University Press.
DOI: 10.1093/oso/9780190061241.003.0009.

The workplace is especially prone to the psychological processes governing obedience. Organized in a hierarchical fashion with steep penalties when staff deviate from orders, employees obey their bosses—or at least appear to do so. Such processes allow for the production of goods and the fulfillment of services, yet can equally go awry when bosses make unethical decisions or when employees follow blindly what they are told to do. The ramifications can lead to white-collar crime and the downfall of an organization. You do not need to look too far back to find examples of collapse resulting from unchecked obedience, as at Enron and Arthur Anderson, where employees followed through on their bosses' directives.

Milgram studied the topic of obedience through an ingenious experimental design that would likely never pass the strict ethical rules of higher education that exist today. Forty participants were recruited from the community in and around New Haven, Connecticut and paid $4.50 for their participation in the experiment. The participants were all male, between the ages of 20 and 50, and represented a wide range of occupations and educational levels. They were recruited through both a newspaper advertisement and direct mail and were instructed that, no matter what happened in the laboratory, the money was theirs to keep.

The experiment took place on the grounds of Yale University, in an elegant and impressive laboratory. The participants were greeted by the same experimenter; a 31-year-old high school biology teacher wearing a gray technician's coat. His demeanor was described by Milgram as both impassive and somewhat stern.

The participants were not alone when they entered the lab. A second participant (an accomplice of Milgram's) was on hand to take part in the experiment. The accomplice was a 47-year-old accountant who was described as mild-mannered and likable. The two participants were seated and given the following cover story:

> But actually, we know very little about the effect of punishment on learning, because almost no truly scientific studies have been made of it in human beings. For instance, we don't know how much punishment is best for learning—and we don't know how much difference it makes as to who is giving the punishment, whether an adult learns best from a younger or an older person than himself—or many things of that sort.

From there, one of two roles were assigned by selecting a scrap of paper in a hat. The selection was rigged and the true participant was always assigned as the teacher, while the accomplice was assigned as the learner. The teacher then watched the learner get strapped into an "electric chair" apparatus, which was explained to prevent excessive movement while the learner got shocked. An electrode was placed on the learner's wrist to reduce blisters and burners. The good news is that the teacher was informed that "Although shocks can be extremely painful, they cause no permanent tissue damage."

The participant's job as teacher was to lead a paired-association learning task, where a series of words were read aloud. The first word of the pair was then repeated along with four new words. The learner was required to indicate which word was in the original pairing. Example pairs from the experiment included Blue—Box, Nice—Day, and Wild—Duck. For the first pair, the options of Sky, Ink, Box, and Lamp were provided. The teacher saw the learner's selection via a series of four lights that would illuminate based on which word was chosen.

The participant sat in front of a shock generator that consisted of 30 lever switches in a horizontal line. Each switch was labeled by both a voltage designation that ranged from 15 to 450 volts and the labels Slight Shock, Moderate Shock, Strong Shock, Very Strong Shock, Intense Shock, Extreme Intensity Shock, and Danger: Severe Shock. The final two switches were simply labeled XXX. The apparent authenticity of the device was confirmed by the participants after the experiment, who truly believed that they were delivering shocks to the learner. To increase the theatricality of the instrument, red lights would illuminate when a lever was pressed, an electric buzz sounded, another blue light labeled "voltage energizer" flashed, the dial on the voltage meter swung to the right, and a variety of relay clicks were heard. A made-up manufacturing stamp was engraved on the device, "Shock Generator, Type ZLB, Dyson Instrument Company, Waltham, Mass. Output 15 Volts—450 Volts."

Before the experiment began, the teacher was given a slight shock from the generator to prove its authenticity. The third lever, corresponding to 45 volts, was pressed and a shock was delivered to the wrist of the participant. Once done, the experiment was ready to begin. The teacher was instructed to shock the learner every time he failed to select the correct word pair and to call out the voltage level just prior to administering the shock. The participant was then to move to a progressively higher shock level for the next incorrect answer. The participant was to "continue giving shocks, until the learner has learned all the pairs correctly."

Following a prearranged sequence of approximately three wrong answers to one correct answer, the learner showed no sign of protest until 300 volts, when a banging sound was heard on the laboratory wall. From that point onward, the learner stopped providing answers to the questions. The experimenter urged the teacher to continue in the absence of response and consider it as a wrong answer. The learner's pounding was then repeated at the 315-volt level for the last time. Whenever a teacher questioned the experimenter on what was happening, the experimenter responded with a series of escalating phrases: "Please continue," "The experiment requires that you continue," "It is absolutely essential that you continue," and "You have no other choice, you must go on." If the teacher refused after this fourth instruction, the experiment was terminated and the participant recorded as being noncompliant.

What interested Milgram was how many of the participants would comply all the way to the end of the experiment, using the full number of levers available to them, even the ones labeled XXX. He also assessed the participant's state of mind, with open-ended questions about what they experienced alongside measures of attitude. With awareness of what he subjected his participants to, Milgram arranged for reconciliation between the accomplice and participant to ensure that no physical harm was done, as well as to reduce any tension or anxiety left over from the experiment.

Milgram discovered something astounding: specifically, that 65% of participants continued the experiment to the very end, obeying the experimenter's orders to continue. Only five participants refused to continue at the first signs of distress (at the 300-volt level). Four more stopped with a second pounding on the wall. One of these participants stated

> I think he's trying to communicate, he's knocking. . . . Well it's not fair to shock the guy . . . these are terrific volts. I don't think this is very humane. . . .
> Oh, I can't go on with this; no, this isn't right. It's a hell of an experiment. The guy is suffering in there. No, I don't want to go on. This is crazy.

Milgram also noted the physical and psychological state of participants undergoing the experiment. Profuse sweating, trembling, and stuttering were all signs of emotional disturbance with what was going on, as well as bouts of nervous laughter. Full-blown, uncontrollable seizures were observed for three participants, one bad enough for Milgram to stop the experiment. Bringing the experiment to life, one of Milgram's visitors to the lab related

> I observed a mature and initially poised businessman enter the laboratory smiling and confident. Within 20 minutes he was reduced to a twitching, stuttering wreck, who was rapidly approaching a point of nervous collapse. He constantly pulled on his earlobe, and twisted his hands. At one point, he pushed his fist into his forehead and muttered: "Oh God, let's stop it." And yet he continued to respond to every word of the experimenter, and obeyed to the end.

After the initial experiment, Milgram went on to create 15 variations of the basic experimental design, involving more than 1,000 participants in his research. The first change to the design included adding vocal protests from the learner that were heard through the wall. This change did not radically alter the level of compliance, falling from 65% to 62.5%. The next variation had a stronger effect, with the learner being placed in the same room as the teacher to provide visual cues. Compliance dropped to 40% in this condition. Making things even harder on the teacher, they were asked to physically give the shocks to the learner by placing the learner's palm on the electrical panel. Only 30% complied fully in this condition.

A new baseline condition was established in the fifth experiment whereby the learner's protests were standardized and the issue of a heart condition was introduced. At 270 volts, the learner produced an agonized scream, stating "Let me out of here." At 300 volts, this escalated to "I absolutely refuse to answer any more. Get me out of here. You can't hold me here. Get me out. Get me out of here." At 330 volts, a particularly prolonged agonized scream was followed with "Let me out of here. Let me out of here. My heart's bothering me. Let me out, I tell you." The absence of any reaction to this content, where there is no longer any mystery as to what was happening in the other room, is startling: 65% complied fully, the same as the first experiment.

The other variations included increasing the separation of the experimenter from the teacher (they communicated by telephone, with a drop in compliance to 20.5%), involving women as participants (no effect, with 65% still in compliance), changing experimental consent with the learner reserving the right to terminate the experiment (40% compliance), removing affiliation to Yale University (47.5% compliance), and eliminating the experimenter and replacing his role with an ordinary man (20% compliance).

In the latter stages of his research, Milgram played around with the social dynamics of the situation. In one variation, he had two experimenters (two bosses) giving mixed signals to the participant, creating doubt in what was happening, and, as a result, all participants refused to continue. In a more complex version, one of the experimenters stepped into the role of learner. As soon as the change occurred, the power of the position was lost and participants complied similarly to the base condition, accepting the orders of the lone experimenter who remained in the room. In a variation involving a peer teacher, where the participant no longer had to press the levers, compliance rose to 92.5%. In this variation, it was far easier for participants to shrug personal responsibility and carry on with the experiment.

The Purpose Behind the Shock Box

There is no grand theory underlying Milgram's work; instead, his experiments stand as a demonstration of what humans are capable of doing given the right context. Milgram's interest in obedience was a personal one, having been born of parents who immigrated from Europe prior to World War II. He used his experiments as a way of rationalizing the Holocaust. He wrote in his 1963 paper,

> It has been reliably established that from 1933–1945, millions of innocent persons were systematically slaughtered on command. Gas chambers were built, death camps were guarded; daily quotas of corpses were produced with the same efficiency as the manufacture of appliances. These inhumane policies may have originated in the mind of a single person, but they could only be carried out on a massive scale if a very large number of persons obeyed orders.

In a telling letter written to his schoolmate John Shaffer in 1958, Milgram stated that he "should have born into the German-speaking Jewish community in Prague in 1922 and died in a gas chamber some 20 years later. How I came to be born in the Bronx Hospital, I'll never quite understand."

Milgram found his way into psychology after initially studying political science, which is no surprise considering the preceding quote in how he positioned his research. Working alongside some of the most well-known psychologists of the day, Milgram initially explored issues of conformity, following the work of Solomon Asch. After completing his doctorate from Harvard in June 1960, Milgram took up an assistant professorship in the department of psychology at Yale University and began his work on obedience, with the aim of demonstrating the power of social influence. Milgram returned to Harvard shortly after, yet was not granted tenure. Several of his colleagues felt uneasy about Milgram's work and the ramifications it had on the department's reputation. Milgram left Harvard to become the head of social psychology at the City University of New York, where he remained until his death in 1984. Beyond the topic of obedience, Milgram was responsible for the identifying the "small world" effect, which itself would challenge college sobriety with the drinking game 6 Degrees of Separation for Kevin Bacon.

Milgram defined obedience as the "psychological mechanism that links individual action to political purpose. It is the dispositional cement that binds men to systems of authority." Obedience is not necessarily a bad thing, and, in many ways, it paves the way for civilization to exist. It is when the aims of obedience are unethical or malevolent that following one's duty to obey can lead to dark places. What Milgram did for us is demonstrate how strong the psychological mechanisms behind obedience are, leading the US Military Academy to stress in its leadership classes the importance of balancing the power of obedience with the responsibility to make well-considered and morally sound decisions.

Yet obedience does not act in isolation, and individuals are influenced by an array of psychological processes. Notably, obedience to a superior's orders can coexist alongside peer pressures to conform and adopt similar habits and routines. Which process wins out depends on the context: the social environment that individuals find themselves in and the strength of personality of those exerting their influence. Such issues characterize Milgram's later studies, where he created variations in the social dynamics experienced by the participant.

Beyond the core experimental design, Milgram captured expectations from a wide range of people about what they would do if they found themselves in the same scenario. This information provides great insight into what people think they would do when asked to obey orders that they personally disagreed with. On the scale ranging from 1 (Slight Shock at 15 volts) to 30 (XXX Shock at 450 volts), college students predicted that the average participant would stop at 9 (Strong Shock at 135 volts). Remember that strong protests are not heard from the participant until 270 volts (Intense Shock). A similar opinion was held by a group of middle-class adults, while psychiatrists went a little easier on folks, predicting that they would stop at 8 (Moderate Shock at 120 volts). The quotes taken from survey respondents were telling, with one person commenting "I can't stand to see people suffer. If the learner wanted to get out, I would free him so as not to make him suffer pain."

It is hard for people to visualize themselves doing harm to another person and yet the majority of participants obeyed orders. Milgram took transcripts of the interchange between experimenter and teacher, providing additional glimpses into the tension experienced by participants as they balanced in their minds the harm inflicted on the learner and their responsibility to follow through on commands. Bruno Batta was one such participant; he was described as showing little emotion and dissociating from the learner's complaints. The experimental variation he participated in required the teacher to put the learner's hand on the shock plate. Even after the learner begged to stop, Bruno continued the experiment in a robotic fashion while remaining highly receptive to the experimenter. When the learner stopped responding, Bruno commented, "You better answer and get it over with. We can't stay here all night." Later, he described the learner as stubborn and difficult.

Yet other participants acted in a way consistent with their self-image and resisted the authority of the experimenter. Jan Rensaleer began questioning the experiment at the first signs of distress and, at 255 volts, pushed his chair away from the shock generator and stated, "Oh, I can't continue this way; it's a voluntary program, if the man doesn't want to go on with it." When the experimenter stated that they did not have a choice, Jan responded, "I do have a choice. Why don't I have a choice? I came here on my own free will. I thought I could help in a research project. But if I have to hurt somebody to do that, or if I was in his place, too, I wouldn't stay there. I can't continue. I'm very sorry. I think I've gone too far already, probably." It is notable that Jan emigrated from Holland just after World War II.

Jan was not alone in resisting the experiment, and although most individuals continued all the way to the end in the base design, participants showed displeasure in what they were doing. Matthew Hollander transcribed 117 audio recordings of Milgram's participants, discovering six distinct forms of resistance. Three implicit forms of resistance included the use of silence/hesitation, cursing, and laughter (interpreted by many as participants having difficulty coping with the situation). In addition, three explicit forms of resistance were found, specifically asking the learner if they wanted to continue, questioning the experimenter, and stating that they wanted to stop.

Of those who completed the full experiment, only 19% attempted to stop the experiment in an explicit way. As a final data point on the power of the experiment, Thomas Blass compared replications of the experiment conducted by researchers around the world. Blass found no relationship between when the study was conducted and the amount of obedience it yielded. Similarly, rates of obedience were similar across cultures, with about two-thirds of participants complying fully with the experimenter.

What Milgram's experiments did for us is to expose the situational variables that result in obedience. Although not exhaustive, the variables listed here played an important part in the experiment and provide a glimpse at explaining why individuals can be brought to do something that is counter to their personal principles.

- *Legitimacy of authority*: In the experiment, Yale's prominence as an esteemed academic institution, as well as the experimenter's attire and professional demeanor, played a part in convincing participants that rules should be followed.
- *Established obligations*: The participants made a commitment to take part in the experiment (albeit for a relatively small amount of money). Breaking this commitment would create tension that participants were motivated to avoid.
- *Worthy goals*: The participants were informed about how the experiment would aid in the advancement of science and that, therefore, their participation would be meaningful. The short discomfort of learners was rationalized as less important than the enduring contribution that the participants would be making to science.
- *Vague ethical guidelines*: In the experiment, there is a fair amount of ambiguity as to what is a fair request, as well as the individual rights of participants. In addition, the participants found themselves in a closed environment where they could not check with external parties about the ethics of the situation.
- *Limited time for reflection*: Not only were they operating in a closed environment, but the participants also found themselves under time pressure to make decisions on the spot.
- *No way to compromise*: Participants found themselves in a mutually exclusive situation, whereby they could attend to the learner or experimenter, but not to both. There is no immediate compromise that would resolve the situation fully.

From Laboratory to the Workplace

The six environmental characteristics experimentally manipulated by Milgram have immediate relevance for the workplace and accurately describe the situation that many of us find ourselves in every day. Unless we have the luxury of being self-employed, reporting to a boss fulfills the first ingredient for obedient behavior. If we do not act in a way that proves that we are contributing to the performance of the organization, we could lose our job and the financial security that goes with it. Even in the gig economy, where relationships are tenuous and fluid, employers retain authority over workers for at least the short term. The company (or client) pays our bills and therefore always has a base level of legitimate authority. Even stronger behavior can be expected if we truly believe that the company we work for should have authority over us.

The same goes for the second ingredient of established obligations. From the moment of accepting an offer of employment or a contract for services, workers have committed themselves to the organization and have opened the door for obedient behavior. Quitting a job, especially when there is no immediate alternative that appears to be a better choice, creates tension. There is risk in making the switch (what happens if the new job doesn't work out?). Awkward conversations are likely to ensue as obligations are unwound, while the very act of change creates a certain level of anxiety as workers voyage into the unknown.

To help put this in context, the Holmes and Rahe Stress Scale compares different levels of stress caused by life events. On this scale, dismissal from work scores 47 out of a possible 100 points (the top end of scale is defined as the most stressful experience possible, specifically the death of a spouse). Dismissal from work sits at a similar level of stress as getting married. Business readjustment creates less stress at a score of 39 (a similar score to pregnancy), while changing to a different line of work attains a score of 36 (a level equivalent to the death of close friend). Taken together, sticking to the current employer is the easiest way to avoid the tension that comes with change.

This is not the same thing as saying that workers value the aims of the company or believe that their employers are smart, visionary, or deserving of respect. Companies go to great lengths to build their brand reputation, from building new skyscrapers for their corporate headquarters to buying the naming rights for a new stadium. Beyond wooing customers, this branding builds credibility in the minds of employees and confirms that they are working for a meaningful and important employer. The products and services they provide play a part in enriching the lives of customers. Beyond the immediate connection to work, corporate-sponsored service days take on causes that better the lives of people. From building wells in Africa to picking up garbage on the side of the road, such actions create the impression that the company is striving to accomplish worthy societal goals.

The remaining three ingredients of obedience are more contextual. Uncertainty in what is ethical behavior can occur in a variety of ways. For example, new technology can push the boundaries of what society has deemed good and just. Nowhere is this more evident than with health technology companies, where intellectual property has been argued to extend to the human genome while cloning provides the potential for life-saving therapies. Ambiguity can also occur in industries where rules have yet to be defined or where companies operate across legal jurisdictions, leaving employees to question whether to follow local customs or seek guidance from the head office. For example, one person's gift can be considered another person's bribe depending on one's vantage point and what is deemed culturally acceptable.

To this, closed environments can increase the chances for obedience. Nowhere is this more evident than in company towns, where the local economy depends on a single large employer. Thirty or forty years of tenure is common among employees, and nepotism becomes virtually unavoidable. With relatively few individuals joining the company from outside the community, there can be a lack of ethical reference points. Employees cannot draw on previous work experience or tap their friends to determine what is right.

For workers in high-stress situations with limited time for deep contemplation around what is ethically correct, obedience to established rules or authority can be the easiest way for employees to reduce stress. Alternatively, there are some situations when the stakes are too high for employees to question apparently unethical behavior, thus leading to a state of delusion that what they are doing is right. There are plenty of examples of corporate fraud, from Enron's forced blackouts to manipulate energy costs to Lehman Brothers' shaky accounting practices when dealing with subprime mortgages. Beyond the puppet masters who know the full extent of the legal or ethical boundaries being crossed, employees act on their bosses' direction and end up breaking the law along the way.

Even if they suspect that something is not kosher, employees may not know what to do, fearing that they are putting their own job security in jeopardy. And what happens if nothing unethical is going on? Will their boss ever look at them the same way again? These situations are reminiscent of John Grisham's *The Firm*, where the protagonist attempts to figure out who he can trust in a web of co-conspirators. Challenging authority is sometimes a one-way street, and, once embarked on, there is no turning back.

Against these six ingredients of obedience, the average workplace fulfills the majority of them. Even stronger alignment can occur when employees are under increased pressure to perform in closed environments and dealing with ambiguous situations. But bowing to authority is not necessarily a bad thing. Even Milgram pointed out that obedience serves a purpose and allows humanity to organize itself to productive ends. What worked well for a loosely connected band of friends when they started a business in a garage may not hold as the business scales in size. Early on, knowledge differences are minimal and decisions can be made by consensus. This only works for a time, and, as a business begins to become more profitable, the time and energy needed to seek consensus can stifle growth. Moreover, multiple leaders can lead to a great deal of ambiguity about direction and priorities. As every parent knows, children are adept at exploiting inconsistencies in decision-making. If Mom says no, just ask Dad. Both parents have the authority to grant a child's wishes and are likely not 100% aligned on every possible request.

Obedience becomes an issue when the goals and objectives of the authority figure are unethical or can do significant harm to others. At the far end of the continuum are the wartime atrocities that prompted Milgram to research the topic. Yet blind obedience in the workplace can still put lives at risk: from orders to ignore safety precautions in a factory setting to ignoring potentially harmful contaminants when processing food or purchasing cheap alternatives when constructing a building, employees or customers are put at risk. It is no wonder that governments worldwide have attempted to set health and safety standards, as well as financial and regulatory statutes, to safeguard workplace behavior and ease whistleblowing.

When a boss knows better and yet forces his or her employees to follow misguided orders, the same psychological processes that Milgram eloquently created in the laboratory become a reality. Just like the experimenter, the boss may hold ultimate responsibility for the outcomes of their actions. They may also make multiple requests of their staff to obey and remind them of the employment relationship by threatening a bad performance rating. Employees themselves become the teacher in the experiment, following through on orders with an occasional hesitation, curse, or nervous laugh.

It is not a huge leap to anticipate that two-thirds of employees will go along with authority in somewhat dubious situations. This figure might actually be higher, as the ramifications for their actions would never be as evident as hearing someone scream out in pain in an adjacent room. Remember, too, that obedience went much higher when the participant did not have to pull the lever. Being an observer was easier than being an instigator. Arguably the pressure to obey might be less for freelancers who view their employer more as a customer than a boss, yet, as mentioned previously, the six ingredients towards obedience are still in play.

The greatest ramification of Milgram's research for the workplace is that whistleblowers can be expected to be in the far minority of employees. This is potentially why whistleblowers gain so much publicity when they do speak out. When a revelation is big enough, the attention is warranted and people will take notice no matter who the individual is or what the context is that prompted them to speak out. Edward Snowden illustrates this point perfectly. Yet lesser known evils still have the power to captivate and make for big Hollywood films. Films like the *Insider*, *Erin Brockovich*, and *The Informant* all captivated us because they focused on a single individual with the power to bring down a powerful organization. Part of the story's attraction results from the tension created by not following orders and acting in a disobedient way. If whistleblowers were common, they wouldn't make for good protagonists, and we would be watching different types of movies.

As with many other psychological processes, the tension to speak out as a whistleblower must be greater than the pressure to follow orders. For Jan in Milgram's experiment, it was his experience in Europe following World War II that tipped the balance and made him stop shocking the learner. For the protagonist in *The Insider* (Jeff Wigand), increased pressure from his employer made him go rogue. Yet whistleblowing is not the norm and employees generally follow what they are told. The pressure to toe the line is higher than the ethical discomfort caused by what the organization is doing. Keeping one's job, avoiding personal conflict, or simply not caring enough about the company's infraction all provide incentives for employees to act in an obedient way.

To combat the imbalance, large companies typically have a whistleblowing policy in place that attempts to safeguard employees from speaking out on unethical behavior. They are promised confidentiality, a third party to talk to, and no repercussions for their actions. Yet these policies probably do more to demonstrate that the company is proactive and has ethical standards in place than provide a true vehicle to unearth bad practices. This is especially the case when employees are not fully aware of the extent of the company's infractions, feel weakly attached to the workplace, or believe that the whole organization is rotten and that no one would provide an objective outlet.

What Milgram showed us is that the pressure to obey largely overpowers other behaviors; it is the path of least resistance for workers to follow. When used for benevolent purposes, obedience can lead to a well-structured, effective organization that can serve the needs of its customers and the larger community. Employees are not employees without some level of hierarchy; otherwise, they would be owners or partners. It is when the psychological processes of obedience are bent toward unethical or selfish ends that tension is created in the workplace. Whether employees rebel against their employer depends a lot on who the employee is and whether they feel embittered or passionate enough to take on the fight. If we believe the results of Milgram's experiment, we shouldn't be surprised if it takes a while for someone to stand up and stop taking orders.

10

Conformity

It is a fresh Monday morning at Paddington Station in west London. The great Victorian terminal is springing to life as commuters arrive from all parts of southwest England and beyond. As the first passengers arrive, the station staff are preparing for the day. Over in one part of the station, Claire is readying her shop to open. As an outlet of a major fashion retailer, Claire ensures that the merchandise is well presented and checks that the right signs are in place announcing the summer sale. For her part, Claire is wearing three items from the shop as a subtle demonstration of how the shop's accessories can be mixed and matched. Although the choice is hers regarding which items she wears on a given day, the company has a policy in place that at least three items are to be worn at work every day. Adhering to this policy is mandatory, and, in turn, her employer provides a hefty discount for staff to buy clothing.

Down toward the train platform, Paul is cleaning the coffee machine after a wave of customers who just arrived from Bristol. Paul wears the easily recognizable red colored shirt and apron that have made his coffee chain popular over the past decade. Paul was provided three branded shirts and one apron during his first day on the job. The same can be said for Gurdit, who works for London Underground. Gurdit is currently standing in the ticket hall, underneath the main station, helping customers buy tickets and navigate to the correct train line. He proudly wears the blue and red colors that have become iconic of the oldest underground railway in the world. Yet his uniform differs in one distinct way: as a recognition of his Sikh faith, Gurdit wears a blue turban instead of the more common conductor's cap.

Uniforms are the most visible way that companies distinguish employees from the customers they serve. Needless to say, it can be rather awkward when a regular shopper is confused for an employee and asked for help. Beyond this basic purpose, uniforms also provide an opportunity for companies to brand their service (like Paul at the coffee shop) or subtly promote sales (like Claire in the clothing store). They also encourage staff to adopt a

Punching the Clock. Joe Ungemah, Oxford University Press (2021). © Oxford University Press.
DOI: 10.1093/oso/9780190061241.003.0010.

common identity and think of themselves as employees. With room to accommodate cultural and religious differences (such as with Gurdit's turban), employees conform to the social norm of wearing uniforms as a condition of their employment and, in so doing, communicate to customers and staff that they are part of the team.

Wearing a uniform is just one example of the type of conformity that occurs on a daily basis within the workplace, and typically, the company never needs to explicitly ask for employees to adopt social norms. How much effort should be exerted on the average day, what time it is normal to arrive at work, and can senior staff be approached on a purely social basis are examples of social norms that are often established without any form of official guidance. Individual workers take their cues from others in their work environment and, in so doing, embed the social norms further. Guiding the acceptance of social norms are deeply rooted psychological processes that govern conformity.

Solomon Asch conducted a series of experiments that sought to uncover how impressionable people are to social pressure. Writing in the 1950s, he was particularly concerned with the emerging potential for technology to deliberately manipulate opinion on a large scale. In previous psychological studies on conformity, a change in opinion was encouraged by presenting individuals with information about how many people agreed or disagreed with them or by providing the opinion of someone they respected. However, Asch questioned whether individuals truly changed their opinion or whether they simply went with the flow. He mused that opinions are more stable than previous psychologists had considered and that individuals would change behavior according to the group consensus irrespectively if they agreed wholeheartedly with them.

In his base experiment, Asch assembled an average of eight young men in a room to take part in an experiment that he explained was geared at exploring visual judgment. The task was simple and rather tedious. Two white cards were presented to the group. On one card, a single vertical black line was drawn. On the other card, a series of three vertical black lines were displayed that were to be compared to the original line. These lines varied substantially in length, ranging from three-quarters of an inch to an inch and three-quarters, with one line always matching the original line from the first card. The participant's job was easy: pick out the line from the series that was exactly the same length as the original line. The group then had to do this again over multiple trials.

In reality, only one of the men was a true participant. All others were confederates of Asch and directed to respond in a certain way. For the first two trials, each of the men took turns choosing the line that best matched the standard for comparison, with the true participant going last. With such a simple task, it is no surprise that the judgments were unanimous, with the correct line chosen across the group members. But then something started to go wrong. On the third trial, the participant finds himself alone in choosing the obviously correct line. All others have gone a different direction and chosen the completely wrong line. Then it happens again on the fourth trial. The participant is in a predicament. In this open group forum made up of his peers, he either must stick to his conviction about what is an obvious fact or bend to the opinion of the group, even though they are completely wrong in their judgment. Not surprising, the participants showed discomfort with the situation, hesitating before making their choices, speaking in a low voice, or smiling in embarrassment. To keep the experiment running for as long as possible, the group was wired to occasionally make the right choice and, across 18 trials, six were answered correctly.

A total of 123 participants took part in the experiment, from three educational institutions. Across the trials, participants went against their best judgment and agreed with the consensus view in 36.8% of the trials. A total of 75% of participants did this at least once in the 18 trials, whereas 25% were completely independent of the group and never agreed with the group's erroneous judgments. Once the trials were under way, the path an individual took was fairly consistent. Either they stuck to their convictions throughout the experiment or succumbed to group pressure.

Regarding the independent participants, Asch commented that these individuals did indeed feel pressure to conform but were successful in building up confidence in their opinion. Other independent participants stated that they came to believe that the group was right and they were wrong, yet they felt an obligation to answer the task consistently with what they personally judged as the correct answer. Among those who largely succumbed to group pressure, they, too, believed that the group was in the right. Even when participants suspected something strange was afoot, they decided to go along with the group (to reduce awkwardness) rather than question the merits of the exercise.

To dig further on the topic, Asch changed the experimental context. First, he altered the group size to see if this would affect the amount of pressure experienced by the participant. Each participant joined a group of confederates ranging in size from 1 to 15 others. In this version of the experiment, participants acted independently when confronted with just one confederate. When outnumbered 2 to 1, the pressure began to mount and the participant went with the group consensus 13.6% of the time. When joined by three confederates, the rate of conformity went up to 31.8%, near to the amount witnessed in the original experiment. From these results, it appears that social pressure tops out at a ratio of 3 to 1, and only when the numbers get really large does the pressure dissipate (people start to suspect that someone, somewhere must agree with them).

In another experiment, Asch introduced a supporting partner to diminish the outright power the group had in the original experiment. Having someone on their side depleted participant conformity by 75%. In other words, the participant went with the group consensus only 25% of the time witnessed under the base experiment. When asked about the partner following the experiment, participants often credited the partner with building their confidence.

In another variation, the partner chose the line between the obviously correct answer and the group's completely wrong answer as a means of testing out compromise. In this set-up, the participant was joined by another dissenter to the group, yet they were not in complete agreement about the correct answer. When performed, the rate of conformity dropped by approximately a third from the base condition, and the choice made by participants moderated. The participants went for the middle ground, to align themselves more with the other dissenter (i.e., they showed compromise).

In two final variations, Asch toiled around with the effects of desertion by the partner. After six trials, the partner changed tactics and joined the majority in making poor judgments. In turn, the participant accommodated this move and began going along with the majority at approximately the same rate as if there was no partner to begin with. In the final variation, the partner left the experiment halfway through, apparently to make a previously arranged appointment with the Dean. Unlike when the partner became a turncoat, the effect of the absent partner outlived his physical presence in the room. Errors did occur more frequently, with participants succumbing to group pressure, but less than when the partner completely turned his back on the participant. Just in case you were wondering, Asch did test whether the length of the lines had any effect on the results and, even with a gross discrepancy of 7 inches, the effects of conformity were still witnessed.

Asch's experiments struck a nerve with psychologists. They demonstrated how group pressure can cause individuals to make public choices that go against what they know is obvious and true. Internally, personal opinion is unlikely to have changed, yet the public behavior of individuals changed nonetheless. Recent critique of Asch's work has taken fault not with the original experiment, but rather with how it has been misconstrued by psychologists teaching the principles of conformity. Specifically, the narrative taught in textbooks overemphasizes the amount of conformity that occurred among participants. For example, few psychologists mention that 95% of participants rebelled against the group at least once during the experiment, focusing instead on the statistic that 75% conformed in at least one of the trials. With this argument aside, Asch's work remains influential for demonstrating that group pressure can change behavior (independent of a person's true opinion) toward baseless conclusions.

The Group at All Costs

Conformity can come in many different shapes and sizes. On the harmless side of the continuum, group members may begin using similar types of phrases, watch the same TV programs, or laugh at a certain kind of joke. Such changes in behavior glue the group further together and generally makes interactions more enjoyable. Yet the pendulum can go too far, to the extent that harmony within the group takes on importance above all else, sometimes with catastrophic consequences.

On April 17, 1961, one of the greatest botches in political and military strategy was under way. One thousand four hundred Cuban exiles were sent to overthrow Fidel Castro, beginning their invasion at a location called the Bay of Pigs. Although authorized by President Kennedy, the plan was developed years earlier under the watch of President Eisenhower, who was wary of Castro's relationship to Nikita Khrushchev, then leader of the Soviet Union. The government made an assumption that a significant portion of the Cuban military and the population in general were unsatisfied with Castro and therefore would join in an uprising against him. Training camps were set up in Guatemala to prepare a small invasion force that, once landed, would transition to guerrilla warfare.

The plan looked great on paper. The attack would take Castro by surprise with multiple deceptions incorporated throughout. Even the landing point at the Bay of Pigs was thought to be ingenious, being in a remote swampy area on the southern coast that could easily be overlooked as an invasion point (it was also more than 80 miles away from a safe haven if anything went wrong). Two air strikes were to occur just before landfall, taking out the relatively small Cuban Air Force, while paratroopers would be dropped over land to disrupt transportation links. To hide US involvement, B-26 bombers were painted to look like stolen Cuban planes. To further confuse the Cubans, a smaller force would attack from the east, to draw attention away from the main army. Once the invading force was established, a provisional government was to be set up to rally the Cuban populace to the cause, creating the momentum necessary to overthrow Castro's government.

The reality was that news travels fast among Cuban exiles in Miami, and Castro was well aware of the army, its training in Guatemala, and basically everything that the United States government was planning. Knowing that planes were on their way from a base in Nicaragua, Castro moved his Air Force into safety and later redeployed them against the invasion force. It didn't help that the chosen planes were quite old (from World War II) and ineffective at hitting their intended targets. The crews were also late in arriving to the fight, having not accounted for the change in time zone between Nicaragua and Cuba. As news broke about the air attack, the link to the United States was so apparent that Kennedy cancelled the second planned air strike.

Things were not much better on the ground. When the invasion force landed, they were spotted by a radio station operator who broadcasted every aspect of the landing across the island. Even the landing itself went wrong, with unexpected coral reefs sinking a number of the landing boats and the Cuban Air Force taking out two escort ships as well as half of the air support. As for the paratroopers, they ended up in the wrong place and didn't do much to disrupt transportation links. The ground force experienced bad weather and found themselves ill-equipped as well as short on ammunition. Castro had amassed a force of 20,000 troops, leaving the ground force outnumbered 20 to 1. In less than a day, Castro had put an end to the invasion, killing more than 100 exiles and capturing roughly 1,200 more. The captured soldiers stayed in captivity for 20 months, until a deal was struck with Castro to exchange the prisoners for $53 million worth of baby food and medicine. The plan could not have gone any worse.

Irving Janis studied the Bay of Pigs fiasco in depth and used it to coin the phrase *groupthink*. Based on the disastrous outcomes of the attack, it would be easy to assume that the team working on the invasion were not up to the task, but this would be the wrong assumption. The team behind the Bay of Pigs involved many of the greatest names in US politics and strategy at the time. This team simply failed to live up to its potential. What Janis came to realize was that the social conformity experienced by the group clouded judgment by putting pressure on its members and discouraging dissident thinking. Like what Asch witnessed in the laboratory, Kennedy's advisors changed their behavior to better align themselves to the group. Team morale triumphed over the critical evaluation of the plan and the realistic appraisal of alternative courses of action.

When cohesive groups experience groupthink, group members tend to go soft on their leader and each other, failing to challenge opinions and the information on which they are founded. At the same time, the group tends to take a hard stance on out-group members, adopting stereotypes and attitudes that others are inferior. All this is done without deliberate suppression by outside forces; the group members suppress their own criticisms of what is occurring and internalize prevailing social norms. They don't necessarily feel inhibited to express their thoughts and criticisms, but rather accept group suggestions at face value and with a bias that the team comes up with great ideas.

Janis identified that highly cohesive groups will get the impression that they are invulnerable, and therefore, members will underestimate risks and overestimate the possibility of success. This was exemplified by Kennedy's belief that the meager American forces would prevail to both establish a beachhead and convince others to join the uprising. Not only did they overestimate capability, but also the chances that the plan would be kept secret, take Castro by surprise, and conceal that the United States was behind the attack. Group members rationalize away threats and discount warning signs.

Feelings toward the group run strong, and members tend to believe in the morality of what they are doing in an unquestioning fashion. For example, with the Bay of Pigs, two prominent leaders, Arthur Schlesinger Jr. and Senator J. Fulbright, had misgivings about the plan but were basically ignored by Kennedy, who did not take seriously their perspectives and even failed to allow Schlesinger a vote when approving the plan. Instead, he gave prominent roles to CIA representatives in his meetings and allowed these advisors to effectively quash any doubts raised about the merits of the strategy. The end result is self-censorship among dissidents as they become aware that they are the lone voice of reason, thus giving the impression to others that the group is unanimous in its beliefs.

At the same time, strong opinions are held about out-group members, thinking of them as evil, inept, or similar. Castro's Air Force was underestimated to the extent that Kennedy's team thought obsolete B-26s could knock it out. Equally misguided was the belief that a small, recently trained brigade was all that was needed against an established army and that Castro would be inept at putting down a local uprising. To quell any disbelief and to maintain the superiority of the group, a few members may take on the role of protector. Robert F. Kennedy was one such person; he confronted Schlesinger and requested that he stop putting pressure on the president.

To Kennedy's credit, he learned from the Bay of Pigs and changed the way his leadership team dealt with future threats. When dealing with the Cuban Missile Crisis, Kennedy established a new way of working. First, each member was encouraged to be critical of suggestions and to openly air objections and doubts. A devil's advocate was assigned whenever a critical juncture was reached. Leaders themselves were asked to conceal their initial thoughts or preferences so as not to taint the discussion. Outside parties, who could provide objectivity, were brought into the fold to either work the same issue or provide expert opinion. Meetings were set aside to survey all available warning signs and to consider the intentions of rivals from multiple standpoints. Finally, when a decision was looming, a second-chance meeting was held to air out any remaining doubts or misgivings. Through these deliberate changes in how the group worked together, Kennedy's team lived up to its potential and saved the world from a nuclear disaster.

It Gets in Your Head

So far, we have looked at overt signs of conformity, from agreeing to go along with group consensus to minimizing internal group conflict. What we have yet to explore is how the psychological processes governing conformity impact our internal attitudes and beliefs. Leon Festinger and James Carlsmith investigated this very thing and in the process coined the phrase *cognitive dissonance* to describe what they found. Cognitive dissonance refers to situations where two or more cognitions are psychologically inconsistent, which in turn causes discomfort and stress to the individual holding the cognitions. The researchers were specifically interested in understanding what happens to an individual's private opinion if they are forced to act in a way that is contrary to how he or she would normally behave. In the discussion about Asch, an assumption was made that participants didn't really change their opinion about what the right answer was. The research by Festinger and Carlsmith challenges that assumption.

At Stanford University in the late 1950s, 71 male undergraduates were invited to take part in one of the most boring and tedious experiments dreamed up by psychologists. First, they were instructed to place 12 spools onto a tray, remove them, and then start again, using only one hand. They did this for half an hour. To the chagrin of participants who were hoping for relief, they were asked to begin a second tedious task. This time, the participants were asked to turn 48 square pegs on a board by 90 degrees, one at a time. After another 30 minutes had passed, the task was called complete, with absolutely nothing accomplished for an hour's worth of time and energy. The participants at this point were probably thinking that the course credit wasn't worth it and potentially were considering a different major.

All throughout the tasks, an experimenter was pretending that the participants' actions were very interesting, using a stopwatch and notepad to capture every moment. When time was stopped, the experimenter came clean and spoke openly about the apparent purpose of the study, specifically to measure performance across two groups of participants. One group was told essentially nothing about the tasks and served as a control group (the participants were all told that they were part of this group). The other group was given an introduction by a confederate who described the experiment using the phrases "It was very enjoyable," "I had a lot of fun," "I enjoyed myself," "It was very interesting," "It was intriguing, and "It was exciting." The purpose of the experiment was explained as testing what this description would do to the level of effort exerted by the participants.

After this confession by the experimenter, the real study began. Participants were offered the opportunity to work for the experimenter and act as the confederate. After explaining that the normal confederate had phoned in sick, the experimenter asked the participant whether he would be willing to go into a second room and talk about the experiment to another student. They were to use the stock phrases ("It was very interesting, I had a lot of fun") to share how much they enjoyed the tasks. As an incentive, the participant was either offered $1 or $20 for his time, as well as the opportunity to be called on for future experiments.

If the participant agreed, he entered the second room where he found a fellow student waiting (the real confederate in the experiment). After the participant mentioned the experiment and how much fun he had, the other student responded by stating she was surprised to hear that the experiment was enjoyable. She stated that a friend of hers had taken the experiment a week ago and encouraged her to get out of it. To this challenge, most participants stated something like, "Oh, no, it's really very interesting. I'm sure you'll enjoy it." After 2 minutes, the experimenter cut the conversation short and invited the participant to come down the hall to share their impressions of the experimental process with a faculty member from introductory psychology. This interview was positioned as an independent check-in to ensure that the experiment was a good way of receiving course credit and an appropriate use of time. Each participant was asked the same four questions, with both verbal responses and numerical ratings captured: (1) Were the tasks interesting and enjoyable? (2) Did the experiment give you an opportunity to learn about your own ability to perform these tasks? (3) From what you know about the experiment and the tasks involved in it, would you say the experiment was measuring anything important? That is, do you think the results may have scientific value? And (4), would you have any desire to participate in another similar experiment?

Of the 71 participants, data from 11 individuals had to discarded, either because they guessed the real purpose behind the experiment, refused to be hired, or were excessively open with the student, explaining that they found the experiment boring but were paid to say the opposite. One final participant went way too far by asking for the student's phone number and offering to meet up with her casually after the experiment was over. Apparently, he viewed the experiment as a good way to meet potential dates.

The results from the experiment are counterintuitive and provide great insight into the psychological processes governing conformity. The experiment purposefully created cognitive dissonance by requiring participants to openly state something that they knew was untrue: specifically, that they enjoyed a tedious series of tasks. To reduce the dissonance, participants persuaded themselves that the tasks were indeed both interesting and enjoyable. Initially hard to understand about the experiment is the fact that participants were most likely to change opinions when paid just a dollar for their time. Participants who received $20 were able to rationalize their worries away, figuring that any discomfort experienced was justified by the reward they received. At just a dollar, lying to another individual just doesn't seem worth it, causing the participants to search for an alternative reason to justify their behavior.

The experimental results found that participants who received $1 rated the tasks as more enjoyable, both in relative terms to those who were paid $20 and in absolute terms, giving the tasks a moderate rating of 1.35 on a scale running from −5 (extremely dull and boring) to +5 (extremely interesting and enjoyable). Moreover, the participants who were paid $1 stated that they were more willing than their higher paid counterparts to participate in similar experiments in the future. What these results demonstrate is a tendency for individuals to rationalize away situations in which they acted against their privately held opinions. To diminish the discomfort and stress experienced, the individual changes his or her opinion to come in line with what he or she has said or done. Moreover, the pressure to change opinions is greatest when the reward is meager or when the individual is hesitating the most in agreeing to act. In this way, conforming to the group can have a lasting impact on the individual by displacing previously held beliefs.

Consensus Is Not Always a Good Thing

From Asch's experiments and the real case study provided by the Bay of Pigs, we have learned how the group can influence its members away from an objective truth for the benefit of preserving group unity. Reacting to what they perceive about other group members, individuals can be brought to publicly support an opinion that they do not believe in. Alternatively, they can be forced to keep silent, reserving their discomfort for the sake of maintaining group consensus. This is a different phenomenon than obedience in that an authority figure is not required to change individual behavior. The individual acts alone in conforming to the group. Moreover, if the individual is convinced to publicly support a position that they do not necessary believe in, there is a chance that he or she will actually reevaluate his or her opinion to resolve the cognitive dissonance caused by actions not aligning to beliefs. Chances are this change will occur when the payoff is the smallest or, in other words, when there is very little reason for the individual to have agreed in the first place.

A degree of conformity is helpful for any social group and especially for those belonging to the same workplace. After all, people from a variety of different backgrounds are brought together to serve a single organizational purpose, from transporting people and goods across a railway system to selling food or clothing. Like the employees described at the outset of this chapter, uniforms and other signs of group membership convey to each other and the customers that they serve that certain goods will be provided and that the employees can be relied on for help. On a subtler level, the unspoken social norms that we abide by allow employees to engage with each other effectively without having to work out new rules and procedures from scratch.

As the workplace evolves, we are seeing signs that these unspoken rules are up for renegotiation, with everything from dress codes, working hours, and virtual workplaces adapting to the desires of Millennials as they become established in the workforce. With the advent of the gig economy, even the rules that make it into the employee handbook are up for grabs. Without close supervision, workers have the freedom to explore multiple approaches for accomplishing a task or interacting with peers. With much more noise in the system, opportunities for conformity (right or wrong) are disappearing, leaving workers to guess what is expected of them.

With conformity comes baggage. As Kennedy learned the hard way, too much conformity within the group can lead to disaster and potentially endanger much more than the immediate team. Outside the world of politics, the processes underlying groupthink can result in industrial spills, loss of retirements savings, or anything else that is governed by a group of people. The first step in combating the negative side effects of conformity is to become cognizant of the situation that the group finds itself within. For example, conformity will be higher when an answer to a problem is unknown. In Asch's experiment, the lines were obviously different, but the participants found themselves questioning their own judgment and going along with the group consensus. Second, the size of the group matters. At a ratio of 3:1 or higher, the pressure of conformity exerts itself the strongest. This power holds up until the group size gets really large and people start taking comfort in their anonymity. Last, having other dissenters in the mix, even for a short time, can moderate the effects of conformity and allow individuals to speak their mind.

As a facilitator or leader of a work group, understanding how these dynamics affect dialogue and, ultimately, the support garnered for a group's position can allow for better problem-solving. If a work group falls within these high-risk parameters— specifically, by discussing a problem with no clear solution among four or more members, with no opportunity to voice dissent, and public pressure to show cohesiveness—the group leader should employ different tactics to safeguard against groupthink. Kennedy was a quick learner and took corrective action after the Bay of Pigs, thus saving the world from a potential nuclear war. We can learn from his example.

Dynamic tension should be encouraged, whereby it is the responsibility of each group member to voice openly objections, doubts, and new perspectives. Outside experts can be invited to take part in discussions to maintain a degree of objectivity, especially if the group is fairly homogenous in its makeup. Beyond involving experts, other forms of data should be sought to help identify hidden risks. If appropriate, a devil's advocate can be assigned at critical junctures to ensure that the path forward really is the best alternative. As decisions get closer, a second-chance meeting can be held to provide one last opportunity to air doubts or misgivings about the group's direction. All throughout the group's interactions, the role of the leader or facilitator should be carefully watched. Knowing that the leader's opinion can sway the group, his or her true opinions and preferences should be concealed as much as possible until a final opinion is required.

In reading this, the time and scrutiny required to safeguard against conformity can appear unproductive. Groups can easily get caught up in the bureaucracy of endless meetings, putting off decisions for the sake of inclusiveness and thorough analysis. For Kennedy and the Cuban Missile Crisis, delaying a decision indefinitely was simply not an option. The missiles were on their way, and the administration needed to respond. Instead, the challenge was force-fitting the preceding decision-making process to a very urgent and important deadline. This is probably why Kennedy's approach was successful. Preserving a sense of urgency, to the extent of creating false deadlines, appears as important as the techniques themselves. The alternative is to allow the power of conformity to transform capable individuals into poor decision-makers and even change their internal beliefs about what is known to be true. Building and then preserving group unity without this baggage is ideal and, in reality, very hard to achieve.

11

Identity

Can an individual exist in isolation from the social world? If so, what does this type of life feel like? After all the social roles, labels, and stereotypes that bind an individual to the social world are stripped away, what's left over? Would such a person have meaning in his or her life, beyond the act of living? These are the types of questions probably best reserved for a quiet conversation over a bottle of wine and chocolate truffles, yet they tap a fundamental topic in psychology that influences how humans interact without each other in everyday encounters. How people describe themselves has a bearing on the social relationships they gravitate toward, as well as those that they might try to avoid.

From time to time, a story emerges about an individual who fell off the social grid. These extreme examples can teach us a great deal about the human condition and, specifically, the topic of identity. Of all the examples, none quite compares to the story of Christopher Thomas Knight who was caught in the act of stealing supplies from the Pine Tree Kitchen in rural Maine on April 4, 2013. Christopher was better known as the North Pond Hermit and was very much the subject of local legend. For decades, he had evaded the police, successfully breaking into and stealing food, clothes, and other necessities from the summer cabins that litter the countryside in central Maine. Beyond getting caught, there was nothing particularly noteworthy about the break-in; it was one of approximately 40 robberies he committed in a typical year. Among the things he routinely scored were food, kitchenware, propane, and clothes. With more than 1,000 break-ins under his belt, it is not surprising that the local community were fed up and sought to capture the hermit.

On the night he was arrested, a newly installed motion-detector alerted his entry into the Pine Tree Kitchen, a place that Christopher had raided in the past. On a previous raid, he had obtained a key to the walk-in freezer, and he used it this night to take burgers and bacon, along with a cornucopia of marshmallows, candy, coffee, and potato chips. Monitoring the motion detector was Sergeant Terry Hughes, who was intent on apprehending the

Punching the Clock. Joe Ungemah, Oxford University Press (2021). © Oxford University Press.
DOI: 10.1093/oso/9780190061241.003.0011.

hermit. When Christopher exited the kitchen with his loot, he found him-self on the other end of Terry's .357 handgun pointed squarely at his nose. Christopher showed no resistance and laid on the ground until state trooper Diane Perkins-Vance (who also actively hunted the hermit) arrived and placed him in custody.

Christopher's physical appearance was odd in comparison to what would normally be expected for a hermit: Christopher was well kept. He was clean, shaven, and wore a fairly new Columbia jacket, Lands' End jeans, and a good pair of boots. The only thing that seemed out of place was his glasses, which turned out to be the only object that he had difficulty finding in the cabins. Although he found the odd pair of glasses, none was as strong as his current prescription, and he was left to wear the out-of-date plastic pair he fashioned when he first went into the woods. They were also the exact pair he wore for his senior high school picture.

Christopher took a few hours to find his voice. When asked where he lived, he stated simply "the woods." When asked how long, he responded by asking when the Chernobyl nuclear plant disaster occurred. This exchange revealed that Christopher had lived in the woods for a much longer time than initially thought; almost 30 years had passed since he left civilization. Christopher's experience with the modern world stopped in 1986. In all that time, he had only one chance encounter with a hiker in the 1990s, when they respectively said "hi" to each other as they passed on a trail. Other than that, he had not spoken or touched another human being in 27 years. Even among hermits, Christopher was particularly isolated.

Shortly after his arrest, Christopher allowed himself to be interviewed by Michael Finkel from GQ Magazine, first with an exchange of letters and later by meeting in person. Christopher described the moment when he be-came a hermit. Christopher was working as an alarm systems technician (which no doubt enabled him to evade the police as a hermit) in Waltham Massachusetts. One day, he decided to quit his job and drive his car through his hometown of Albion, Maine, to take "one last look around" before driving into the countryside. He stated, "I drove until I was nearly out of gas. I took a small road. Then a small road off that small road. Then a trail off that." He got out of the car. "I had a backpack and minimal stuff. I had no plans. I had no map. I didn't know where I was going. I just walked away."

Christopher did not immediately turn toward burglarizing cabins, but realized soon into his new lifestyle that foraging would only get him so far, especially with the brutal winters that he endured. Initially he moved around quite a bit, but after 2 years, he came across a campsite that would become his home for the next 25 years. That particular patch of land had the perfect combination of concealment and shelter from the elements. When Christopher led the police to his campsite, they found an established living area, inclusive of a tent, bedframe, mattress and box spring, toilet paper, hand sanitizer, Coleman two-burner stove, deodorant, grooming materials, and more. He even had an emergency bag packed with essentials in case he was discovered and needed to leave in a hurry. Christopher's only connection to society was through radio and books. He had stolen a radio, antenna, and earphones, such that he could listen to music, talk radio, and popular TV shows, although he had to image what was happening on the screen. He also stole hundreds of books and magazines over the years, which he double purposed as building materials to prop up his camp as makeshift bricks once he finished reading them. Although connected to society, the relationship was unidirectional; Christopher consumed society but did not interact with it.

Christopher developed a series of tactics to survive in the woods. Getting fat in the summer was a priority, and he did this by eating anything with a high sugar or alcohol content. He also learned how to stock up on his provisions for the winter, to grow and maintain a beard of the ideal length, and to survive the nights without freezing to death while asleep. For 6 months out of the year, Christopher did not stray far from his campsite and had to make do with whatever he was able to steal prior to the winter. Some years, he came perilously close to death by running out of food and fuel too early. Despite it all, Christopher decided that the only way he would leave the forest was by force. He yearned to spend the remainder of his life isolated from society.

Christopher did not adjust well when he was taken into custody. His attempts to interact with fellow inmates and guards failed miserably. He had nothing in common with them, finding a major gap between the current world and the one he left 27 years prior. Christopher wrote, "I am retreating into silence as a defensive move. . . . I am surprised by the amount of respect this garners me. That silence intimidates and puzzles me. Silence is to me normal, comfortable." In jail, his physical and mental health deteriorated as he grappled with how to reconnect to the world. Not only was casual conservation an issue, but even looking at others was problematic, "I'm not used to seeing people's faces. There's too much information there. . . . Too much, too fast." He was concerned that his sanity was starting to slip in jail, writing "I suspect more damage has been done to my sanity in jail, in months; than years, decades, in the woods."

Christopher was sentenced to 7 months in jail, which was basically the same as the time he served waiting for his case to be heard. A longer jail term was argued by the prosecutor as particularly cruel for Christopher as his readjustment to society was already difficult enough. Before his release, Christopher spoke to Michael Finkel about his experience, the trial, and his readjustment. He stated, "I don't know your world. Only my world, and memories of the world before I went into the woods. What life is today? What is proper? I have to figure out how to live." He continued, "Sitting here in jail, I don't like what I see in the society I'm about to enter. I don't think I'm going to fit in."

In returning to society, Christopher's sense of self was turned on its head. The 47-year-old man in jail had little connection to the recent high school graduate who quit his job and headed into the woods. The person Christopher became was created in isolation from the rest of society, with no reference point about what is normal or acceptable. His cultural knowledge had atrophied to a point where he held nothing in common with those around him. Yet Christopher found himself in a position where he needed to assimilate into society. Under the terms of his release, he was barred from disappearing back into the woods and continuing his life as the North Pond Hermit.

Christopher's readjustment is just half of the story. The community was faced with accepting a man who had lived on the fringes of their society. Although the material loss from Christopher's looting sprees may not have been hugely significant, he violated the safety of his neighbors. For nearly three decades, they felt threatened by an intruder who broke into their homes and left little trace about who he was or his motive. Even if considered more of a hermit than a thief, Christopher faced a community who might not accept him. Early in his interactions with Finkel, Christopher commented that he found it surprising how others thought of him, writing "When I came out of the woods they applied the label hermit to me. Strange idea to me. I had never thought of myself as a hermit. Then I got worried. For I knew with the label hermit comes the idea of crazy."

Christopher's story provides a tangible example of what it means to have a social identity. In the absence of others to connect and share experience with, a person's sense of self changes dramatically. It makes you question what remains after all the labels and relationships are gone. How human can we be when we are removed from society? In a rare moment, Christopher became introspective and described what happened when he lost society as a reference point. "I did examine myself. Solitude did increase my perception. But here's the tricky thing—when I applied my increased perception to myself, I lost my identity. With no audience, no one to perform for, I was just there. There was no need to define myself; I became irrelevant. . . . I was completely free."

Who Are You?

In 1952, a pair of researchers named Manford Kuhn and Thomas McPartland created one of the simplest yet most powerful psychological experiments ever conducted. Participants were asked to complete a single task: answer the question "Who am I?" as a means of establishing a reliable measure for evaluating the concept of self. How a person thought of him- or herself was very much the point of the experiment, and, for whatever reason, it took until the 1950s for psychologists to seek consensus on a method for measuring the meaning we ascribe ourselves in the social world.

It is actually a worthwhile task, and I encourage you to try out the experiment right now. You'll first need a blank sheet of paper. From there, write the numbers 1–20 in a single column down the left side of the page. Once done, follow the original instructions provided in the experiment:

> There are twenty numbered blanks on the page. Please write twenty answers to the simple question "Who am I?" in the blanks. Just give twenty different answers to this question. Answer as if you were giving the answers to yourself, not to somebody else. Write the answers in the order that they occur to you. Don't worry about logic or "importance." Go along fairly fast, for time is limited.

Mark the time when you start and give yourself 12 minutes to complete the task.

Look back over your list. Do you see any themes that underlie the responses? For example, did you identify yourself in relation to your family, potentially as a father, mother, grandparent, or sibling. Did you write down your occupation, education, or demographic information, like your age, ethnicity, or gender. How about where you live, your citizenship, or religion? What about social affiliations, such as being a fan of your local sports club, alumni of a university, or member of a community group?

Beyond themes, was there something about the order of your answers? How easy was the task for you as you went down the list? Did you get stuck for a description, or did you fill up the page? Was there anything surprising that you came up with or that doesn't really make much sense now that you are looking over your responses?

If you have the time, have your partner or friend complete the same task. Compare your results and see what trends emerge. Does the list surprise you in any way by revealing something you did not already know? How about the areas of similarity and difference between your lists or potentially the order by which the items were written? Does this make sense for how you two interact? Hopefully, if you are in a serious relationship, the description of partner, wife, husband, fiancé, or similar made the list (sorry if this is not the case and the experiment just made your relationship a bit awkward).

Generally speaking, responses to the Twenty Statements Test are bucketed into five thematic categories, the first of which was originally pinpointed by Kuhn and McPartland. *Consensual statements* designate membership to social groups or a particular social status. They are easily recognized, and the conditions of memberships are well known, like being a woman, member of the Rotary Club, or working as an astronaut. Consensual statements appear early in the Twenty Statements Test relative to the remaining four categories, which are harder to nail down and require interpretation about what is exactly meant by the description. These include *ideological beliefs* (religious or philosophical orientations), *aspirations* (future-oriented goals and achievements), *preferences* (personal interests and aversions), and *self-evaluations* (physical, mental, or personality judgments). For example, if you wrote down "cheerful," the word itself needs to be interpreted. Who exactly are you comparing yourself to?

For any individual, there is a great range of responses that can appear on the list, but there are no hard rules about the appropriate number or specific items. Rather, the full list provides a snapshot of your identity as perceived by you at this particular moment in time. Having done the task myself a few times over the past 15 years (and encouraging my wife to do the same), my list has changed quite radically depending on the twists and turns that life has taken. Living outside the United States was reflected in my national identity appearing on the list and disappearing again when I moved back, while a new job forced a change in both the relative importance of my occupation and a new classification that didn't exist before. By far the biggest change was in becoming a father and all the descriptions that go along with it.

The Twenty Statements Test helps identify social statuses and the attributes that underlie them, which in turn exposes why people act the way they do. We seek out people who can embellish certain roles that we cherish while actively avoiding others who may hold significantly different views and challenge the way we like to think of ourselves. In between, personal drives toward inclusivity encourage us to interact and appreciate individuals who would likely hold a very different set of answers to the Twenty Statements Test. The social identities revealed through the test play out in a complex dance of behavior that can include attraction, avoidance, tolerance, and ambivalence toward others. Considering the multiple identities that we all hold, this dance changes shape depending on the context of our interactions. As a case in point, the work Christmas party creates a perfect recipe for conflict between personal identities. Without warning, you realize that a coworker you greatly enjoy working with would not be the type of friend you would make otherwise.

Bleeding Blue

It is a balmy, record-setting day for heat in Houston. This is saying a lot for a city that builds tunnels under its downtown so that its citizenry can survive the summers in relative comfort. As I approach a cafe close to the heart of the Galleria, I am reminded why I choose to live on the other side of the country. I have been outside for 5 minutes and am already a sweaty mess. The same cannot be said for Tim Fischer, who appears unfazed by the melting sidewalks.

I was introduced to Tim because of a curious phrase I overheard in a conversation with an employee at Marathon Oil. In describing the culture from his point of view, he said in passing that they "bleed blue." He went on to explain that the affinity many employees hold toward the company runs so deep that it becomes an integral part of their identity. If an employee sat down to complete the Twenty Statements Test, it would not be unusual for Marathon to feature at the top of it. When asked if I could meet someone who could give me a firsthand account of what it means to bleed blue, I was given Tim's name, and, through my conversations with him, came to understand why.

Tim is neither native to Houston, nor a natural big city dweller. He grew up in La Crosse, Wisconsin, and moved to central Ohio to pursue his education at Cedarville University. With a degree in accounting, Tim was interviewed by his fair share of what were then the Big 8 accounting firms. He was also interviewed by a single company outside the industry, Marathon Oil, which could not have been any more different from the big city, corporate cultures of the accounting firms. At the time of his interview, Marathon was not yet a Houston company, but rather headquartered in Findlay, Ohio.

The personal, tight-knit community feel that Marathon was known for was evident from the start. Instead of meeting in the lobby of the corporate headquarters, Tim's future boss suggested having breakfast off-site. This was a particularly unusual decision considering that Tim was an unexperienced hire among a field of equally fresh graduates. Yet the hiring manager felt compelled to invest the time to get to know Tim personally. His investment paid off, as Tim just celebrated his 25th anniversary with the company a few weeks before our conversation in Houston.

The personal touch that Tim experienced was not strange for Marathon. In many ways, Marathon typified the culture of small towns in the Midwest, where community runs deep and neighbors can rely on each other. Early CEOs at the company had come from the same family and therefore took a paternalistic approach to how employees were treated. This does not mean that Marathon was excessively inwardly focused or stuck in its own ways. The company was one of the first to sign Lyndon Johnson's plan for progress in 1966, which set in motion recognition for the value of diversity and the establishment of policies for equal opportunities. As a second example, Marathon suspended dividends to shareholders during the Great Depression as a means of keeping its staff fully employed. Marathon's cultural roots can be described as doing the right thing, at least according to Tim. He would know, as one of Tim's sideline responsibilities was to act as corporate historian and archivist.

In his first job with the accounting department, Tim was tasked with taking inventory for gas terminals. Despite this very specific and narrow job responsibility, Tim came into contact with a broad range of workmates and experienced a tight-knit community that watched Super Bowls together, played league volleyball and basketball, and celebrated Christmas at each other's houses. Marathon benefited from a naturally inclusive and socially active group of employees. Even without corporate sponsorship, they got together anyway.

Tim's career accelerated rapidly. He was given the opportunity to complete his work toward a CPA degree and gained exposure to a range of special projects. In one such project, Tim worked closely with representatives from the other oil companies and learned just how different his experience was at Marathon. He was more than a number. Beyond the culture, Tim benefited from strong career sponsors who opened doors for him throughout the business.

At the time of our conversation in Houston, Tim got word that one of his sponsors had recently passed away. Fred was the Audit Director early in Tim's career and was notoriously difficult to work with. "At some point or other, everyone in the department was fired." Just before the fired employee took the threat seriously and began packing his or her boxes, Fred would come back and make amends. Despite his high emotions, Fred had a big heart and did his best to recognize and develop staff. When Tim passed his CPA examination, Fred wrote a personal letter of congratulations. As a complete coincidence, Tim found this letter tucked away inside a box over the summer, just around the time of Fred's death. So meaningful was this relationship for Tim that he kept the letter as a keepsake for two decades.

Doors continued to be opened for Tim. He was soon offered a job in Treasury with the then-parent company of Marathon, US Steel. With much anxiety, Tim turned down the promotion after realizing that the job was a poor fit. Instead of going along with the flow and taking the job, Tim trusted his gut instinct and, in so doing, felt that he had just committed career suicide. To the company's credit, Tim's opinion was respected. Part of the company culture and a key feature of what it meant to bleed blue was to speak your mind, which is what Tim did. In response, Tim's superiors followed the code, continued to value Tim for his abilities, and found an opportunity that was better aligned with his ambitions. With one door closed, another opened and so started the second chapter of Tim's career with Marathon. The hitch was that the job was in Pittsburgh.

Beyond giving up a hometown that Tim had grown to enjoy, he was faced with the challenge of working in a completely different office environment. Tim was an outsider and instantly branded the "Marathon guy." Although he made every effort to integrate himself into the social network, Tim found it difficult to break in. His US Steel workmates had existing relationships, and they were not terribly motivated or interested in adding another. Over time, Tim grew to enjoy Pittsburgh and successfully grew strong friendships outside the company, but he did not feel as attached to his workplace as he had in his original job. Tim admitted that, across his career, the only time that he seriously considered switching companies was when he was in Pittsburgh. Far from being job-related, the social glue that held him to the organization was running thin.

Tim's opportunity to return to Marathon came in 2001, when USX divested its energy business. A move back to Ohio was not part of the deal, but rather a job in Houston. For a man who enjoyed small-town environments, Tim was getting progressively away from his comfort zone. He arrived in Houston on the same day as Enron's collapse, a monumental day in the history of the city. Once at the pinnacle of the energy business, Enron fell to pieces in a dramatic way, taking its employees with it, some of whom were rehired by Marathon into the finance department.

The Houston team was built from scratch, enabling Tim, the ex-Enron folks, and the rest of the crew to gel quickly. Although the social activities differed from basketball games and Super Bowl parties, Tim once again found an inviting and congenial group of people to work with. In an urban environment, more effort was needed to ensure that people got together, but new traditions formed nonetheless, such as the annual attendance at Restaurant Week. From a professional standpoint, Enron's collapse provided Tim with a unique opportunity to enact policies with profound impact on how the organization operated, which was both interesting and career-defining. Anecdotally, Tim was now labeled the "Steel guy" among the Houstonians.

The third chapter of Tim's career occurred in 2002, when his personal life was brought closer than ever to his workplace. The CEO was intent to leave a mark on Marathon and decided that a commitment to diversity would be part of his legacy. Although Marathon had a strong history of doing the right thing, the CEO felt that the company fell silent on the issue and did not do enough proactively to build a diverse and inclusive workplace.

As a very public way of coming out to his workmates, Tim decided to apply for the Diversity Council. Up until this point, Tim had kept this aspect of his personal life separate from Marathon. He agonized over filling out the application for the council, which explicitly asked why he would like to join the group. He knew that this was a one-way street and that once his sexual orientation was known, there was no going back. Not knowing what the reaction would be among his workmates, Tim felt strongly about taking part and turned in his application.

Once again, Tim put his faith in Marathon to do the right thing and respect who he was as an individual. Tim was accepted on the council and became a focal point for representing the LGBT community. Marathon had proved itself again as the personal and ethical employer that Tim wished it to be. The appointment on the council began the fourth chapter of Tim's career with Marathon. In 2005, he was given an opportunity for a career change, making diversity his full-time job. What initially was a 3-month stint as diversity and inclusion advisor became a second career that led to the position of Corporate Development and Diversity Manager. Normally an introvert, Tim's interest in the topic pushed him from a development expert into the public eye, representing Marathon within the community. Although Marathon was progressive in many ways, change did not always come quickly. Tim preferred to work within the culture and take baby steps toward his goals. It was evident that Tim's belief that Marathon's culture of doing the right thing would prevail and push the organization toward progressive ends. Unlike much of his career, he was now in a leadership position and could help make change a reality.

Tim bled blue. His identity had been strongly influenced by his relationship with Marathon. Working for the company extended beyond his job as an auditor or diversity advisor. He saw himself as part of a strong social unit, one that shared common interests, invested in work together, and genuinely cared for each other. There are many aspects of Tim's specific experience as an employee that set the foundation for having a strong identify. First, Tim benefited from managers and advocates who took a personal approach in their interactions with him. Conducting an interview over breakfast and writing personal letters of congratulations take effort beyond normal work responsibilities. These leaders felt that a personal touch was worth the investment. Coming full circle, Tim eventually found himself in their shoes as a leader who had the power to make a personal mark on someone else's career.

As an organization, Marathon had a unique cultural history of supporting employees and encouraging them to look after each other. Locating its headquarters in the small town of Findlay, Ohio, provided opportunities for employees to interact with and engage each other in casual and unexpected ways. The community extended beyond the office, to the corner grocery store and post office. When things got tough, the community pulled together and leadership took progressive steps to ensure the well-being of employees, such as deferring the payment of shareholder dividends during the Great Depression. Such signs of loyalty encouraged employees to invest their time and energy in the organization.

This is not to say that Tim's identity was completely dominated by being a part of Marathon. For example, it took until 2002 before Tim's identity as a gay man coexisted with his identity as an employee of Marathon. We all have a range of identities that are active at any given point in our lives. They move up and down our list of importance, with implications on who we seek out to socialize with and the way we treat each other. Sometimes new identities move onto the list, especially with significant life events like being married, becoming a parent, or relocating between cities. Tim's identity as a financial professional moved down a notch as he found his passion for diversity and inclusion. Moreover, he found comfort in public speaking, something that he actively avoided earlier in his career.

Identity is also shaped by what we are not. Tim experienced resistance when he attempted to break into new workgroups, being labeled as the "Marathon guy" in Pittsburgh or the "Steel guy" in Houston. It should not be a surprise that Tim felt less connected to Marathon at these points in his career. The glue that bound him to the organization was not as sticky as it once was. Tim's affinity for the organization was rekindled only when his immediate workgroup began to form new traditions and establish a set of social norms.

As the economy changes toward more temporary and contingent assignments, Tim's experience in Pittsburgh is likely to be the norm. Coming in and out of work environments, without a shared history or social connections, works against a common workplace identity. Instead, gig workers will likely identify with their vocation or peers who work outside of their current employer. The knock-on effects of a low workplace identity can be expected in a reduction of pro-social and organizational citizenship behavior, off-setting the efficiency or productivity gains expected from tapping contingent labor pools.

Between our meeting in Houston and the write-up of his story, Tim's career with Marathon reached its final chapter. On November 5, 2015, Marathon announced a restructuring in its business to better respond to a collapse in the price of oil. Marathon sought to cut costs through the elimination of non-essential jobs and a reduction in headcount by approximately 200 people. Tim's position was one of those affected by the change, and his last day with Marathon was set for New Year's Eve.

For 25 years, Tim's identity had been defined in part by his connection to Marathon. In the later phases of his career, his role required a high degree of visibility into his relationship with the company, working as a corporate ambassador for topics involving diversity and inclusion. With the end of his employment, Tim's professional identity was separated from Marathon for the first time. He had not worked for any other employer since graduating from college. In many ways, Tim was free to explore an identity for himself as an expert in Corporate Development and Diversity, independent of the confines of how Marathon defined him. Any remaining identification with Marathon would be based on the memories of the organization he grew up in, rather than the current establishment. As the years progress, it is safe to assume the blue will begin to fade away.

Identity makes us feel connected and part of something greater than ourselves. It provides a reason to act altruistically and is the grease that keeps organizations and societies moving in the same direction. As exemplified in Tim's story, creating a shared identity is an effortful process and one that is constantly in flux. A key take-away from his story is that a shared identity should never be taken for granted and should be enjoyed for as long as it lasts.

12

Conflict

Imagine that you are a 12-year-old boy growing up in 1954. Like the summer before (and probably the summer before that), you are heading off to camp. This is not a Harry Potter- or Pokémon-themed camp, but a quintessential "roast your marshmallow over the fire while telling a ghost story" camp. You don't know much about this specific camp, other than that you will be joined by a large group of other boys your age and will take part in a range of physical challenges and games. You say goodbye to your parents, grab your backpack, and head for the bus. Once on, you meet your campmates and camp counselors and drive to what sounds like a promising summer. Even better, the camp is situated near one of Jesse James's hideouts, commonly known as Robbers Cave. How can this not be a great experience?

The only hitch is that this is not really a camp but a carefully crafted experiment by a psychologist at the University of Oklahoma, Muzafer Sherif. He deliberately chose your campmates based on a combination of interviews with family members and teachers, school and medical records, results from personality instruments, observed behavior in class and play, and demographics. The campers were a homogenous lot in every way, representing healthy and well-adjusted prepubescent boys who came from white, Protestant, middle-class homes in Oklahoma City. Children from broken homes or who were in foster care were not accepted. Neither were children who had experienced abrupt changes in school performance, a history of breakdowns, or who tended to run away from home. They all were deemed to be normal in development and able to participate in the physical activities planned for the camp. Sherif even went so far as to balance the level of musical ability, acting skills, previous camp experience, popularity, and membership in youth organizations. Moreover, none of the boys knew each other prior to the camp to ensure that existing friendships would have no influence on the group dynamic.

Selection of the campers was done in a slightly creepy way by today's standards. An observer was sent to a neighborhood school to watch children play at recess. When the observer spotted a boy who appeared to meet

Punching the Clock. Joe Ungemah, Oxford University Press (2021). © Oxford University Press.
DOI: 10.1093/oso/9780190061241.003.0012.

the criteria, he asked for the child's name and then accessed school records concerning IQ, grades, and psychological adjustment, as well perceived popularity and social standing from the homeroom teacher. All this was done without the parents' awareness. From an initial list of 200 names, 50 boys were selected to be interviewed, with the final list made up of 22 campers. In total, 300 hours were spent in selecting boys for the experiment. The boys were sorted into two groups, with careful attention paid to balance the boys' weight, sports ability and skill, popularity, musical and acting skills, cooking ability, swimming, and previous camp experience across the groups.

The camp counselors were psychologists in disguise, there to observe and record the campers' behaviors. The counselors were given strict direction about what they could and could not do. They were instructed to refrain from influencing the boys in any way or to steer them toward activities that were not part of the design. Counselors were instructed not to act as leaders in any capacity, but rather to allow for the prearranged activities to transpire and for the boys to take the initiative in solving problems as they encountered them. Basically, the counselors were positioned to do very little other than look after the basic safety, health, and well-being of the campers and, of course, to record every minutia of their behavior. During the course of the experiment, they racked up approximately 492 hours of observation, took 1,200 pictures, and secretly recorded the boys' conversations.

An equal amount of consideration went into choosing the camp site. A 200-acre Boy Scouts of America camp within the Robbers Cave State Park was chosen for its combination of terrain and ability to initially isolate two groups of boys from each other. This was an important feature of the experimental design, as Sherif wished for the two groups of boys to establish their own internal social norms before discovering that they were not alone at the camp. Like many of the experiments of the era, it is remarkable that Sherif was first allowed to recruit boys and place them in an environment without parental supervision and then experiment without a clear idea of what would actually happen once conflict emerged. More shockingly, the 1954 camp was not the first time Sherif attempted to create real group conflict, having previously performed similar experiments in 1949 and 1953.

On the morning of June 19, 1954, the first group of boys was picked up for camp. A typical bus ride with a "paper-wad" game, songs, and chit-chat led to the arrival at the camp. The boys were allowed to pick their bunks, mingle, and make friends. The following day, a second group of boys were driven to a second campsite. During the following week, the two groups of boys independently explored the area around them and engaged in hikes, over-night campouts (requiring them to secure provisions and pitch tents), treasure hunts, and baseball. The campers were able to earn money to purchase gear from the counselors. Both groups opted to buy caps and T-shirts, which they stenciled their own chosen names of either the "Rattlers" or the "Eagles." Unfortunately for Sherif, two boys from the Eagles became homesick and were sent home prematurely. Despite his careful screens, one of these boys had a history of leaving camps early, while the other had never been to camp before and found it overwhelming.

Although the boys' activities looked to be a typical mix of camp experiences, they were in fact designed to explore how group categorization and structure leads to the emergence of prejudice. The first set of activities was designed to have a common appeal among the camp members, as well as require independent and cooperative effort to accomplish specific goals. In short order, the activities encouraged the boys to create their own jargon, tell and retell jokes, and keep secrets. When a boy within a group did not follow the code, the boys exerted control over him through threats and ostracism. Sherif's goal of creating groups of boys who shared an interdependent status and held a distinct set of social norms to regulate behavior was accomplished for both the Eagles and Rattlers and on schedule.

After a week at camp, the boys learned that they were not the only ones at Robbers Cave. The Rattlers overheard the Eagles practicing on the baseball diamond and immediately sought to "run them off" the field. Over the ensuing hours and days, the boys became obsessed by the other group and began pestering the counselors for the opportunity to compete against them in sports. These demands ushered in the second phase of the experiment, which targeted creating a competitive and frustrating environment for group interaction to occur.

Sherif surmised that prejudice emerges from the dynamic that groups find themselves in. If groups interact with each other in the pursuit of common goals, group members tend to hold positive views toward the other group and anticipate that future interactions will be positive. However, when competing for scarce resources, an opposite pattern emerges, with ethnocentric attitudes that inhibit both current and future interactions. Although this hypothesis seems to be common sense in hindsight, no other psychologist invested the time to see the dynamic play out in a controlled but otherwise normal social context. Moreover, this viewpoint stood in direct contrast to the conventional wisdom of the day, that prejudice emerges from a deficiency in personality and upbringing. Sherif sought to show that prejudice can emerge with well-adjusted individuals given the right situation. This also explains why Sherif went through such pains to ensure that boys chosen for the study were as homogenous as possible.

To build up a competitive spirit among the boys, the counselors began a series of independent, informal conversations about a tournament between the Eagles and Rattlers. The Rattlers were quicker to take the bait and were soon exclaiming how superior they felt they were. The boys' excitement built when they encountered an exhibit in the mess hall that outlined the up-coming tournament. On display was a trophy, medals, and the star prizes for the winning team, specifically a four-bladed knife for each boy, which was probably not the best idea for an experiment aimed at creating conflict.

The tournament was comprised of 15 events, including three baseball games, three tug-of-wars, two tent-pitching competitions, and a touch foot-ball game. The remaining five events were scored by staff members and in-cluded three cabin inspections, a skit and song contest, and a treasure hunt. These last five activities allowed Sherif to manipulate the outcome of the tournament and ensure competition was tight up until the end. Progress was marked by raising thermometers on an official score board in the mess hall, as well as official announcements about points at the end of each day.

When the groups laid eyes on each other for the first time on the base-ball diamond, Sherif did not have to wait long before prejudice emerged. Derogatory name-calling began when a particularly outspoken member from the Eagles called one of the Rattlers a "dirty shirt." As the tournament progressed, the boys had less and less appetite to interact with members of the opposite group. At their first encounter in the mess hall, considerable name-calling and singing of derogatory songs was heard. After an unsuc-cessful bout of tug-of-war, the defeated Eagles decided to snatch the Rattler flag, set it on fire, and rehang it for the other boys to find in the morning. The situation escalated when the Eagles attempted to take a second Rattler flag, ending in an actual fistfight between the boys.

The next escalation occurred when the Rattlers decided to raid the Eagles' cabin following their loss in the second tug-of-war. The Rattlers stormed the Eagles at 10:30 PM, turned over bunks, tore down mosquito netting from the windows, and stole comic books and clothes. The Eagles retaliated the next day by storming the Rattlers' cabin while they were at the mess hall. Armed with sticks and bats, they turned over bunks, scattered dirt and possessions, and then made weapons (socks filled with rocks) in preparation for further retaliation by the Rattlers, which thankfully did not occur.

At the end of the tournament, the Eagles were deemed the winners, helped by some last-minute manipulation by the judges. The Eagles were clearly jubilant in their victory, hugging each other and yelling at the top of their lungs. The Rattlers showed a lack of emotion, deflated by the outcome of the tournament. It was not long before their silence turned into anger. The Rattlers raided the victorious Eagles, taking the prized knives and medals, whereupon the Eagles rushed over to the Rattler cabin and demanded their prizes back. With two lines of boys staring each other down, a fistfight soon broke out and, this time, the camp counselors decided to step in to avoid possible injury (especially now that one of the groups was armed with knives!). Sherif had accomplished what he set out to create: real group conflict as exhibited through the words and actions of an otherwise normal group of boys.

Hostilities remained well beyond the tournament's end. The counselors arranged for some relatively benign opportunities for the groups to come into contact with each other, which largely involved waiting together in close proximity for the mess hall to open. They also rearranged seating in the hall as a way to encourage groups to intermingle. Such efforts did little to reduce hostilities. Name-calling, derogatory remarks ("ladies first" was particularly favored by the Eagles), and food fights were witnessed. Even a special opportunity to shoot firecrackers together to celebrate the Fourth of July failed to result in positive interactions between the groups.

Simply providing contact would not resolve group tensions. Instead, the introduction of common, superordinate goals was necessary. A series of situations were artificially created to compel the boys to work together and eventually undo the arbitrary group memberships imposed by the experiment. The first manufactured catastrophe was a break in the water supply for the camp. The counselors turned off the main valve and hid its location, as well as made the faucet to the water tank inoperable. The boys were initially informed that there was a water shortage in the camp and they should fill their canteens as a precaution. They were also told that this type of shortage sometimes occurs due to vandals messing around with the pipes. Later in the day and when canteens were running dry, the counselors informed the boys that a complete failure in the water supply had occurred and they needed help to track down the cause, whether it was a leak, pump failure, or issue with the tank.

Both groups of boys volunteered. The stretch of pipe between the reservoir and camp was marked off into four segments so that it could be inspected for leaks. A group of Eagles took the furthest stretch by the reservoir. A group of Rattlers took the next segment, followed by the remaining Eagles, while the final segment was given to the Rattlers. Although the groups were not intermixed, both were involved in a collective activity that required interdependence. Of course, no leak was discovered in the pipe and the boys turned their attention to the tank and its attached faucet (which could be used to fill their canteens). After finding a conveniently located ladder and looking into the tank, water was clearly seen. The boys' attention turned to the faucet, whereupon they found a sack shoved up within it. The boys worked together for the first time, attempting to get the material cleared from the faucet. They succeeded and were able to wet their parched lips. At this point, there was a noticeable difference in the amount of intermingling between group members; some boys lost interest completely in the task and were seen catching lizards and making wooden whistles with each other. With attention waning, a staff member reminded the boys that the water supply had not yet been restored to the camp. A few boys took the bait, found the valve, and turned it back on. Despite this minor win, old patterns reemerged during dinner, with insults and food flung between the groups.

A second superordinate goal was introduced. This time, the counselors offered to hold a movie night at the camp. The boys were overjoyed at the prospect of watching *Treasure Island*, but came to realize that neither group individually had enough money to rent the film. The boys negotiated across group lines to work out the fairest way to pay the $15 rental fee. The end solution saw the Eagles pay a bit more per person, as their group had fewer members than the Rattlers. Somehow, the boys convinced the counselors to chip in, arguing that they would probably like the movie, too. From the perspective of both the Rattlers and Eagles, the solution was seen as fair, and group relations showed a noticeable improvement both before and after the movie.

Sherif pushed the limits further by arranging a camp-out 60 miles away in wilderness that was completely unfamiliar to the boys. In preparation for their trip to Cedar Lake, the counselors threw all the provisions and equipment haphazardly into two trucks, which would require the Rattlers and Eagles to work together to sort out. Once at the campsite, a staff member created the illusion that one of the supply trucks broke down. The driver appeared to struggle against the truck, and, for its part, the truck made all sorts of noises. The boys, hungry for lunch, declared that they would help get the truck moving. Having spotted the rope used for the tug-of-war during the tournament (which had magically been packed for the camp-out), the boys tied it to the bumper and began pulling as one collective. When the driver finally allowed the truck to start, the boys exclaimed, "We won the tug-of-war against the truck!" This time, a great deal of intermingling, friendly banter, and backslapping ensued.

The effect carried over to lunch preparation. Although some boys began negotiating whether the Rattlers or Eagles should go first, others simply began chopping the food. The boys sat down and had their first meal together. The collaboration continued when it came time to pitch tents, with supplies gladly swapped between groups. When the food truck predictably broke down again at dinner time, the boys wasted no time in getting the rope, tying it to the bumper, and pulling. The cooperative pattern was now established and required no discussion about what to do.

For Oklahoma boys living in the 1950s, going across the state line to Arkansas was apparently a big deal. When counselors asked the campers whether they were interested in taking a day trip across the border, the boys were enthusiastic. Yet again, there was a hitch. With only one reliable truck, the Eagles and Rattlers were required to ride in the same truck. With the stakes running high, the prospect of riding in the same truck caused much apprehension despite all the good relations from the past few days. Eventually group consensus won out, and the boys agreed to ride together. Once under way, the boys first recounted stories about the tournament, but quickly turned to singing songs, alternating between those preferred by the Rattlers and the Eagles. The merriment continued, and the boys sent postcards back home to prove that they made it to Arkansas.

During their last night at camp, the boys decided to entertain each other by singing and performing the skits first seen during the tournament. The groups continued to take turns in a manner, but unlike before, when it was for their own personal benefit, the groups were alternating to ensure that the other group was entertained. The counselors noted that, by the time of the final campfire, absolutely no derogatory references or insults were heard. The next morning, the boys packed their bags and decided that they wished to return home in the same bus (recall that the boys arrived in two separate buses). The counselors agreed to their request. At the rest stop, the Rattlers realized that they had $5 left in their coffers. Instead of using it to pay for lunch, the Rattlers decided that they would treat the Eagles to a round of malts. With full bellies, the boys got off the bus and returned to their normal lives in Oklahoma City, unaware that they just experienced a totally artificial camp environment that sought to first create and then dispel group conflict.

Beyond Summer Camp

The psychological processes that underlie intergroup conflict play out in very real and tragic ways every day. Adding to long histories of discontent, struggles for scarce resources, and feelings of animosity, how individuals think about their group in relation to competitors fuels conflict and enables it to transcend generations. When people identify strongly with a distinct social group in an environment where demographic lines are drawn very clearly and where everyday interaction fails to occur, conflict can be considered all but inevitable. Such is the case of Northern Ireland and its centuries-long history of conflict.

"The Troubles" in Northern Ireland stem from a long-standing division between people who generally seek to join the Republic of Ireland and those who would prefer to remain part of the United Kingdom. Although the conflict has its origins in events and actions that occurred centuries ago, a relatively recent escalation in violence was witnessed in the 1960s that grabbed the attention of social psychologists. This escalation, termed "The Troubles," led to a deployment of British troops and more than 3,600 deaths and 35,000 injuries resulting from 34,000 shootings and 14,000 bombings. In the end, more than 16,000 people were charged with terrorist offenses. Beyond these tangible aspects of conflict, The Troubles left a mark on the mental health of the people living in Northern Ireland.

Although the high levels of violence experienced during The Troubles have thankfully dissipated in the past two decades, the seeds for conflict remain. The Good Friday Agreement signed on April 10, 1998, and officially enacted on December 2, 1999, might have established a political solution to Irish territorial claims and the creation of more inclusive democratic institutions, yet it did little to directly eliminate divisions in the population. Orangemen Parades continue to be held on July 12, and Sinn Fein stands firm on boycotting Westminster, refusing to take up the seats in the Commons that it legitimately wins through public elections. Issues of social identity run deeper than political change.

Those who argue for or against Irish nationalism represent two very different populations who remain segregated on a variety of levels. Foremost is religion, with Catholics dominating the population seeking one Irish nation, while Protestants make up the majority of the populace wishing to remain in the United Kingdom. Beyond religion, the two groups experience extensive personal segregation, with group members rarely interacting in sport, work, or leisure activities. Marriage across the groups is rare, and more than 95% of children attend denominational schools, setting a precedence for how they will interact as adults. As of 1996, it was estimated that somewhere between 35% and 40% of the Northern Irish population lived in a completely segregated neighborhood. This finding is particularly marked among the working-class or disadvantaged, who experience higher rates of segregation than the affluent middle class.

Trends toward residential segregation occur from the amount of intimidation and conflict experienced within any given population, creating a vicious cycle. Families who either directly or indirectly experience violence or intimidation look for a way out and tend to move into safe havens made up of other people like them. Having a close personal friend or relative experience harm or intimidation can be enough to cause people to act and move away. Threat itself comes in many shapes and sizes, from a physical altercation on the street to religious symbols that act as a visual reminder of the importance of group membership. As people move away, further divisions are made between social groups and provide grounds for greater misunderstanding and distrust. The cycle continues until the two populations become islands unto themselves despite sharing a close physical proximity to each other.

Living in a mixed neighborhood has the potential to break down stereotypes, encourage interaction, and seed the formation of a shared identity. The theory goes that the more people come into contact with each other, the greater the opportunity for intergroup encounters of a positive nature. *Contact theory* has been particularly influential in shaping policy in Northern Ireland, and initiatives toward reconciliation have concentrated on promoting intergroup contact. For example, government departments invested £5.3 million on improving community relations in 1995–1996. By living in close proximity to members of a different social group, people gain firsthand experience about their neighbors, which starts to erode preexisting stereotypes. Yet contact with out-group members may not always go as planned. Despite the social psychological adage that there are more differences within groups than between groups, the next-door neighbor might actually be a very good representation of a stereotype and can work to confirm initial expectations. Alternatively, the individual might subcategorize the neighbor by essentially not considering him or her as a real member of the out-group. He or she might be heard saying "my next-door neighbor is all right, but I could do without the rest of them."

The rub with contact theory is that positive interactions are not guaranteed. Although it can be expected that the majority of interactions will be benign (like a casual interchange at the grocery store) or positive (even if not earth-shattering), there is real potential for conflict given who the other individual is and the context in which they meet. Moreover, the power of one negative interchange may completely counteract all the positive and informal exchanges that occur on an everyday basis. Receptiveness toward out-group members can also differ between people. Previous experience with the out-group, as well as an individual's status, can influence perceptions of threat. Those of a higher social class or with greater educational attainment may have less to lose and therefore have relatively more open attitudes toward out-group members.

Northern Ireland provides an accessible and unique opportunity to test out whether the positives of intergroup contact can make up for the real and perceived threat of living in a mixed neighborhood. As mentioned earlier, there is great convergence of social groupings in Northern Ireland, creating an "us versus them" mentality. The same could not be said for places like New York or London, where countless dialects and accents can be heard during a single ride on a bus or subway. Second, the opportunity for a meaningful shared identity, one in which both the Catholic and Protestant communities could ascribe, has been limited until recently with the devolution of government. Third, the wounds run deep, with the struggle for nationalism against unification being passed down for generations.

Through extensive studies of residents living in a variety of neighborhoods in and around Belfast, the tradeoff in contact was found. Residents in a mixed neighborhood did indeed witness violence and felt more threatened; however, they also reported more positive intergroup interactions, less bias toward their own group, and fewer tendencies toward aggression. This research suggests that the simple solution of mixing communities is not without its hardships. Yes positive exchanges would occur and stereotypes could potentially be unwound—but not every day would be a good day. Residents in mixed neighborhoods require resilience toward the violence and intimidation posed by a significant minority of community members. These encounters may create a setback to the trust and forgiveness gained, but, over time and with a change in circumstance (like an outside threat to the whole of Northern Ireland), group relations might improve. In the meantime, residents would need constant reminders that the good outweighs the bad.

For contact to work effectively, a variety of conditions must generally be met. First, equal social status between groups should exist, such that no group can claim outright superiority. This is especially true when there are a limited number of ways that the groups can be compared to each other or when a convergence occurs across demographics (e.g., when ethnicity, wealth, and power all line up). Second, the group should work toward common goals. It would be great if the goals were for altruistic aims, but, short of this, coming together against a common threat works, too (the phrase "the enemy of my enemy is my friend" comes to mind). Third, official institutions should condone intergroup contact and encourage group members to interact as a means of solidifying relationships. Last, the reasons for contact should be meaningful, with group members given the opportunity to perceive others as sharing common interests and similarities in ambitions, struggles, or the other things that make us all human. It is for this reason that the development of close personal friendships with out-group members is particularly powerful in dismantling prejudice.

In the case of Northern Ireland, social contact has been found effective at breaking down conflict and thus efforts to improve group relations appear warranted. Yet other factors continue to play a part in how effective the contact can be, such as the relative educational and economic status of an individual as well as their personal experience with violence and intimidation. Segregation might provide a short-term reprieve for an individual with direct or indirect experience of conflict, but in time, it fosters group ignorance and suspicion that will likely manifest itself into some future break in relations. Real-world examples such as The Troubles in Northern Ireland remind us that group identity is not always beneficial and, given the right set of variables, plays a major role in splitting a society apart.

Dismantling Conflict

In a lot of ways, creating conflict is far easier than dismantling it. What Sherif demonstrated and countless other real-world examples confirm, is that it is easy for groups to fall prey to self-aggrandizement at the expense of positive interactions with others. When put into competition over scarce resources with little opportunity for positive interaction, a cycle begins that tears apart the social fabric. Stereotypes ensue about what the other group is like, and, with limited knowledge about their relative truth, stereotypes are accepted at face value. Prejudicial feelings emerge and, in extreme cases, altercations and violence result. This pattern is especially true when group membership converges across social categories, like income level, ethnic background, and religion.

Social identity theory attempts to pull all these tendencies under one roof. Underlying the theory is a consideration about how much latitude an individual has to change his or her group membership within a given social context. For example, when individuals find themselves locked into group membership (e.g., based on biological age), they experience greater pressures to accept the group identity. Their view of other groups will also be biased by the amount of social mobility experienced, viewing other groups as either tight-knit units or as loose groups of individuals.

Categorization into social groups is the starting place for social identity theory. Since the early 1980s, research has shown that even the most basic group memberships (where simple labels are assigned randomly to individuals) can trigger intergroup competition and discrimination. The theory describes the mechanism behind conflict whereby individuals strive to maintain or enhance their self-esteem, which is influenced heavily by their group memberships. Favorable group comparisons between their group and a relevant out-group result in greater self-esteem. In situations where their social identity is poor, individuals will attempt to leave the group or attempt to make the group more attractive in some other way by redefining the variables on which they are compared to other groups or unhinging the evaluative context from the defining characteristics. For example, if your university is not so good at basketball, why not compare on hockey, or, even better, make comparisons on academic merit?

Describing how group conflict occurs is only so helpful. The real power of the theory lies in its implications for how group conflict can be reduced and sometimes completely eliminated. The most obvious solution is to reduce perceptions of scarcity. In the work context, pitting departments against each for funding or other finite resources works against the combined health of the organization. This is not to say that the reality of budgeting should be ignored, but rather attention should be paid on how decisions are positioned (e.g., whether it is obvious that if marketing gets its new product campaign then operations will lose its expansion plan). Couching decisions as tradeoffs can only lead to perceptions of scarcity and internal competition. The same goes with how sales commissions are counted (if credit can only be given to one sales rep or account manager), allocation of pay increases (if placed on a normal curve), or setting limits for the number of employees on development programs.

In the past few years, there has been renewed vigor for improving diversity and inclusion in organizations. If defined beyond demographic lines to include characteristics like skills, experiences, and preferred working style, group membership gets blurred and conflict between two well-defined groups becomes harder. The same reasoning applies for the value of collaborative teams that work across the organization. The "us" and "them" mentality is much harder to maintain when you cannot identify exactly who falls into these groups. The gig economy has the potential to drive change further as a greater degree of fluidity between workers increases opportunities for intergroup interaction. Equally, group membership may lose its meaning as barriers between departments and jobs become more permeable to new talent, which together can help eliminate group conflict.

As a final technique, creating superordinate goals draws attention to what groups have in common, rather than dwelling on differences. Having a defined purpose or cause in the workplace can galvanize workers. Sure, Pepsi wishing to "kill Coke" might provide a very clear goal, but what would be left if the company succeeded and Coke stopped being a competitor? People like meaning in their lives, and when it is shared widely with others, organizations thrive. As with the boys at Robbers Cave, simply having contact with each other does not reduce conflict. The interaction must be meaningful as well as positive and repeated across multiple encounters. For those companies who rely on the annual Christmas party to bring employees together, it is a wasted effort and parallels how the shooting off of fireworks on the Fourth of July did little to improve relations between the Eagles and Rattlers. The conflict remains after the distraction of the celebration passes. Every organization needs to find its tug-of-war against the truck and then go for a round of chocolate malts afterward.

13

Misdirection

During the early days of photography, early adopters of the technology were at the mercy of long-exposure times, images that quickly degraded, and expensive chemicals that required a great deal of knowledge to master. Up until 1839, the time required to take a picture could be an hour or more, testing the patience of even the most enthusiastic subject. With the introduction of the *daguerreotype process*, images could be captured in minutes under ideal conditions, fueling a budding interest in portraiture by the middle class. The world of photography opened up further with the advent of the *collodion process*, which allowed for the creation of a negative on a glass plate that could be used to create multiple copies of the same image. While entrepreneurs set up parlors to cash in on the fad, other photographers set out to capture the world around them. Some of the earliest pictures caught glimpses of the Crimean War, the reconstruction of the Crystal Palace in London, and even an aerial view of Boston, taken on a chilly morning by balloon in October 1860 from the height of 1,200 feet.

In 1862, a relative novice in the world of photography set up shop with a rather improbable offering. William Mumler claimed to be able to capture images of the afterlife in his studio. When a subject came for a sitting, the process would progress as normal; with a quick flick of the wrist, the black cloth covering the camera lens would be removed. The subject would sit motionless for a few minutes until a quality image was captured. The magic happened when the photograph's negative was developed. Instead of sitting alone in the picture, the subject was accompanied by a fainter, but still recognizable image of a deceased loved one. Parents, siblings, spouses, and children were all captured, sometimes standing behind the subject and other times to the side. Mumler had seemingly done the impossible by providing reassurance that our loved ones stay with us in the afterlife.

Down the street from Mumler, James Wallace Black ran his own successful photography studio and anecdotally was the aerial photographer who floated above Boston. With 20 years of experience under his belt, Black smelled a con and sought to disprove that Mumler could produce such images. To put

Punching the Clock. Joe Ungemah, Oxford University Press (2021). © Oxford University Press.
DOI: 10.1093/oso/9780190061241.003.0013.

Mumler to the test, he first sent his assistant, Horace Weston, undercover to take part in one of Mumler's paranormal sessions. Weston sat in the corner as instructed by Mumler, who then took his picture, developed it, and produced an image of Weston with his deceased father standing at his side. At this point, Weston fessed up to Mumler, admitting that he could spot nothing unusual about the process and asked whether Black himself could book a session in exchange for 50 dollars. Mumler obliged.

When Black entered Mumler's studio, he welcomed him, "Mr. Black, I heard your generous offer. All I can say is, be thorough in your investigations." He showed Black his studio and equipment, "That is the instrument I propose to take your picture with. You are at liberty to take it to pieces." Black had an air of superiority over Mumler and therefore declined the offer, doubting Mumler's ability to rig the equipment. He did, however, agree to inspect the photographic plate to ensure no visible signs of tampering. Black commented, "I don't lose sight of this plate from this time." The plate was then coated and placed into the camera, ready for use. With Black seated in the studio, the black cloth was swiftly taken away from the camera lens. After a few minutes, Black commented "Mr. Mumler, I should be willing to bet one thing, that you have got my picture."

Mumler led Black to the darkroom so that they could develop the negative. Black turned down the offer to develop the picture, stating "I am not acquainted with the working of your chemicals, and might spoil it. You are not smart enough to put anything on that negative without my detecting it." Brushing off the obvious jab at his capabilities, Mumler opened a bottle of developer and the men together watched the negative emerge. At first, nothing out of the ordinary was seen; there was Black sitting on a chair in Mumler's studio. But soon after, a second image emerged, standing to his side with a hand on Black's shoulder. Black exclaimed, "My God! Is it possible?" for his deceased father was now visibly standing side by side with his son. Jarred by what he saw, Black was lost for words and stayed just long enough to receive a copy of the picture. Black asked, "How much is to pay?" to which, Mumler responded, "Not a cent."

Black failed to expose Mumler as a fake. There was nothing obvious or unusual about the process that Black observed, despite reservations that Mumler was truthfully capturing images from the afterlife. He was not alone, as other photographers attempted and failed to create spirit pictures without overlaying two negatives on top of each other. No complete account of Mumler's trick has been documented, however many suspect that Mumler found a way to control the chemical reactions in a process that was decades ahead of his time. Mumler's reputation kept building after his brief encounter with Black, topping out when former First Lady Mary Todd Lincoln turned up at his door to capture one last image of her recently deceased husband.

Beyond the obvious mystery of how Mumler produced his spirit photographs, the story reveals a slice of human nature at its core: the intense feelings of loss and desire to reconnect with loved ones. Customers entered Mumler's studio empty, looking for one last image of a lost husband, wife, parent, or child. They left relieved, feeling that their loved one was not entirely gone but was instead still present in their life and looking over them. In many ways, it does not matter that Mumler was almost certainly a con man because the comfort he provided to his customers was real. His customers wanted to believe Mumler could work magic and do the impossible. Mumler did little to convince them otherwise, presenting himself as a man of authority over his craft. As will be shown shortly, this combination of intense need coupled with a person of authority is essential to how scammers perform their art.

Never What It Seems

Over the course of hundreds of scams recreated on streets across Britain, the cast of *The Real Hustle* set out to expose how easily conned we all are. First released in 2006, the series ran for seven seasons on BBC Three and followed the exploits of three master scammers, using hidden cameras to capture how things went wrong for each unsuspecting victim caught up in their web. Yet, unlike a real scam, each of the victims was given his or her money back and debriefed, with the goal of educating the mass public on how to spot and avoid everyday scams. An expert in security and privacy at the University of Cambridge named Frank Stajano quickly became a fan of the program and noticed that many of the scammers used a fixed set of techniques to win over their marks. Excited by his revelation, he contacted one of the hosts of the program, Paul Wilson, and collaborated on a report that exposes the psychology behind scams.

Stajano and Wilson used a well-known scam, the Monte, to illustrate how master operators successfully entice their victims to give away their money. The Monte is usually presented as a game involving three cards (equally prevalent is the shell game) in which the player is asked to keep an eye on a target playing card that gets moved around a table. The game begins with the player being shown a target card that is flipped over and then moved around in interlacing patterns with two other cards, in full view of the player. When the operator stops, the player places money on what he or she believes is the winning card. If correct, the player wins and doubles his or her cash. Stajano and Wilson are quick to note that the Monte is not a game at all, but rather involves a sleight-of-hand trick similar to what magicians perform on stage. With a bit of misdirection, the operator ensures that the player has no way of winning.

Yet Stajano and Wilson also make it clear that sleight of hand is only a fraction of the total scam. The real craft is bringing in potential marks to play the game and then increasing their willingness to place high bets. When these games are encountered, there is often a small crowd of people, players and onlookers, surrounding a table. Things are not as they seem; the crowd is made up of shills (accomplices) who are there to entice the mark to play the game. Watching a shill win a profit puts a potential player at ease, as does watching another shill make an obviously wrong guess. Both of these acts provide evidence that the game is not rigged and is winnable.

After watching a few rounds, the mark may decide to give the game a chance, and, to his or her delight, might win the first couple of rounds. When the mark's luck runs out, which it always does, the shills are there to coax the player on. A common technique involves the shills pretending to cheat on behalf of the player, for example by bending the corner of the target card when the operator is seemingly distracted. The shills might also work to separate the mark from family or friends, ensuring that the player doesn't walk away.

When the operator feels that he or she has extracted as much cash as possible from the mark, the game abruptly comes to an end. Pretending to see a police officer is a common tactic. So, too, is faking contempt by accusing the player of cheating. Paul Wilson, who consults with casinos and is himself a magician, emphasizes that it is nearly impossible for a player to spot the sleight of hand used by the operator. Even if a card has been marked in some way, with a pen or bent corner, an experienced operator will work the scenario to a point where the card is switched without being noticed. As mentioned at the start, the Monte is not a game at all because there is no way for the player to beat the operator. The only thing that is uncertain is how much money can be extracted from a player once hooked on the game.

Essential to the Monte is keeping the mark sufficiently distracted to be scammed, which is the first of seven psychological principles that Stajano and

Wilson identified. *Distraction* plays a major part in magic, too, with the illusionist working to keep one step ahead of his or her audience at all times. In the Monte, the operator will wait until the most opportune time to make the switch, sending the target card to an unexpected position. Even if the corner is bent, the operator is one step ahead with a second bent card at the ready to be switched into the game, unnoticed by the mark. Beyond the operator, the shills are all there to direct the attention of the mark away from family and friends who might discourage betting. They have even been known to pickpocket the mark while the game is under way. The shills serve a secondary purpose of encouraging *herd* behavior, the second principle from Stajano and Wilson. With so many others apparently enjoying and believing in the game, how can the mark resist being swept up in the fun?

The Monte's pervasiveness is partly due to the number of psychological principles exploited in the scam, with six of the seven principles playing a part. When the mark becomes complicit in attempting to cheat the operator (by bending the card), he or she has enacted the third principle involving *dishonesty*. The operator takes advantage of the mark's decision to cheat by using it as an excuse to close the game prematurely and keep the cash. The mark's potential argument that the game is a fake is undercut because he or she also rigged the game.

Skilled operators in the Monte do their best to create the illusion of fairness, where any passerby has a chance of correctly finding the target card. The fourth principle of *kindness* is exploited by operators when they allow shills and marks to win the game. Winning dissipates any reservations held by the mark that the game is not what it seems. Once at ease, operators work on the fifth principle, that of exploiting the mark's need and greed in making quick money from an apparently easily winnable game. As losses begin to mount for the mark, the operator might take advantage of his or her desperation, enticing the mark to increase the bet or even encouraging the shills to put in side bets. With such a flurry of activity, the sixth principle kicks in, involving time pressure. Backed into a corner with losses mounting, the mark must make a decision about whether to go double or nothing or simply to walk away. Time pressure kills off the possibility of objectivity in favor of emotion. The final line of each episode of the Hustle sums it up, "If it sounds too good to be true, it probably is!"

Evident in this discussion is the combined effect of placing the mark under considerable cognitive and emotional pressure as a means of undermining his or her capacity for sound decision-making. The seventh principle of *social compliance* is not utilized in the Monte but commonly appears in other scams, whereby an authority figure creates a feeling of trust or normality. Those with a particularly high level of trust may find themselves more susceptible to this principle. From the Nigerian Prince e-mail scam to bogus products promising health or beauty, the seven principles of distraction, social compliance, herding, dishonesty, deception, need, and time create a web that is difficult to escape once entered.

When Mumler's spirit photographs are held against these principles, it is easy to see that he exploited four of the seven effectively. Mumler recognized and took advantage of the intense need of his customers to make a connection with lost loved ones. To this, he layered in an air of authority, with technology and practices that were not commonly experienced or understood by a lay person at the time. Herding played a part, too, in Mumler's success as even the wife of President Lincoln followed the crowd to his studio's door. Last, Mumler took advantage of deception, saying little to convince his customers that the images captured in his pictures were anything other than spirits.

Once the principles of a scam are understood, spotting a potential con and avoiding it becomes infinitely easier. Operators routinely use core human behaviors and drives to their advantage, transforming normally beneficial traits like emotional connection and personal commitment into an Achilles heel for the mark. But, once understood, potential marks can take a deeper look at the situation in front of them, judging for themselves whether it really is too good to be true. This is not to say that people should lose their humanity, but instead they must consider how their conscious and unconscious biases and drives influence the choices they make.

Spotting a Crisis

When the COVID-19 pandemic broke out, several countries appeared to be caught off guard by the crisis despite earlier outbreaks of Middle East respiratory syndrome (MERS) and severe acute respiratory syndrome (SARS). Beyond the medical supplies and equipment necessary to effectively treat large swaths of the population, educating individuals about the risks of illness and how to avoid transmission was essential. Yet this task might have been the more difficult of the two, as ordinary people were asked to sacrifice their normal way of life even though they felt 100% well and did not know a single ill person. Working against health officials and politicians were a range of cognitive biases that can impede well-reasoned, life-saving advice.

There are at least 100 cognitive biases that govern how the world around us is perceived and acted upon. Many of these biases are directly linked to the vulnerabilities exploited by the spirit photographer William Mumler and the scammers profiled by *The Real Hustle*. Under most circumstances, these biases prevail for their ability to speed up reactions and decision-making, which is also their inherent weakness. Under certain circumstances, these short-hand scripts can miss essential details, place emphasis on characteristics that do not deserve it, eliminate factors from consideration, or create an abundance of personal confidence. Documentation of cognitive biases took off in the 1970s, led by the efforts of Amos Tversky and Daniel Kahneman. In an interview with Ben Yagoda, Kahneman takes on a pessimistic tone about the ability of people to effectively identify and change course when confronted with a cognitive bias. He believes that the way to approach bias is from the outside in, by using other vantage points or established protocols to guide decisions. Kahneman advises, "You can't improve intuition. Perhaps, with very long-term training, lots of talk, and exposure to behavioral economics, what you can do is cue reasoning. . . . And for most people, in the heat of argument the rules go out the window."

When COVID-19 broke out, governments tapped their established protocols for dealing with a pandemic. Countries that had a recent history of dealing with similar crises, such as Singapore or South Korea, took swift and decisive action, closing down nonessential activities, testing the population broadly for infection, and mandating social distancing. To circumvent natural human inclinations toward poor decision-making, these policies and procedures took personal choice out the equation. Rather than tackling the cognitive bias itself, which is highly resistant to change, these approaches prevented people from acting on biased thoughts. Similar techniques are used across a diverse range of disciplines, from checklists used by doctors in medical procedures to automatic deductions made by employers for retirement.

Countries that lacked well-trained muscle in dealing with pandemics, notably the United Kingdom and the United States, dithered in their initial reaction and, in so doing, lost precious time to fight the infection. Even after stay-at-home orders were put in place, a vocal subsection of society protested against the orders, believing that the economic harm and lack of free movement outweighed the health risk posed by the pandemic. Three major cognitive biases played a part in both the lackluster response and second-guessing of established protocol. Leaders, TV personalities, and citizens alike demonstrated the *optimism bias*, where beliefs about a rosy future clouded hard evidence, resulting in citizens ignoring precautions to limit their exposure to the illness. They also showed signs of *outcome bias*, where learning from previous crises was undervalued (e.g., when Ebola was contained in Africa rather than becoming a worldwide pandemic). When confronted with mounting evidence about the perils of COVID-19, evidence- seeking was closed down for people wishing for normality as a sign of confirmation bias. Rural state leaders declared that they were not New York, but these areas later experienced hotspots of rampant infection. Younger people also reiterated that they would not get a serious illness and therefore played down the risk to themselves and their loved ones.

Throughout the pandemic, health officials routinely talked about "flattening the curve," where infection rates are prevented from ballooning out of control and overwhelming health resources. The policies toward restricting movement and limiting social contact aimed to slow the doubling rate of the virus. Ethan Siegel, writing for *Forbes*, recaps the problem, "Think about these two sequences of numbers, one of which shows linear growth and one of which shows exponential growth. 2, 4, 6, 8, 10, 12, 14, 16, 18, 20 etc. 2, 4, 8, 16, 32, 64, 128, 256, 512, 1024, etc. Exponential growth is so powerful not because it's necessarily fast, but because it's relentless." Yet, understanding the difference between these two sets of numbers is subject to the *exponential growth bias*.

In most situations, linear thinking works absolutely fine. For example, if a person has room in her fridge for a six-pack of soda on each shelf, she will need three shelves to accommodate 18 cans. Notably, this same type of thinking falls down when applied to personal finance. Noninvestors have a tendency to systematically underestimate both the cost of borrowing and the return of long-term saving, transposing the true relationship of compounding interest into linear terms. Such bias has been shown to have real-life implications for both retirement savings and personal debt. Making matters worse, people display overconfidence in their ability to think in exponential ways and routinely turn down advice from professionals or tools that combat their limitations. Understanding the potential impact of this cognitive bias, it is no wonder that health officials and political leaders took more drastic action to flatten the curve for COVID-19.

By mid-March, some health officials believed that the point of containment had past, accepting that, over time, approximately 100 million people in the United States would contract the virus with similar impact across the world. In the near term, decisive action was needed to flatten the curve, to spread out the doubling time of infection from every 2 or 3 days to a more manageable level. Beyond the cognitive biases detailed earlier, many of the psychological drivers found elsewhere in this book were working against them. Whether a population would accept the information provided by health officials and political leaders depended in part on what type of role modeling was demonstrated, whether compassionate or dismissive. Providing confidence in people's capability to do the right thing and rewarding action that promoted health and safety despite personal sacrifice would enable change, as would freeing up cognitive resources by reducing the number and complexity of personal choices. Without such clarity, individuals would be paralyzed by indecision and carry on with their risky behaviors. Taking a cue from the *bystander effect*, providing clear direction on who and how individuals could help in a crisis would pave the way for accountability and action while sharing how others are supporting the cause could create a self-fulfilling prophecy, as a positive version of obedience and conformity. All these psychological drives were in play as countries around the world attempted to contain the outbreak of COVID-19. Skillful navigation of them would require a firm understanding of the approaches and techniques unearthed over the past century of psychological research.

The COVID-19 pandemic accelerated changes already under way in how society operates. The lessons learned from the pandemic informed and augmented the trajectory of the Future of Work by providing a real-life experiment of remote working at scale as well as a glimpse at the possible. Future-focused companies reacted to the pandemic by challenging established norms about their operating model, questioning how data and technology would allow them to jump the "s-curve" into a post-pandemic world. The Future of Work emerges from the crisis emboldened, and it will continue to blur the lines about who exactly is an employee as increasing numbers of workers become free agents or work multiple gigs. The barriers, both economic and social, that directed workers into long-term employment will continue to disappear, with fewer workers considering themselves to be a "company woman" or "company man." Alongside these shifts in worker types, office environments will continue to transform. Working from home will be an accepted norm, seen as an effective way to get the job done for major employers who themselves are destroying traditional office environments in favor of open-plan, activity-based working. Technology will continue to play a part in deconstructing jobs and creating greater breadth in the mechanics of work as fueled by the expectations and desires of workers. Advancing in the corporate hierarchy and becoming financially wealthy will increasingly be less important than finding fulfilling work.

The transition to the Future of Work and the gig economy is not clean-cut from a psychological perspective, but rather is a story of tradeoffs. As explored over the preceding dozen chapters, the new style of working will likely result in a number of positive implications. For example, a greater sense of control and autonomy should emerge among workers at the same time as a reduction in blind obedience and the chances for conformity to run wild. The flaring of group conflict will likely decrease with the intermingling of new and different types of workers. On the flip side of the coin, the gig economy does not provide the same opportunity for rapport building and shared purpose among workers that currently exists in traditional workplaces. Moreover, temporary assignments counteract incentives to help and mentor others and hinder a deeper understanding of what others value and need. Gig workers may operate blindly in the absence of established social norms.

With the blurring of lines between the professional and personal, as well as the office and home, understanding the basic drives and biases of people becomes even more important. As the barriers fall, the potential for misunderstanding has increased as coworkers attempt to find their own specific flow in how to work together. What the recent pandemic exposed, as reinforced by the stories found in this book, is that although the social fabric changes, our psyche remains relatively constant. Understanding the how and why of social interactions can provide some comfort in an otherwise turbulent time, as we navigate this new world of work together.

Further Reading

The Future of Work in a Post-Pandemic World

Cellan-Jones, R. (2020, March 28). Coronavirus: What if this had happened in 2005? BBC News. /www.bbc.com/news/technology-52052502

Davenport, C., Gregg, A., and Timberg, C. (2020, March 22). Working from home reveals another fault line in America's racial and educational divide. *The Washington Post*. https://www.washingtonpost.com/business/2020/03/22/working-home-reveals-another-fault-line-americas-racial-educational-divide/

Domm, P. (2020, April 15). Another 5 million unemployment claims could be tallied, but the job-loss trend may be peaking. CNBC. https://www.cnbc.com/2020/04/15/another-5-million-unemployment-claims-could-be-tallied-but-the-job-loss-trend-may-be-peaking.html.

Editors. (2016, August 1). Some of the world's most boring jobs. *BBC Magazine*. https://www.bbc.com/news/magazine-36902572

Editors. (2016, November 28). Office worker survey: Moaners and noisy eaters among top gripes. *BBC Business*. https://www.bbc.com/news/business-38125619

Hern, A. (2020, March 13). Covid-19 could cause permanent shift towards home working. *The Guardian*. https://www.theguardian.com/technology/2020/mar/13/covid-19-could-cause-permanent-shift-towards-home-working

Thompson, D. (2020, March 13). The coronavirus is creating a huge, stressful experiment in working from home. *The Atlantic*. https://www.theatlantic.com/ideas/archive/2020/03/coronavirus-creating-huge-stressful-experiment-working-home/607945/

World Health Organization (WHO). (2020, April 8). WHO timeline: COVID-19. www.who.int/newsroom.

Chapter 1: Imitation

Bandura, A., Ross, D., and Ross, S. (1961). Transmission of aggression through imitation of aggressive models. *Journal of Abnormal and Social Psychology, 63*, 575–582.

Conger, K. (2019, 18 December). Uber settles federal investigation into workplace culture. *New York Times*. https://www.nytimes.com/2019/12/18/technology/uber-settles-eeoc-investigation-workplace-culture.html

Isaac, M. (2017, 22 February). Inside Uber's aggressive, unrestrained culture. *New York Times*. https://www.nytimes.com/2017/02/22/technology/uber-workplace-culture.html

Picchi, A. (2017, 10 April). Does "bro" culture spark sexual harassment? CBS News. https://www.cbsnews.com/news/does-bro-culture-spark-sexual-harassment/

Rosenthal, R. (2002). Covert communication in classrooms, clinics, courtrooms, and cubicles. *American Psychologist, 57*, 839–849.

Rosenthal, R., and Jacobson, L. (1966). Teachers' expectancies: Determinants of pupils' IQ gains. *Psychological Reports, 19*, 115–118.

Siddiqui, F. (2019, 29 August). Internal data shows Uber's reputation hasn't changed much since. *Washington Post.* https://www.washingtonpost.com/technology/2019/08/29/even-after-ubers-ipo-long-shadow-deleteuber-still-looms/

Solon, O. (2017, 30 August). New Uber CEO meets staff as emotional Travis Kalanick gets standing ovation. *The Guardian.* https://www.theguardian.com/technology/2017/aug/30/uber-new-ceo-dara-khosrowshahi-all-staff-meeting

Solon, O., and Wong, J. C. (2017, 21 June). With Uber's Travis Kalanick out, will Silicon Valley clean up its bro culture? *The Guardian.* https://www.theguardian.com/technology/2017/jun/21/uber-travis-kalanick-what-next-silicon-valley

Timber, C., and Dwoskin, E. (2017, 6 June). Uber fires 20 employees as part of harassment investigation. *Washington Post.* https://www.washingtonpost.com/news/the-switch/wp/2017/06/06/uber-fires-more-than-20-employees-as-part-of-sexual-harassment-investigation/

Chapter 2: Connection

Abraham, L. (2010, March 8). Can you really predict the success of a marriage in 15 minutes? Slate. https://slate.com/human-interest/2010/03/a-dissection-of-john-gottman-s-love-lab.html

Ainsworth, M., Bell, S., and Stayton, D. (1971). Individual differences in Strange Situation behaviour of one-year-olds. In H. Shaffer (Ed.), *The origins of human social relations.* New York: Academic Press.

Benson, K. (2017, October 4). The magic relationship ratio, according to science. https://www.gottman.com/blog/the-magic-relationship-ratio-according-science/#:~:text=Kyle%20Benson%20October%204%2C%202017%20That%20E2%80%9Cmagic%20ratio%E2%80%9D,happy%20marriage%20has%20five%20%28or%20more%29%20positive%20interactions.

Bretherton, I. (1992). The origins of attachment theory: John Bowlby and Mary Ainsworth. *Developmental Psychology, 28*, 759–775.

Gottman, J., et al. (1998). Predicting marital happiness and stability from newlywed interactions. *Journal of Marriage and the Family, 60*, 5–22.

Chapter 3: Reward

Mischel, W., Shoda, Y., and Rodriguez, M. (1989). Delay of gratification in children. *Science, 244*, 933–938.

Pavlov, I. (1927). *Conditioned reflexes.* London: Oxford University Press.

Seligman, M., and Maier, S. (1967). Failure to escape traumatic shock. *Journal of Experimental Psychology, 74*, 1–9.

Skinner, B. F. (1948). Superstition in the pigeon. *Journal of Experimental Psychology, 38*, 168–172.

Chapter 4: Choice

Bellaby, M. (2017, May 6). 80 years later, what caused the Hindenburg fire? *Florida Today*. https://www.whas11.com/article/news/80-years-later-what-caused-the-hindenburg-fire/417-437346523

Langer, E., and Rodin, J. (1976). The effects of choice and enhanced personal responsibility for the aged: A field experiment in an institutional setting. *Journal of Personality and Social Psychology, 34*, 191–198.

Porter, J. (2014, June 4). Why having too many choices is making you unhappy. *Fast Company*. https://www.fastcompany.com/3031364/why-having-too-many-choices-is-making-you-unhappy

Rotter, J. (1966). Generalized expectancies for internal versus external control of reinforcement. *Psychological Monographs: General and Applied, 80*, 1–28.

Tugend, A. (2010, February 26). Too many choices: A problem that can paralyze. *The New York Times*. https://www.nytimes.com/2010/02/27/your-money/27shortcuts.html

Walters, J. (2017, May 7). The Hindenburg disaster, 80 years on: A "perfect storm of circumstances." *The Guardian*. https://www.theguardian.com/us-news/2017/may/07/hindenburg-disaster-80th-anniversary

Webster, D. (2017, May 4). What really felled the Hindenburg? *Smithsonian*. https://www.smithsonianmag.com/smithsonian-institution/80th-anniversary-hindenburg-disaster-mysteries-remain-180963107/

Chapter 5: Confidence

BBC News. (1999, June 22). How Leeson broke the bank. http://news.bbc.co.uk/2/hi/business/375259.stm

BBC News. (2009, January 16). Pilot hailed for "Hudson Miracle." http://news.bbc.co.uk/2/hi/americas/7832439.stm

Chua-Eoan, H. (2007, March 1). Crimes of the century. *Time*. http://content.time.com/time/specials/packages/article/0,28804,1937349_1937350_1937488,00.html

Lowy, J. and Sniffen, M. (2009, February 24). Controller thought plane that ditched was doomed. The San Diego Union-Tribune. https://www.sandiegouniontribune.com/sdut-plane-splashdown-hearing-022409-2009feb24-story.html#:~:text=Controller%20thought%20plane%20that%20ditched%20was%20doomed%20US,testify%20before%20the%20House%20Transportation%20and%20Infrastructure%20Committee.

Marr, J., and Thau, S. (2014). Falling from great (and not-so-great) heights: How initial status position influences performance after status loss. *Academy of Management Journal, 57*, 223–248.

McFadden, R (2009, January 15). Pilot is hailed after jetliner's icy plunge. *The New York Times*. https://www.nytimes.com/2009/01/16/nyregion/16crash.html

Nick Leeson Official Website (2016). (http://www.nickleeson.com). Accessed March 3, 2016.

Rivera, R. (2009, January 17). A pilot becomes a hero years in the making. *The New York Times*. https://www.nytimes.com/2009/01/17/nyregion/17pilot.html

Rodrigues, J. (2015, February 24). Barings collapse at 20: How rogue trader Nick Leeson broke the bank. *The Guardian*. https://www.theguardian.com/business/from-the-archive-blog/2015/feb/24/nick-leeson-barings-bank-1995-20-archive

Titcomb, J. (2015, February 23). Barings: The collapse that erased 232 years of history. *The Telegraph*. https://www.telegraph.co.uk/finance/newsbysector/banksandfinance/11427501/Barings-the-collapse-that-erased-232-years-of-history.html

Vine, S. et al. (2015). Individual reactions to stress predict performance during a critical aviation incident. *Anxiety, Stress, and Coping, 28*, 467–477.

Wald, M. (2009, February 5). Was flight 1549's pilot fearful? If so, his voice didn't let on. *The New York Times*. https://www.nytimes.com/2009/02/06/nyregion/06crash.html

Chapter 6: Power

Alcorn, C. (2020, February 4). Hollywood is more diverse than ever. So why are the Oscars still so white? CNN Business. https://www.cnn.com/2020/02/04/media/hollywood-diversity-report-2019/index.html

BBC News (2016, January 19). Oscars head acts over lack of nominees' diversity. https://www.bbc.com/news/world-us-canada-35348062

BBC News. (2016, February 22). Hollywood has "inclusion crisis" suggests study. https://www.bbc.com/news/entertainment-arts-35629523

BBC News. (2016, January 23). Academy to double female and minority members by 2020. https://www.bbc.com/news/entertainment-arts-35387639

BBC News. (2016, January 27). Animal House actor Stephen Furst laments Academy role changes. https://www.bbc.com/news/entertainment-arts-35418010

BBC News. (2016, January 19). How to become an Academy member. https://www.bbc.com/news/entertainment-arts-35352506

Bruney, G. (2020, January 13). The very white 2020 Oscar nominations deserve all the shit they're getting. *Esquire*. https://www.esquire.com/entertainment/movies/a30496916/oscars-so-white-nominations-2020-reactions/

Haney, C., Banks, C., and Zimbardo, P. (1973). Interpersonal dynamics in a simulated prison. *International Journal of Criminology and Penology, 1*, 69–97.

Jones, E. (2020, February 1). Three years after *Moonlight*, why are awards shows still so white? *The Guardian*. https://www.theguardian.com/film/2020/feb/01/three-years-after-moonlight-why-are-awards-shows-still-so-white

Stanford Prison Experiment. (2015, December 15). http://www.prisonexp.org.

Wells, M. (2002, January 24). BBC halts "prison experiment." *The Guardian*. https://www.theguardian.com/uk/2002/jan/24/bbc.socialsciences

Zimbardo, P. (1973, April 8). The mind is a formidable jailor: A Pirandellian prison. *The New York Times Magazine*. https://www.nytimes.com/1973/04/08/archives/a-pirandellian-prison-the-mind-is-a-formidable-jailer.html

Chapter 7: Helping

Darley, J., and Latane, B. (1968). Bystander intervention in emergencies: Diffusion of responsibility. *Journal of Personality and Social Psychology, 8*, 377–383.

Heyden, T. (2015, June 4). When 100 people lift a bus. *BBC News Magazine*. https://www.bbc.com/news/magazine-32993891

Latane, B., and Darley, J. (1968). Group inhibition of bystander intervention in emergencies. *Journal of Personality and Social Psychology, 10*, 215–221.

Manning, R., Levine, M., and Collins, A. (2007). The Kitty Genovese murder and the social psychology of helping: The parable of the 38 witnesses. *American Psychologist, 62*, 555–562.

Chapter 8: Intent

BBC News. (2016, May 14). Renting while black. https://www.bbc.com/news/blogs-trending-35464634

Bohannon, J. (2016, April 7). For real this time: Talking to people about gay and transgender issues can change their prejudices. *Science Magazine*. https://www.sciencemag.org/news/2016/04/real-time-talking-people-about-gay-and-transgender-issues-can-change-their-prejudices

Broockman, D., and Kalla, J. (2016). Durably reducing transphobia: A field experiment on door-to-door canvassing. *Science, 352*, 220–224.

Denzet-Lewis, B. (2016, April 7). How do you change voters' minds? Have a conversation. *The New York Times Magazine*. https://www.nytimes.com/2016/04/10/magazine/how-do-you-change-voters-minds-have-a-conversation.html

Eberhardt, J. (2019, June 12). Can Airbnb train hosts not to be racists? *Daily Beast*. https://www.thedailybeast.com/can-airbnb-train-hosts-not-to-be-racists

Edelman, B., Luca, M., and Svirsky, D. (2016). *Racial discrimination in the sharing economy: Evidence from a field experiment*. Cambridge, MA: Harvard Business School, Working Paper Series.

Glusac, E. (2016, June 21). As Airbnb grows, so do claims of discrimination. *The New York Times*. https://www.nytimes.com/2016/06/26/travel/airbnb-discrimination-lawsuit.html

LaPiere, R. (1934). Attitudes vs. actions. *Social Forces, 13*, 230–237.

Singal, J. (2015, May 29). The case of the amazing gay-marriage data: How a graduate student reluctantly uncovered a huge scientific fraud. New York Magazine. https://www.thecut.com/2015/05/how-a-grad-student-uncovered-a-huge-fraud.html?wpsrc=nymag

Chapter 9: Obedience

Blass, T. (2002, March 1). The man who shocked the world. *Psychology Today*. https://www.psychologytoday.com/us/articles/200203/the-man-who-shocked-the-world

Hollander, M. M. (2015). The repertoire of resistance: Non-compliance with directives in Milgram's 'obedience' experiments. *Social Psychology, 54*, 425–444.

Holmes, T. and Rahe, R. (1967). The social readjustment rating scale. *Journal of Psychosomatic Research, 11*, 213–218.

Milgram, S. (1963). Behavioral study of obedience. *Journal of Abnormal and Social Psychology, 67*, 371–378.

Milgram, S. (1974). *Obedience to authority: An experimental view*. New York: Harper and Row.

Chapter 10: Conformity

Asch, S. (1955). Opinions and social pressure. *Scientific American, 193*, 31–35.

Festinger, L., and Carlsmith, J. (1959). Cognitive consequences of forced compliance. *Journal of Abnormal and Social Psychology, 58*, 203–210.

Griggs, R. (2015). The disappearance of independence in textbook coverage of Asch's social pressure experiments. *Teaching of Psychology, 42*, 137–142.

Janis, I. (1971). Groupthink: The desperate drive for consensus at any cost. *Psychology Today, 5*, 43–46, 74–76.

Chapter 11: Identity

Finkel, M. (2014, August 5). The strange & curious tale of the last true hermit. *GQ*. https://www.gq.com/story/the-last-true-hermit

Kuhn, M., and McPartland, T. (1954). An empirical investigation of self-attitudes. *American Sociological Review, 19*, 68–76.

Chapter 12: Conflict

Hewstone, M., et al. (2006). Intergroup contact, forgiveness, and experience of "The Troubles" in *Northern Ireland. Journal of Social Issues, 62*, 99–120.

Schmid, K., et al. (2008). The effects of living in segregated vs. mixed areas in Northern Ireland: A simultaneous analysis of contact and threat effects in the context of micro-level neighborhoods. *International Journal of Conflict and Violence, 2*, 56–71.

Sherif, M., et al. (1954). *Intergroup conflict and cooperation: The Robbers Cave Experiment*. Original full research report. http://psychclassics.yorku.ca/Sherif

Chapter 13: Misdirection

Levy, M., and Tasoff, J. (2017). Exponential-growth bias and overconfidence. *Journal of Economic Psychology, 58*, 1–14.

Manseau, P. (2017, October 10). Meet Mr. Mumler, the man who "captured" Lincoln's ghost on camera. *Smithsonian*. https://www.smithsonianmag.com/smithsonian-institution/meet-mr-mumler-man-who-captured-lincolns-ghost-camera-180965090/

Marshall, M. (2020, April 14). Why we find it difficult to recognize a crisis. *BBC Future*. https://www.bbc.com/future/article/20200409-why-we-find-it-difficult-to-recognise-a-crisis

Siegel, E. (2020, March 17). Why "exponential growth" is so scary for the COVID-19 coronavirus. *Forbes*. https://www.forbes.com/sites/startswithabang/2020/

03/17/why-exponential-growth-is-so-scary-for-the-covid-19-coronavirus/
?sh=1c0688aa4e9b

Stajano, F., and Wilson, P. (2009, August). *Understanding scam victims: Seven principles for systems security*. University of Cambridge Computer Laboratory Technical Report.

Stango, V., and Zinman, J. (2009). Exponential growth bias and household finance. *The Journal of Finance, 64*, 2807–2849.

Yagoda, B. (2018, September Issue). The cognitive biases tricking your brain. *The Atlantic*. https://www.theatlantic.com/magazine/archive/2018/09/cognitive-bias/565775/

Index

For the benefit of digital users, indexed terms that span two pages (e.g., 52–53) may, on occasion, appear on only one of those pages.

Academy Awards boycott 2016, 83–86, 88
Ailes, Roger, 3
Ainsworth, Mary, 17–20
Airbnb, 104–7, 113
AirbnbWhileBlack, 106
artificial intelligence (AI), viii
Asch, Solomon, 130–33, 140
authority. *See* conformity; obedience
Automattic, x–xi

Bain, Addison, 56
Bandura, Albert, 4, 14–15
Barings Bank, 65–69
baseball arbitration, 70–72
Batta, Bruno, 122
Bay of Pigs, 133–36
behavioral learning development, 38–40
behavioral scripts, 81–83, 88
behaviorism, 38–42
behaviors, origins of, 3–9
Benchmark Capital, 3
bias in crisis spotting, 173–77
Black, James Wallace, 168–70
Blass, Thomas, 122–23
bleeding blue, 148–54
Bobo Doll study, 4–9
Boggs, Wade, 38–39
Bowlby, John, 17
Broockman, David, 109–12
bullying, 83. *See also* power
butterfly effect, 57
bystander effect, 98, 176

canvassing studies, 108–12
Cherry, Ronnia, 106
Chesky, Brian, 106
Chinese couple road trip study, 102–7, 113

choice
    attributions, 58–59
    butterfly effect, 57
    cause and effect perceptions, 54–60
    cognitive resources allocation, 49–51, 59
    decision-making effects, 48–51
    failed retail model, 47–48
    fundamental attribution error, 58
    impulsivity, 50
    information overload, 49–50
    leaders role in regulating, 59–60
    personal control and, 51–54, 59
    staff engagement/productivity, 54, 59–60
Clarke, Kenneth, 68
classical conditioning, 35
cognitive biases in crisis spotting, 173–77
cognitive engagement studies, 51–54
cognitive overload, 48, 49–50, 59–60
cognitive scripts
    disruption of, 112–14
    in intent, 107–12
    power relationships, 81–83, 88
    in scamming, 174
Collins, Alan, 90
collodion process, 168
conditioning, 33–38
confidence
    choking under pressure, 64, 72–73
    composure, 63–64, 68
    ego threat, 69–73
    failure and, 65–69
    overconfidence, 65–69, 175
    resiliency, 69
    role modeling in, 176
    stress perceptions/performance relationships, 61–65

confirmation bias, 174–75
conflict. *See also* stereotypes
    contact in reduction of, 159, 163–65
    contact theory, 163–64
    dismantling, 165–67
    Irish nationalism, 162–65
    mixed neighborhoods, 163–65
    personal/residential segregation, 163
    prejudice emergence study, 155–62
    superordinate goals in reduction of,
        159–62, 167
conformity
    Asch experiments, 130–33, 140
    cognitive dissonance, 136–39
    consensus in workplace, 139–41
    groupthink, 133–36, 140
    objectivity and, 141
    out-group members, 136
    self-censorship, 135
    social norms, 130, 139–40
    social pressure, 130–33
    support of dissension, 132, 140
    uniforms, 129–30, 139–40
cons/scams, 170–73
consumer choice. *See* choice
contact theory, 163–64
Cooperative Campaign Analysis
        Project, 110–11
corporate culture. *See also* Uber
    bleeding blue, 148–54
    culture of appreciation/respect, 30
    leader's role in development, 13–15
COVID-19 pandemic, viii–xi, 173–77
crisis spotting, 173–77
Ctrip study, x
Cuban Missile Crisis, 141

daguerreotype process, 168
Darley, John, 91–96, 98
deception in scamming, 172
decision-making. *See* choice
Denizet-Lewis, Benoit, 108
desperation in scamming, 172
discrimination
    attitudes/action relationships
        study, 102–7
    gender-based, 111–12
    indirect, 84–85, 86, 87–88

LGBT, 108–12
    prejudice emergence study, 155–62
    racial/Airbnb, 104–7, 113
dishonesty in scamming, 172
distraction in scamming, 171–72
Doehner, Werner, 56

expectancy effect, 9–14
exponential growth bias, 175

Fischer, Tim, 148–54
fixed-interval reinforcement, 36, 37
Fleischer, Dave, 108, 110, 111
Fleming, Alexander, 33
flying moor, 55–56
Four Horsemen, 27–31
Fowler, Susan, 2
Fox News, 3
Furst, Stephen, 86
future of work, viii–xi, 176–77

Genovese, Kitty, 89–90, 92, 98
gig economy
    adaptation to, viii–xi, 177
    confidence/feedback
        relationships, 72–73
    conformity in, 140
    diversity and inclusion, 167
    help requests, 98–100
    perceptions of scarcity, 166–67
    staff engagement/productivity,
        54, 59–60
Gottman, John, 22–25, 26–27, 29, 30–31
Grant, Stefan, 106
group dynamics. *See* conflict

harassment. *See* conflict; Uber
Harvard Test of Inflected Acquisition, 10
helping behaviors
    bystander effect, 98, 176
    case studies, 89–91
    collaboration, 100
    diffusion of responsibility, 92, 94, 96
    experimental studies/
        emergencies, 91–97
    gender differences, 94–95
    leader effects, 99
    message interpretation, 99–100

personal distance effects, 98
predicting, 96–97
public requests, 100
social norms *vs.* repercussions,
     91–92, 94
social pressure, 98–99, 100
workplace environment/help
     requests, 97–100
herd behavior in scamming, 171–72
Hindenburg disaster, 54–60
Holder, Eric H., 2
Hollander, Matthew, 122–23
Huffington, Arianna, 2

identity
   aspirations, 147
   bleeding blue, 148–54
   consensual statements, 147
   factors shaping, 152–53
   group affiliation, 148–54
   ideological beliefs, 147
   in isolation from society, 142–46
   power and, 76, 80
   preferences, 147
   readjustment to society, 144–45
   self-concept, 146–48
   self-evaluations, 147
   social identity, 145–46
   workplace, 153–54
imitation. *See* role modeling
Incredible Universe, 47–48
Instant Booking service, 106
intent
   attitudes/action relationships study,
      102–7, 113
   cognitive script, 107–12
   cognitive script disruption, 112–14
   racial discrimination/Airbnb, 104–7
   social norms, 101–2
   social pressure, 113–14
IQ testing study, 9–12
Isaacs, Cheryl Boone, 85–86
Ishfaq, Zoheb, 90–91
Iyengar, Sheena, 49

Jacobson, Lenore, 10
Jaffe, David, 75
jam buying studies, 49

Janis, Irving, 134–35
Jordan, Michael, 38–39

Kahneman, Daniel, 174
Kalanick, Travis, 1–3, 13. *See also* Uber
Kalla, Joshua, 109–12
Khosrowshahi, Dara, 14–15
Knight, Christopher Thomas, 142–46
Kuhn, Manford, 146

LaCour, Michael, 108–11
Langer, Ellen, 51–54
LaPiere, Richard, 102–7, 113
Latane, Bibb, 91–96, 98
Leadership LAB, 110, 111–12
leader's role
   in corporate culture
      development, 13–15
   helping behaviors, 99
   in regulating choice, 59–60
learned helplessness, 40–42, 45–46
Leeson, Nick, 65–70
LevelUp, 113
Levine, Mark, 90
LGBT, 108–12, 151–52
Love Lab, 22–26. *See also* Gottman, John;
     relationships
Lyft, 14–15

Maier, Steven, 40
Manning, Rachel, 90
Marathon Oil, 148–54
Marr, Jennifer Carson, 70–71
Marshmallow study, 42–46
Maslach, Christina, 80
McPartland, Thomas, 146
microwave, 33
Milgrim, Stanley/Milgram experiments.
     See obedience
Miracle on the Hudson, 61–65
Mischel, Walter, 42–43
Monte scam, 170–73
Morrison, Herbert, 54–55
Moseley, Winston. *See* Genovese, Kitty
mother/child interaction
     studies, 17–22
Mumler, William, 168–70, 173, 174
Myers Briggs Personality Type, 50

North Pond hermit, 142–46

obedience
  compliance statistics, 118, 119,
    121–22
  defined, 121
  emotional disturbances, 118–19, 122
  established obligations, 123, 124
  ethical guidelines, 123, 125
  legitimacy of authority, 123, 124
  limited time for reflection, 123, 125
  Milgram experiments, 115–20
  Milgram's motivations, 120–23
  no way to compromise, 123, 125
  psychological processes coexisting
    with, 121
  self-image/resistance to
    authority, 122–23
  shock box, 117, 120–23
  situational variables affecting, 123
  social pressure, 118
  as virtue, 115, 121, 126
  whistleblowers, 127–28
  in workplace, 116, 124–28
  worthy goals, 123, 124–25
operant conditioning, 35–36
optimism bias, 174–75
O'Reilly, Bill, 3
OscarsSoWhite, 83–88
outcome bias, 174–75
Overmier, J. Bruce, 40

Paterson, David, 62
Pavlov, Ivan Petrovich, 33–35, 45
penicillin, 33
Peterson, Jason, 110
plant sitting studies, 51–54
Porter, Jane, 48–49
power
  authority, 76–77
  behavioral scripts, 81–83, 88
  bullying, 83
  coping strategies, 81–82
  discrimination, 83–88
  diversity and inclusion, 84–88
  emotional effects, 78–79, 81–82
  ethics, 82
  guards' roles, 80–83

identity and, 76, 80
rebellion, 77, 78
reward/punishment, 76–77
role immersion effects, 74–80
role modeling, 83
social norms, 82
solitary confinement, 79–80
visitation, 78–79
prejudice emergence study, 155–62.
    See also discrimination
productivity, factors affecting, x
profiling, 104–7, 113
punishment, 40–42. See also reward
    systems
Pygmalion effect, 9–14

Rampling, Charlotte, 84
rapport establishment, remote work
    effects on, x
Real Hustle, The, 170–73, 174
relationships
  active listening skills, 23–24, 25
  attachment theory, 17–20
  avoidant behavior, 21
  case study, 16–17
  complaining without blame, 29
  connection in, 21–22
  contempt effects, 16–17, 22–23,
    27, 28, 30
  criticism effects, 16–17, 24, 25,
    26, 28, 29
  culture of appreciation/respect, 30
  de-escalation, 24–25, 29–30
  defensiveness effects, 16–17, 22–23, 27,
    28, 29–30
  failing, downhill trajectory of, 24–26
  magic ratio, 27–31
  marriage outcome studies, 22–26
  negativity effects, 24–25, 28
  openness to influence/personal
    power, 26
  reinforcement schedules, 37
  secure vs. insecure adults, 20–22
  stability, predicting, 24–25
  stonewalling/withdrawal, 29, 30
  timeout, 30
remote working, adaptation to, viii–xi
Rensaleer, Jan, 122

reward systems
  behaviorism, 38–42
  conditioning, 33–38
  delayed gratification, 43–45
  employee incentivization, 45–46
  impulses and behaviors, 32–33
  learned helplessness, 40–42, 45–46
  punishments, 40–42
  reinforcement, positive, 36–38
  self-control development, 42–46
  self-distraction, 44
  superstitions and, 38–42, 45
  temptation, xi, 32, 43–44, 45
Robbers Cave experiment, 155–62
robotic process automation (RPA), viii
Rodin, Judith, 51–54
role modeling
  in aggressive behaviors
    development, 3–9
  in confidence, 176
  expectations/biases in behavioral
    development, 9–13
  gender differences, 6–7, 8–9, 13–14
  leader's role in culture
    development, 13–15
Rosenthal, Robert, 9–10, 12, 13–14
Rotter, Julian, 58–59

salivation studies, 33–35
Samsung survey, vii–viii
Selden, Gregory, 106
Seligman, Martin, 40–42
Sherif, Muzafer, 155–62
Shields, Anthony, 90–91, 98
Shierholz, Heidi, ix
shock box. See obedience
Skinner, B. F., 38–40, 45
social categorization. See conflict;
    discrimination
social compliance in scamming, 172–73
social identity theory, 166–67
social isolation/loneliness, x
social roles, gender differences, 7
Sophocieous, Alex, 90
Spencer, Percy, 33
Spirit Photographer, 168–70, 173, 174

Stajano, Frank, 170–72
Stanford prison experiment, 74–83, 88
stereotypes. See also conflict
  expectancy effects, 12–13
  intent/action relationships, 104
  Irish nationalism and, 162–65
Strange Situation experiment, 17–22
Sullenberger, Chesley, 61–65, 69–70
superstition, 38–42, 45

talent management, 73, 86–87, 167
teacher–student interactions studies,
    9–12, 13–14
Tests of General Ability, 10
Thau, Stefan, 70–71
The Troubles (Northern Ireland), 162–65
time pressure
  in obedience, 123, 125
  in scamming, 172
transgender. See LGBT
Tversky, Amos, 174
Twenty Statements Test, 147–48

Uber
  bullying, learning, 3–9
  cognitive script disruption, 113
  expectancy effect, 9–14
  harassment investigations, 2–3
  leader's role in culture
    development, 13–15
  misconduct allegations, 1–2
  sexism/'bro' culture, 1–3, 14–15

variable-interval reinforcement, 36,
    37–38
variable-ratio reinforcement, 36–37
Vine, Samuel, 64

well-being, personal control and, 51–54
Wendell, Turk, 38–39
whistleblowing, 110–11
Wilson, Paul, 170–72
work psychology/employee engagement,
    vii–viii

Zimbardo, Philip, 74–80, 82